KU-181-826

MAORI YOUTH

A Psychoethnological Study of Cultural Deprivation

David P. Ausubel
University of Illinois

Holt,
Rinehart
and
Winston, Inc.

New York - Chicago - San Francisco - Toronto - London

6 00 160357 5   TELEPEN

HB3692.SP6

Yes

20/-

Maori
Youth

**To my
friends of
Ngati-Awa
and
Whakatohea**

E tipu, e rea, mo nga ra o tou ao.
Ko to ringa ki nga rakau a te pakeha hei ora mo to tinana.
Ko to ngakau ki nga taonga a o tipuna hei tikitiki mo to mahunga.
Ko to wairua ki te Atua, nana nei nga mea katoa.

Grow, tender shoot, for the days of your world!
Turn your hand to the tools of the pakeha for the well-being of
    your body.
Turn your heart to the treasures of your ancestors as a crown for
    your head.
Give your soul unto God, the author of all things.

Sir Apirana Ngata
From a Maori schoolgirl's autograph book.

UNIVERSITY
LIBRARY
NOTTINGHAM

Preface to American Edition Copyright © 1965 by
Holt, Rinehart and Winston, Inc.

© 1961 by David P. Ausubel

Library of Congress Catalog Card Number: 65–25670

20608–0215

Printed in the United States of America

First published 1961 by Price Milburn and Co. Ltd., New Zealand

Foreword

IN THIS STUDY PROFESSOR AUSUBEL HAS GIVEN HIMSELF A three-fold task. He has set out to make a careful investigation of the educational and vocational aspirations of two groups of Maori youth (an urban, and a rural or semi-rural group) and to compare these aspirations with those of a pakeha (European) control group. Secondly, he has used his qualitative data to show the significance of his quantitative material for an understanding of the place of Maori youth in contemporary New Zealand society. Finally, Dr Ausubel interprets his results with reference on the one hand to the recent historical development of Maori society and on the other hand to a psychological theory of the development of Maori personality. The presentation of data and its interpretation give a closely woven argument which is masterly in its synthesis and impressive in its final achievement.

Dr Ausubel's study fits very aptly into the pattern of Maori investigations sponsored over the past few years by Victoria University. He has tackled a problem foreshadowed as important in the original Rakau enquiries. Taken in conjunction with Williams' work on Maori achievement motivation, we now have an analysis of some of the major difficulties that face Maori youth in the complex process of growing to maturity in contemporary New Zealand society. Full integration of the Maori into this society is likely to be an arduous task for Maori and pakeha alike. Social Science investigation such as this of Ausubel's will give us all a better understanding of the difficulties involved. It is characteristic of Ausubel's approach that it hides in no ivory-tower isolation (though it will need no stressing that this study constitutes in many respects an important contribution to the theory of how personality is formed in a given culture). Equally prominent therefore are Ausubel's practical recommendations. He obviously thinks that something needs to be done about helping Maori youth realise their educational and vocational aspirations. What needs doing he states clearly and unequivocally.

Foreword

This study therefore can be read both as a contribution to the theory of psychological acculturation and as a blue-print for action by teachers, administrators and others concerned with the difficulties of Maori young people. It is a measure of Dr Ausubel's ability that in both respects he has given the data and argued a case that will command the attention of both the academic student of the subject and of the practical person who is driven into action by the needs of Maori youth seeking a part to play in New Zealand life today.

ERNEST BEAGLEHOLE

Victoria University
Wellington
New Zealand

Preface to the American Edition

EDUCATORS, PSYCHOLOGISTS, ANTHROPOLOGISTS, AND CIVIL servants are much concerned these days with the problems of "culturally deprived" youth. This research study explores in some depth the psychological and ethnographic dynamics of cultural deprivation. How do culturally disadvantaged youth get to be the way they are? Through what psychological and social mechanisms are the educational and vocational aspirations of a culturally deprived ethnic group transmitted to the youth of that group?

In short, *Maori Youth* is a research study, *in situ,* of cultural deprivation. The methods it employs are historical analyses of cultural values, psychological interviews with parents and youth, objective psychological tests, and "participant observation."

The findings of *Maori Youth* have relevance, therefore, to the struggle against poverty and ignorance in the United States, to the work of the Peace Corps in the economically undeveloped nations of Asia and Africa, and to the education of ethnic minority and lower social class groups in the great urban centers of the United States and other countries. *Maori Youth* can be used as a primer in the training of special teachers for such work, as well as supplementary reading for students in courses on adolescent psychology and cultural anthropology.

DAVID P. AUSUBEL

Urbana, Illinois
November, 1965

Preface

THE RESEARCH ON WHICH THIS REPORT IS BASED CONSISTED OF eleven months of intensive field work in New Zealand, principally in two North Island communities. It was carried out in 1957–1958 during the tenure of a Fulbright research grant, when I was affiliated with the Department of Psychology, Victoria University of Wellington. I am indebted to my colleagues at Victoria University, Professor Ernest Beaglehole, Mr J. E. Ritchie, and Mrs Jane Ritchie, and to Mr George Parkyn and Mr John Watson of the New Zealand Council for Educational Research for practical suggestions and assistance in the field; and to the United States Educational Foundation in New Zealand and to the Graduate Research Board and the Bureau of Educational Research of the University of Illinois for financial support of the project. I have to thank the Maori Purposes Fund Board of New Zealand for a substantial contribution towards the costs of publication.

I also wish to acknowledge the gracious co-operation of the headmasters, teachers, and pupils of the two schools in which the research was carried out and the valuable assistance of Robert M. Tomlinson, graduate fellow in industrial education at the University of Illinois, and of my wife, Pearl Ausubel, in the scoring, tabulation and statistical analysis of the data.

The opinions and conclusions expressed herein are solely my own, and should not be construed as necessarily representing the views of any of the institutions associated with the sponsorship, financial support or publication of this research.

DAVID P. AUSUBEL

Champaign, Illinois
July, 1959

Contents

I INTRODUCTION

The Problem --- --- --- --- --- --- --- 13
Relation to Previous Research --- --- --- --- --- 13
Importance of Aspirational Changes in Adolescence --- --- 15
Values and Pitfalls of a Cross-Cultural Approach --- --- 16
Cross-Cultural Research in a Setting of Acculturation --- --- 17
  Methodological Precautions --- --- --- --- --- 19
Relevant Findings about Maori Adolescence from Prior Research 21
  General Characteristics --- --- --- --- --- --- 21
  Aspirational Pattern --- --- --- --- --- --- 22
  Supportive Traits --- --- --- --- --- --- 24
  The Urban Maori Adolescent --- --- --- --- --- 25
Hypotheses --- --- --- --- --- --- --- --- 26
Research Design --- --- --- --- --- --- --- 27
  Research Methods --- --- --- --- --- --- 28

II THE LOCAL SETTINGS

The Urban Setting --- --- --- --- --- --- --- 36
  Residence of Pupils --- --- --- --- --- --- 37
  Occupations of Pupils' Fathers --- --- --- --- --- 38
  Tribal Organisation and Social Life --- --- --- --- 39
  Religious Affiliations --- --- --- --- --- --- 40
  Housing --- --- --- --- --- --- --- --- 42
  Race Relations --- --- --- --- --- --- --- 42
  The School Environment --- --- --- --- --- 44
The Rural Setting --- --- --- --- --- --- --- 45
  Residence of Pupils --- --- --- --- --- --- 46
  Tribal Organisation and Social Life --- --- --- --- 47
  Religious Affiliations --- --- --- --- --- --- 48
  Housing --- --- --- --- --- --- --- --- 48
  Race Relations --- --- --- --- --- --- --- 49
  The School Environment --- --- --- --- --- 50
Organisation of Remaining Chapters --- --- --- --- 51

III IMPLICATIONS FOR VOCATIONAL ACHIEVEMENT

Maori-Pakeha Uniformities and Differences --- --- --- 53
Urban-Rural Uniformities and Differences --- --- --- 56
  Reasons for the Urban Drift of Maori Population --- --- 57

Contents

General Trends in Urban-Rural Differences 58
Maori-Pakeha versus Urban-Rural Differences 60
Factors Affecting Maori Vocational Achievement 60
    Expressed Vocational Aspirations 60
    Parental Influences 63
    Peer Group Influences 67
    Maori Cultural Factors 68
    General Factors in New Zealand Culture 74
    Racial Prejudice and Discrimination 75

IV FACTORS AFFECTING MAORI EDUCATIONAL ACHIEVEMENT

Expressed Academic Aspirations 78
Home Influences 80
Peer Group Influences 83
Maori Cultural Factors 84
Difficulties in Adapting to Secondary School 87
Racial Prejudice 89
Stunting of Verbal Intelligence 90
Bilingualism 93
Absenteeism 94

V ACCULTURATIONAL HISTORY AND MOTIVATIONAL DEVELOPMENT

Stages in Maori Acculturation 96
    Pre-Colonisation (1769-1839) 96
    Colonisation (1840-1859) 98
    War (1860-1872) and Withdrawal (1872-1939) 100
    Post-withdrawal (1940-) 109
    Sources of Maori-Pakeha differences in Aspirational and
        Motivational Traits 118
    Pre-Pakeha Maori Achievement Ideology 119
    Post-Pakeha Maori Achievement Ideology 120
    Childhood and Adolescent Experience 124
    Social Class and I.Q. 126
Transmission of Motivational and Supportive Traits 126
    Examples of Transmitting Mechanisms in the Maori Situation 128
    The Role of Early Childhood Experience 129
Outlook for the Future 131
Maori Social and Economic Organisation 132
Cultural Values Regarding Achivement 134

VI RECOMMENDATIONS

Vocational Guidance 135
    Inadequacies of Present System 139
    Maori Vocational Guidance Officers 140
    Hostels 142

Contents

Education   142
   Maori Schools   145
Identification of Youth with Maori Culture   146
   Teaching of the Maori Language   148
Improvement of Race Relations   153
   Equality of Vocational Opportunity   154
   Equality in Housing   156
   The Maori's Responsibility in Improving Race Relations   158

VII SUMMARY AND CONCLUSIONS

Problem and Research Design   160
   The Findings   162
   Factors Affecting Maori Vocational Achievement   166
   Factors Affecting Maori Educational Achievements   169
   Acculturational History and Personality Development   172
Recommendations   179

APPENDIX I   PROCEDURES AND INSTRUMENTS

Structured Interview   183
Tests and Rating Scales   185
Categorisation of Variables   186

APPENDIX II   COMPARISON OF MAORI AND PAKEHA ASPIRATIONAL PATTERNS

Maori-Pakeha Uniformities and Differences   189
   Stated Academic Aspirations   189
   Stated Vocational Aspirations   191
   Prestige Motivation   192
   Task-Oriented Motivation   194
   Group Welfare Motivation   195
   Traits Important for Implementing Achievement Goals   195
   Perceived Family Pressures for School Success   196
   Perceived Family Pressures for Vocational Success   197
   Perceived Influence of Others in Vocational Choice   198
   Perceived Peer Group Pressures for School Success   199
   Perceived Opportunity for Vocational Success   199
Summary of Maori-Pakeha Uniformities and Differences   200
   Conclusion   202
Urban versus Rural Intercultural Differences   204

Contents

APPENDIX III   COMPARISON OF URBAN AND RURAL
ASPIRATIONAL PATTERNS

Urban-Rural Uniformities and Differences 205
Stated Academic Aspirations 206
Stated Vocational Aspirations 206
Prestige Motivation 207
Task-Oriented Motivation 208
Group Welfare Motivation 208
Traits Important for Implementing Achievement Goals 208
Perceived Family Pressures for School Success 209
Perceived Family Pressures for Vocational Success 210
Perceived Influence of Others in Vocational Choice 210
Perceived Peer Group Pressures for School Success 211
Perceived Opportunity for Vocational Success 211
Summary: Comparison of Urban and Rural Maori Pupils 211
Summary: Comparison of Urban and Rural Pakeha pupils 213
Maori versus Pakeha Interlocational Differences 214
Urban-Rural versus Maori-Pakeha Differences 215

REFERENCES 217

GLOSSARY 219

INDEX 221

TABLES

Table I: Form, Age and I.Q. of Subjects 28

Table II: Occupations of Subjects' Fathers in Urban and Rural
Samples 38

Table III: Religious Affiliations of Subjects in Urban and Rural
Samples 41

Table IV: Stated Vocational Aspirations of Urban and Rural
Samples 191

Table V: Mean Rank Values of Factors Influencing Vocational
Choice 192

Table VI: Reasons Given for Desiring Vocational Success 193

Table VII: Mean Rank Value of Reasons Given for Desiring
Vocational Success 194

CHAPTER ONE

Introduction

THE PROBLEM

IN GENERAL THIS RESEARCH IS CONCERNED WITH CULTURALLY determined uniformities and differences in the personality structure and development of Maori and pakeha adolescents and how they are transmitted to the developing individual. More specifically it seeks (a) to identify Maori-pakeha uniformities and differences in expressed and internalised levels of academic and vocational aspiration and in the kinds of motivations underlying these aspirations; (b) to identify Maori-pakeha uniformities and differences in supportive personality traits important for the realisation of achievement goals; and (c) to relate these motivational and other personality differences to cultural and interpersonal factors and mechanisms that account for their transmission from one generation to the next.

Another focus of research concern is on urban-rural differences in aspirational pattern among Maori adolescents and on the relative magnitude of Maori-pakeha differences in urban and rural areas. An attempt is also made to assess the relative magnitude and significance of Maori-pakeha differences by comparing them to urban-rural differences.

In addition to their theoretical significance for general problems of adolescent personality development (e.g., cross-cultural uniformities and differences; the impact of acculturation), findings such as these obviously have important implications for the direction and organisation of education and vocational guidance for Maori youth. The data have particular relevance for the serious problem of keeping Maori youth in school beyond the age of fifteen and of increasing Maori representation in the professions and skilled trades.

RELATION TO PREVIOUS RESEARCH

Research on the social anthropology of the Maori has generally been of two kinds. Anthropologists such as Raymond Firth,[17]

17 These numbers refer to the books listed on pages 217 and 218.

13

Peter Buck,[14] and Elsdon Best[12] have attempted a reconstruction of pre-pakeha Maori culture by analysing oral traditions and early records preserved by Maori elders, early accounts of Maori life by European missionaries and explorers, and residual cultural practices still extant among the more isolated Maori tribes. The second type of research—intensive and global field studies of modern Maori communities—is exemplified by the investigations of Hawthorn,[19] the Beagleholes,[8] and Ritchie.[34] Three less global studies of particular age segments of Maori personality development in the same rural community previously studied by Ritchie have been conducted by Mulligan,[30] Earle,[16] and Jane Ritchie.[36] Metge has also made two preliminary reports on a study of the urban Maori of Auckland City.[26, 27]

The present study differs from previous research both in scope and methodology. It is much less global—not only being restricted to male adolescent development, but also to a limited aspect of this development, i.e., academic and vocational aspirations and their underlying motivations, supportive personality traits, and perceived pressures for achievement in the cultural environment. Methodologically it differs (a) in placing greater reliance on objective measures and structured interviews than on informal interviews and projective techniques; (b) in studying both urban and rural populations, thus making possible a test of the generality of Maori-pakeha differences in diverse settings, a determination of urban-rural differences, and an assessment of Maori-pakeha differences; and (c) in employing a pakeha control group in each setting. The latter feature permits identification of those aspects of the aspirational traits of Maori adolescents that are distinctive of present-day Maori culture rather than reflections of the general New Zealand culture of which it is a part. It also makes possible the separation of genuine Maori-pakeha differences from those that are attributable to social class and urban-rural factors.

An earlier study by McQueen[25] explored the same broad area of education and vocations for Maori youth encompassed by this research project, but more from the standpoint of surveying the existing situation in New Zealand as a whole, reporting recent trends, and making recommendations. Quite unlike the present investigation it was not an experimental field study of only two communities focussing on psychocultural aspects of academic and vocational achievement.

IMPORTANCE OF ASPIRATIONAL CHANGES IN ADOLESCENCE

Changes in aspirational traits are among the most important aspects of adolescent personality development. Almost universally during the adolescent period primary status becomes a more important source of self-esteem and displaces derived status as the principal determinant of the individual's feeling of adequacy as a person.[3] With the onset of pubescence, children are expected to strive more for *primary status* based on their own efforts, competence and performance ability, and to strive less for *derived status* predicated on their personal qualities and on their dependent relationship to and intrinsic acceptance by parents, relatives, parent surrogates and peers.

Concomitantly, in support of this shift in the relative importance and availability of primary and derived status, adolescents are expected to be less dependent than children on the approval of their elders and to play a more active role in formulating their own goals and in making their own decisions. They are under greater pressure to persevere in goal-striving despite serious setbacks, to postpone immediate hedonistic gratification in favour of achieving long-range objectives, and to exercise more initiative, foresight, executive independence, responsibility, self-criticism, and respect for the demands of reality. In assimilating values and norms of conduct it is expected that they will be guided less by uncritical impulses of personal loyalty, implicit acceptance of authority and absolutistic notions of unilateral obligation, and will be influenced more by considerations of ego-enhancement and expediency and by functional concepts of equity and reciprocity of obligations.[3]

These motivational and supportive changes in personality organisation are prerequisite for the developing person's achievement of that degree of more equal status and responsible membership in the adult community that is necessary for both the perpetuation of a given cultural pattern and the survival of its individual carriers. Hence it can be anticipated that in their general aspects the personality changes outlined above will characterise adolescent development in almost any cultural setting. Superimposed on these uniformities, important intercultural differences in adolescent personality development may be expected on the basis of the duration, abruptness, explicitness and anxiety of adolescent transition; the availability and kinds of primary status open to adolescents; the degree of discontinuity between child and adult worlds; social class and caste factors; acculturation pressures; general cultural values; and the rate of cultural change. Other intercultural differences will depend on whether adolescent socialisation is primarily regulated by peers or by adults; whether during early and middle childhood children receive the major portion of their derived status from parents or peers; whether derived status continues as a significant source of self-esteem during adult life; and whether an ego-aggrandising type of primary status prevails (emphasis on personal prestige, hierarchical position, competitive advantage, etc.).

VALUES AND PITFALLS OF A CROSS-CULTURAL APPROACH

The most striking advantage of the cross-cultural approach to the study of personality is that only by this method is it possible to discover intercultural uniformities and differences in personality development as well as the determinants and processes underlying these uniformities and differences. This advantage does not accrue, of course, if the investigator is bound by the relativistic position that every culture is completely unique and a law unto itself, since he is prevented by *a priori* strictures from perceiving intercultural uniformities that exist at higher levels of abstraction and transcend specific differences in content and patterning. In fact until quite recently, the chief conclusion drawn by psychologists from the study of cross-cultural materials on adolescence was that there are no universal problems or principles of adolescent development, and that adolescence is largely a unique psychological problem reflective of the special complexities attending the achievement of adult status in Western civilisation.

An even more serious hazard associated with the anthropological approach to personality has been the tendency to attribute intercultural differences in adult personality structure to specific items of child rearing or childhood experience without taking other current, intervening or concomitantly operative cultural influences into account, and without holding other relevant variables constant. The widely accepted sex repression theory of adolescent emotional instability, for example, is often supported by an attempt to link the stressfulness of American adolescence to Victorian standards of sex conduct, and the alleged tranquillity of Samoan adolescence to virtually unrestricted access to premarital intercourse. Totally ignored in this argument,* for example, are the facts (a) that a similar situation of relatively low adolescent stress is associated with restrictive or non-promiscuous sex practices in other primitive cultures, (b) that stressfulness is still high for lower-class adolescents in the United States who by and large are no less sexually promiscuous than their Samoan counterparts, and (c) that in addition to differences in sex norms, American culture is characterised by greater prolongation of sub-adulthood, by a multiplicity of value systems and vocational alternatives, by a more rapid rate of social change, by a relatively long interval between marriage and the attainment of pubescent status, etc.

Thus, whereas the important methodological device of a control group or of "holding other relevant variables constant" is obviously unnecessary in purely descriptive ethnological research within a single isolated culture, it is essential either in testing postulated causal relationships between antecedent cultural conditions and consequent personality outcomes or in making cross-cultural comparisons.

CROSS-CULTURAL RESEARCH IN A SETTING OF ACCULTURATION

The problem of comparability of general cultural setting can be circumvented to some extent by making intercultural comparisons in a situation of acculturation or culture contact. Because of cultural overlap and common exposure to many cultural determinants within a single framework embracing both cultures, intercultural differences and their determinants can be identified with greater confidence that other relevant cultural variables are comparable than would otherwise be the case in cross-cultural research. In dealing with two independent and geographically separated cultures, on the other hand, the same cultural determinants do not overlap in their impact on the respective populations and can therefore be rendered comparable only with great arbitrariness.

A second great advantage of the acculturation approach is the frequent availability of a continuum of sub-populations representing different gradations of acculturation of the indigenous culture. This creates the possibility of relating *continuous* variability in a given determinant of personality to continuous variability in a given personality trait, and of avoiding the disadvantages of analysing

---

* This, of course, is a widespread misinterpretation of Margaret Mead's findings and conclusions in *Coming of Age in Samoa* (New York: Morrow, 1928).

relationships between a dichotomous cultural determinant, on the one hand, and dichotomous personality outcomes, on the other. The validity of extreme differences in personality outcomes between two discrete cultural groups, attributable to the operation of the extremes of a given personality variable, is obviously en-hanced if intermediate differences can be obtained in comparing groups that are less discrepant from each other.

Since situations of culture contact vary greatly from one another in terms of historical evolution, the major properties of the inter-acting cultures, current social, economic and political factors impinging on the interaction, and the inter-group attitudes of the populations involved, few over-all *a priori* generalisations can possibly have any validity. Without empirical investigation of the particular acculturation setting in question it is impossible, for example, to determine whether attachment to certain traditional ceremonial elements is simply symbolic of defiance and resent-ment of the dominant introduced culture (e.g., native "adjustment cults") but otherwise has little psychological viability in its own right, or is reflective of a vigorous, genuinely felt and currently functional identification with the traditional values and way of life.

The concept of an "acculturation continuum" is an indispensable and self-evident theoretical construct for culture contact studies. It only assumes (a) that personality changes in the indigenous culture (from pre- to post-contact stages or from earlier to later stages of contact) reflect in part the influence of cultural deter-minants emanating from the introduced culture; (b) that different groups and individuals are exposed to and adopt various features of the introduced culture in varying degrees; and hence (c) that differences in degree of acculturation are related to both differences in exposure to and familiarity with the introduced culture and to individual differences in temperament, personality and experience. It does not assume that the introduced culture is superior to, more desirable than, and passively accepted or totally uninfluenced by the indigenous culture. Neither does it assume that acculturation is an irreversible or unidimensional process or that parallelism in rate of acculturation occurs for all components of personality in a given individual. Thus, efflorescence of native values or practices may take place after they have already undergone considerable acculturation, and a particular individual can simultaneously occupy opposite ends of the continuum with respect to different dimensions.

The acculturation continuum construct is also consistent with the possibility that for the indigenous culture considered as a whole, different components of personality and behaviour may be characterised by marked differences in degree of acculturation. Among the Maori, for example, an appreciable amount of acculturation has occurred in such outward manifestations of culture as language, dress, religion, economic pursuits and recreation. In some parts of New Zealand, especially in urban areas, even many of the more tenacious residual components of traditional Maori life are being gradually abandoned. These include the Maori language; such Maori arts and crafts as wood carving, weaving, *taniko* work, and the *haka;* knowledge of genealogies and tribal history; the *tangi, hui,* and *hongi; tapu* restrictions; deference to elders; and lavish hospitality.[26, 27] Nevertheless there are many indications that the more immaterial expressions of Maoritanga are still quite vital and that relatively few Maoris have completely identified with the *Weltanschauung* of the pakeha.[8, 19, 26, 27, 34] In his characteristic aspirations for primary and derived status, his supportive personality traits, his attitudes toward children and sex, his organisation of interpersonal relations, his regard for kinship obligations, and his need for a personal and intimate type of psychological support from his fellows in everyday vocational activities, this modern Maori is still a very far cry from a coloured pakeha.

Methodological Precautions

Use of a Control Group. Although common exposure to many cultural determinants in an acculturational setting solves some of the problems of comparability in cross-cultural research, it also creates new methodological problems. First, just in describing the properties of the indigenous culture, quite apart from any intercultural comparisons, how is one to ascertain which characteristics are distinctive of it and which characteristics have simply been assimilated from the introduced culture in which it is embedded? Despite the technical difficulties involved and the virtual impossibility of employing it in many situations, the only convincing technique of identifying the unique properties of the indigenous culture that are currently functional is to use a matched control group composed of individuals drawn from the introduced culture. Thus, although one can safely employ the criterion of self-designation in choosing a population of Maori subjects, one cannot be sure that simply because these individuals regard themselves as Maoris they necessarily manifest traits that are characteristic of contemporaneous Maori society.

Secondly, it only rarely happens in a situation of culture contact that the distribution of the indigenous population in such categories as occupation, social class, urban-rural residence and I.Q. parallels the distribution of the European population in these same categories. Almost invariably the indigenous population is disproportionately concentrated in rural areas, in unskilled occupations, in lower social class groups and in the below average range of I.Q. scores. Hence in the absence of a control group it is very easy to confound a cluster of traits associated with rural residence, low I.Q., manual labour and low social class status with genuinely distinctive ethnic characteristics. This difficulty is further compounded by the investigator's quite understandable tendency to compare his description of the indigenous population with a mental image of "average" individuals in his own culture or often of the intellectually and economically above average persons in his own social milieu.

Finally, from a methodological standpoint, before one can confidently identify the personality change occurring in an acculturation setting, one must first have reliable knowledge of the introduced culture toward which the indigenous culture is moving as well as knowledge of successive serial stages of such movement. In practice this means that one cannot take the properties of the introduced culture for granted but must study it explicitly, and also include in the population of the indigenous group different segments varying in position on the *acculturation continuum.*

Sampling Considerations. The use of urban and rural populations permits the sampling of groups occupying different points along an acculturational gradient. Unfortunately, however, our sampling problems are much more complicated. "Typical" Maori communities, either rural or urban, simply do not exist. In addition to pronounced urban-rural differences, the pace of Maori acculturation—as well as the vocational and educational aspirations of Maori youth—can be expected to show much regional variability related to such factors as tribal history, extent of "detribalisation" of social structure, community social morale, religious affiliations, and effectiveness of leadership; the presence or absence of residual resentment from the so-called Maori Wars and the quality of contemporaneous race relations; the organisation of pakeha-type economic enterprises and the prevailing degree of economic prosperity and vocational opportunity; geographical isolation, the density and flow of Maori population, proximity to urban centres, and exposure to tourists; and the predominance of dispersed or nucleated settlement, the amount of Maori-owned land, and the recency of tribal settlement in the area.

All of this makes the problem of sampling and representativeness of population important if conclusions are to be drawn for the Maori people as a whole rather than for particular Maori communities. Before making general statements about Maori acculturation or about the aspirations of Maori youth, it would be necessary to study a number of Maori communities, at least a half-dozen, that were representative of the principal "general types throughout New Zealand."[9] Such a project, however, is obviously beyond the resources of a single investigator with only a year at his disposal.

RELEVANT FINDINGS ABOUT MAORI ADOLESCENCE FROM PRIOR RESEARCH

The following three sections (general characteristics, aspirational pattern and supportive traits) are based on the *Rakau* material of Ritchie[34] and Mulligan.[30] They describe adolescence in an isolated and relatively backward rural Maori community that suddenly became the centre of a large scale logging industry and the site of a newly constructed town, housing many newly arrived Maori and pakeha workers. Since much of this descriptive material is applicable in a general way to Maori adolescence in many rural areas, including the area selected for this study, it is abstracted in some detail. Ways in which this account does not apply to the unique conditions prevailing in the latter area are pointed out in later chapters.

General Characteristics

As the Maori boy enters pubescence, the adult community concerns itself more actively with his behaviour and imposes greater discipline and pressure to conform to adult standards. The free-roaming, undisciplined period of the middle years (during which time the peer group is virtually independent of adult control) is brought to a close. The adolescent perceives the peer group as less dependable and less capable than formerly of satisfying his needs for security and status. Accordingly, quite unlike the situation in pakeha culture, which is characterised by rather abrupt emancipation from parents, rapprochement with home and family takes place, emotional ties to parents are strengthened, and identification with peers becomes more superficial.

A short transitional period of one to two years follows in which the adolescent shifts his group and value identifications and learns the new role of young adult. It is undoubtedly a period of marginality, disorientation and anxiety, but compared to the long interim period of pakeha subadulthood it is relatively short and untraumatic. It is characterised by varying degrees of shyness, loss of poise, sullenness, moroseness, intractibility, and withdrawal behaviour.

After this brief transitional interlude, the adolescent acquires the status of junior male adult enjoyed by the majority of unmarried (or even married) men under the age of twenty-five, and regains his poise and sociability. He has limited family and community responsibilities, pursues a somewhat indefinite and unsettled vocational course punctuated by frequent periods of idleness and change of employment, and participates in beer parties, rapidly shifting fads, and a relatively casual, direct and socially uncontrolled type of sex experience. The status of junior adulthood, however, is definitely linked with the main stream of activities and concerns in the adult community and is in no sense comparable to the peripheral, sub-adult, peer group status enjoyed by pakeha teenagers.

Aspirational Pattern

Among the Maori, the importance of *derived status* is not de-emphasised to the same extent during and after adolescence as is customary in Western civilisation. Adolescents and adults continue to obtain a substantial portion of their self-esteem from a broad-based system of mutual psychological support, emotional interdependence, and reciprocal obligations. Simply by virtue of the intrinsic acceptance they are accorded for their personal qualities, their group membership, their genealogical position in a kinship structure, their wholehearted participation in an interlocking network of highly personal obligations and relationships, and their conformity to the basic norms of the group, they enjoy a reassuring sense of personal adequacy that is quite independent of their competence and performance ability.

This continued emphasis on derived status throughout the lifetime of the individual is a surviving heritage of pre-pakeha Maori culture and is characteristic of most primitive societies with highly developed kinship systems. In modern times, however, because of the declining importance of tribal organisation and the extended family group, and because of fewer opportunities for differentiated role playing in communal activities, the base of derived status is somewhat narrower, hereditary status counts for less, and the range of personal qualities and relationships (on which group acceptance of the individual is predicated) is less varied and particularised. On the other hand, because of disorganisation in traditional patterns of acquiring primary status and because of marginality, disorientation and anxiety associated with acculturation tensions, dependence on psychological support and direction from the group has increased. Hence, derived status has tended to become an even more significant source of the modern Maori's fund of self-esteem, while concomitantly, freedom for the development of individual autonomy and the expression of individual personality differences has tended to decline in the face of the group's increasing power to exact conformity from the individual.

Aspirations for *primary status* increase during adolescence but the predominant pattern is one of relatively low achievement motivation.[8, 30, 34] The ancient Maori emphasis on craftsmanship and individual accomplishment as important sources of adult status in the community[14, 17] appears to be negatively sanctioned in Rakau now that the channels and socio-economic organisation through which such status was formerly attained are no longer functional. Pakeha channels for achieving primary status, the self-aggrandising features of pakeha primary status (e.g., personal ambition, drive for success, prestige and power), and the supportive traits necessary for achieving this status are actively rejected as alien to the Maori value system, as personally uncongenial, and as threatening to group cohesiveness and the individual's need for group psychological support. Some of this negative valence has probably even carried over to the more task-oriented type of primary status that is traditionally Maori. But the traditional group orientation to primary status (although attenuated in its more

active, group enhancing aspects) remains: regard for kinship
obligations, co-operative sharing of many economic burdens and
vicissitudes, emphasis on personal-social goals in economic enterprise, and aversion to solitary work or work in an unfamiliar,
impersonal context. To compensate for the declining significance
of primary status in the economy of ego-organisation, the relative
importance of derived status has increased.

Most boys at 16 or 17 are prepared to seek employment locally
in unskilled forestry occupations, but do not contemplate marriage
until the age of 25 or 26. They prefer the immediate security of
such local employment to the adventure and less certain outcome
of more ambitious vocational ventures outside the district. Their
expressed vocational aspirations, however, are misleading since
they almost invariably name totally unrealistic occupations (e.g.,
medicine, engineering, mechanic) which most of them have no
genuine intention of ever pursuing and in fact never do.

Supportive Traits

Consistent with the Maori adolescent's low aspirations for
primary status are such supportive traits as (a) low frustration
tolerance and goal tenacity;[30, 34] (b) distractibility and lack of
perseverance;[34] (c) preoccupation with immediate hedonistic
gratification, lack of volitional independence, unwillingness to plan
for remote, difficult, and long-range goals,[8, 34] and disinclination
for prolonged vocational preparation;[8, 25, 34] and (d) paucity of
initiative, foresight, executive independence, responsibility, thrift,
punctuality, and methodicalness.[8, 34] He is typically perceived by
pakehas as shiftless, slipshod, careless, improvident, easygoing, and
casual.[8, 25, 34] His low level of achievement motivation makes for
relatively little ego-involvement in and superficial relatedness to
problems of adaptation. Rather than face up to and come to grips
with difficulty, stress and conflict in the environment, he prefers
to constrict his perceptual and behavioural fields, to ignore the
existence of troublesome problems, and to withdraw from threatening situations;[34] his withdrawal, however, is characterised by direct
hedonistic gratification in reality—not by flight into fantasy or by
symbolical mediation of experience.[34] Because he is not highly
motivated by the self-aggrandising aspects of primary status, he
manifests little competitiveness, acquisitiveness, compulsive need

to work, or anxiety concerning prestigeful achievement.

Another cluster of supportive personality traits follows from his high valuation of derived status and his group orientation to primary status: helpfulness, generosity, hospitality, enjoyment of sociability, and fear of loneliness and separation from the group.[8, 34] His exaggerated dependence on the group for derived status makes him hypersensitive to the threat of group disapproval and rejection and disposes him to over-conform to group direction and to surrender his volitional and ideational autonomy.[34] Anxiety regarding the dreaded withdrawal of group support favours the cultivation of a jovial, outgoing and inoffensive personality and leads to over-controlled, overvigilant, stereotyped and ultra-safe behaviour.[34] Whatever feelings of hostility he entertains must obviously be directed outside the group.[34]

The Urban Maori Adolescent*

Many plausible reasons exist for postulating that the aspirational patterns of urban adolescent Maoris are closer to the middle-class pakeha norm than are those of Maori adolescents in rural areas First is the matter of selective migration to the city of persons who have absorbed the achieving pattern of social mobility and who are seeking educational and vocational skills in order to qualify for more ambitious, higher status, pakeha-type jobs. Second, long-standing urban dwellers are probably more acculturated in terms of their aspirational patterns than are rural Maoris and thus are more likely to transmit such patterns to their children. Third, as pointed out above, many of the external manifestations of Maoritanga, and even traditional canons of hospitality, are necessarily attenuated in the city. Fourth, children and adolescents have less opportunity for obtaining derived status from their peers in an urban setting (due to dispersion of the Maori population), and hence are more dependent on primary status for their self-esteem. Furthermore, because of this restricted contact

---

*This description of urban Maori adolescence is based on Metge's Auckland material.[26, 27] In our smaller urban centres (see Chapter II), adjacent Maori families were more often members of the same extended family group, *hapu* or tribe, were dispersed over a smaller urban area, were less distantly removed from their home district, and were more frequently engaged in agricultural occupations. Many of our urban subjects also lived in small nucleated settlements outside the city.

with other Maori children, as well as with Maori elders, they are less extensively exposed to traditional Maori values. Lastly, the authority of elders and the force of public opinion are weaker in the city. Thus, there is less pressure to conform to traditional ways of life and greater freedom to adopt pakeha values. Many young persons, therefore, tend to repudiate the Maori cultural pattern as incompatible with modern life.

Nevertheless, considerable diversity of urban aspirational patterns may be anticipated on the basis of the varied reasons Maoris have for migrating to the city. The city not only attracts earnest young people with serious vocational goals but also loafers and drifters; youth in search of pleasure, excitement, or high wages for rough, unskilled labour; and rural workers and would-be farmers discouraged by lack of steady employment, land and capital in their home districts. Furthermore, as already indicated above, many signs point to the conclusion that urban Maoris have not yet been completely integrated into city life and have not yet abandoned their central core of traditional values. Their social contacts with the pakeha majority are very limited and are largely restricted to lower-class elements. Many trained and educated Maoris still prefer unskilled gang work to the skilled trades or white collar jobs for which they are qualified in order that they may work in the more congenial personal-social context of their own people.

HYPOTHESES

General theoretical considerations and analysis of the relevant literature on pre-pakeha as well as modern Maori culture led to the formulation of the following hypotheses as a means of structuring the scope, design and theoretical substrate of this study:

1. Pakeha secondary school pupils would express higher academic and vocational aspirations than Maori secondary school pupils, and would be more highly motivated by prestige factors but less highly motivated by task-oriented and group welfare factors.

2. Pakeha pupils would manifest to a greater degree those personality traits important for implementing high achievement goals, and would perceive greater family and peer group pressures as well as greater opportunity for such achievement.

3. Although the direction of Maori-pakeha differences would be similar, the differences would be more conspicuous in the urban than in the rural sample. (Despite being more highly acculturated than rural Maoris, urban Maoris have not yet assimilated the urban pakeha pattern as completely as rural Maoris have assimilated the rural pakeha pattern.)

4. Urban-rural differences would be in the same direction as hypothesised pakeha-Maori differences. That is, urban Maoris would differ from rural Maoris in much the same ways that pakehas generally differ from Maoris, and rural pakehas would be closer than urban pakehas to the Maori pattern.

5. Urban-rural differences, although similar in direction for both samples, would be less marked in the Maori than in the pakeha sample because of relatively less complete assimilation of the urban pattern by the Maori group.

6. Intercultural (Maori-pakeha) differences would be greater than interlocational (urban-rural) differences.

RESEARCH DESIGN

The general plan was to utilise a rural and an urban group of Maori adolescents and comparable groups of pakeha adolescents from the same localities. Partly because of the advantage of ready accessibility to subjects, and partly because one focus of inquiry was on academic aspirations, only young adolescents attending school were studied.

In order to keep the research project within the limits of available time and resources, the sex variable was eliminated. Previous research had shown that the aspirational patterns of adolescent boys and girls are markedly different from each other;[6, 23] and since more significant and discontinuous aspirational changes occur in boys during the adolescent period, the population of this study was restricted to male adolescents.

Maori and pakeha subjects in each sample (urban and rural) were drawn from the same secondary school and were matched individually on the basis of form, course, stream (ability group), and father's occupation. The number of Maori and pakeha subjects in each locational setting (classified by form), as well as their mean age and score on the Otis Group Test of Intelligence are shown in Table I. IQ was not used for matching purposes since this variable had been taken into consideration in the pupil's assignment to a particular stream. Rematching of urban and rural subjects in both the Maori and pakeha samples was necessary, of course, before urban-rural comparisons could be made (see Appendix III).

TABLE I
FORM, AGE, AND I.Q. OF SUBJECTS

| | Number of Pupils | | | |
| Form Age and I.Q. | Urban Sample | | Rural Sample | |
	Maori	Pakeha	Maori	Pakeha
3rd Form	31	31	21	21
4th Form	14	14	14	14
5th Form	3	3	15	15
Total Pupils	48	48	50	50
Mean Age (years-months)	15–1	14–7	15–5	15–0
Otis I.Q.	90.3	94.3	84.9	92.8

Sufficient time was not available for studying secondary school pupils in more than one urban or rural district. Thus, because of this limitation in the range and representativeness of the research sample, conclusions applicable to Maori adolescent boys as a whole and conclusions regarding the total range of Maori acculturation in this area of inquiry are not warranted.

Research Methods

Generally speaking, two principal kinds of evidence were gathered to test the hypotheses set forth above: (a) quantitative data consisting of pupils' replies to structured interview questions and their test scores on objectively measurable personality traits; and (b) qualitative, descriptive data based on systematic and extended participant observation and informal interviews. The methods associated with the first type of evidence are considerably more technical and are of less general interest than those associated with the second type of evidence. For the benefit of the more general reader, therefore, only the latter methods are considered below; formal description of the quantitative methods will be deferred until later (see Appendix I). The professional reader, however, might prefer to turn to the description of the structured interview and of the personality tests and rating scales before proceeding with Chapter II.

The methods of participant observation and informal interview are indispensable in most types of ethnological or sociological research in which it is important to ascertain various aspects of social structure, different kinds of role behaviour, the flavour of interpersonal and intergroup relationships, and the more implicit attitudes, beliefs and practices of a particular community. Access to such data and insight into their meaning can only be gained by living in the community under observation, by participating in community life, and by interacting and conversing with the inhabitants in a wide variety of formal and informal situations.

This is particularly true if one studies an alien culture markedly different from one's own, works with adults rather than children, and is interested in attitudes or practices dealing with sensitive or delicate issues. Under these conditions structured interview questions typically evoke withdrawal or resistiveness. Furthermore, in order to obtain valid replies to such inquiries, one must not only put them informally and unobtrusively, but must first establish adequate personal rapport and overcome formidable barriers of reserve and suspicion erected against any outsider, and particularly an inquisitive representative of a different culture. These latter tasks obviously require considerable time and patience, since they presuppose punctilious observance of social protocol as well as sufficient personal contact under favourable auspices for the development of mutual trust and confidence. All of these considerations (in addition to language difficulties and natural limitations of time) dispose the investigator to cultivate a relatively small number of intimate relationships with intelligent, articulate and strategically placed informants in preference to a larger number of more superficial reationships with less articulate and less well-informed representatives of the culture he is studying.

Since this particular investigation was not a global study of Maori personality, social structure, or interpersonal relationships, but focussed on a restricted aspect of Maori adolescent development, the methods of participant observation and informal interview were less central than in most community studies. They were primarily employed for two purposes: (a) to obtain supplementary data about the origins and implementation of academic and vocational aspirations, and their transmission from one generation to the next (e.g., community morale and leadership, cultural attitudes towards work and achievement, race relations, employment opportunities and practices), that could not be readily obtained through structured interviews or objective measures of personality traits; and (b) to furnish background material of general cultural and regional significance that would make possible the placing of the more quantitative findings in their proper cultural context, and hence facilitate their interpretation.

General Considerations. Maoris are generally very jealous of their cultural privacy, and do not actively encourage efforts made to study their community life and affairs. They keenly resent investigators who collect data for strictly theoretical purposes, without having any intrinsic interest either in Maori culture or in the welfare of the Maori people. Their attitudes toward ethnological research have also been rendered considerably less favourable as a consequence of negative experience both with a spate of superficial, redundant and seemingly purposeless Government "surveys", and with the efforts of certain self-appointed pakeha reformers who assertedly know precisely what is best for the Maori people without even bothering to ask them. If a pakeha research worker, on the other hand, demonstrates that he is "genuinely interested in Maori culture and in Maoris as people, if he manifests genuine humility and does not try to impose his views on them, and if his project has clearly defined, down-to-earth objectives that they can understand, he will receive ample and cordial co-operation, provided that he follows a few simple commonsense rules consonant with the Maori way of life."[5]

The investigator must first be prepared to take plenty of time and to exercise more than the usual amount of patience. If his Maori informants once get the idea that he is impatient or is trying to hurry them, he cannot hope to obtain valid answers to any of his inquiries. They will not, in any case, reveal authentic or significant information until they have had sufficient opportunity to judge his motives and sincerity and are convinced that he is a person to be trusted. Secondly, the investigator must be careful to observe Maori social protocol and to work through recognised social channels. It is important, for example, first to seek out the tribal elders and to be formally welcomed by the community on the *marae* (or introduced at a *tangi, hui,* wedding, or tribal committee meeting), *before* making contact with particular individuals or families. The traditional *marae* welcome with its flowery personal tributes and lofty metaphorical allusions, however, must not be interpreted as indicative of complete or unquestioning acceptance. These oratorical flourishes are merely the customary kinds of formal utterances considered appropriate for such occasions; and by making them, the Maori neither accepts the stranger into his in-group nor engages in deliberate insincerity. He is simply complying with traditional ceremonial decorum.

A third important consideration is the matter of entrée. Only a pakeha with extraordinary social gifts could enter a Maori community unannounced and as a complete stranger and hope to be accepted within a reasonable period of time. Hence it is practically essential to secure appropriate introductions to well-known individuals of status in the local area. In this way trust is generated indirectly by contagion: the people trust the investigator because they have confidence in and respect the judgment both of the outside persons who provided the introductions and of their own leaders.[5]

In first reacting to an American investigator, the individual Maori quite naturally tends to transfer to him his general attitude towards the pakeha; this attitude

is a mixture of shyness and guarded friendliness. The Maori feels both unsure of himself and uncertain of how pakehas will respond to him. Hence he is extremely cautious about entering into intimate social relations with them, e.g., about visiting or eating at their homes or inviting them to his. . .

Superimposed upon this individual shyness is a generalised cultural attitude of suspiciousness towards all out-group members, particularly towards pakehas whom he has good reason to distrust on the basis of sad historical experience. He is prepared to be friendly if the circumstances warrant friendliness, but he refuses to commit himself until he feels quite certain that a particular pakeha can be trusted. This decision takes some time, but when it comes there is a sudden change in his demeanour if it is positive: his reserve melts away and he abruptly stops trying to figure out what your "angle" is. . . .

If, on the other hand, he decides that you are not to be trusted, he tells you in a very courteous and respectful manner exactly what he thinks you want to hear. He does this so convincingly that inexperienced, insensitive or unsuspecting pakehas are easily led astray. The Maori is a past master at this cultural type of "leg pulling". . . .

[Thus] it is important for the investigator not to attach too much importance to a certain abruptness of manner, almost suggestive of sullenness, which he commonly encounters when meeting Maoris for the first time. This is primarily a defensive reaction to cover suspiciousness and feelings of inadequacy, and to ward off questions that might possibly infringe on his privacy; most of it is usually gone by the second meeting.[5]

Language constituted less of a problem than in most cross-cultural studies. English was generally adequate in most instances for ordinary purposes of communication. But although fluent knowledge of the Maori language was by no means indispensable, it certainly would have been helpful, both for establishing greater intimacy of rapport and for communicating subtleties of thought. It must be remembered, of course, that some Maori elders speak little or no English, and that a fair number of middle-aged Maoris have only a crude, functional grasp of the language, which is insufficient for expressing or understanding abstract ideas of any complexity.

Even my very limited command of the Maori language—which consisted of the commonly used colloquialisms in everyday speech and the ceremonial responses that were appropriate when formally introduced to a Maori community on the *marae,* in the meeting house, or at a *tangi,* wedding, *hui,* or birthday party—proved to be a tremendous research asset. It invariably provoked much favourable comment and was greatly appreciated, largely because it offered such an unexpected contrast to the usual practice of translating the remarks of pakeha visitors. As a result of the good-will and excellent group rapport built up in this way, it was much easier to overcome reserve and establish rapport on an individual basis.

Interview and Observational Procedures. The general aim in conducting informal interviews was to conduct them so informally that the persons involved would not realise that they were being interviewed. No leading questions were asked and no written notes were taken. To ensure reasonably uniformity of coverage on a given topic, a check list of questions was memorised, and the latter were injected into the conversation at appropriate moments. The substance of informants' replies was committed to memory with the aid of various mnemonic devices, and then transcribed in private, as fully as possible, at the first opportunity—usually during the same day.

Informants were chosen on the basis of accessibility, articulateness, and familiarity with Maori community life and problems. My pakeha informants, for example, included persons of bi-cultural background (by virtue of inter-marriage or knowledge of both languages), and individuals whose work brought them into intimate contact with Maoris (e.g., public health nurses, visiting teachers, clergymen, employers, vocational guidance officers, agricultural supervisors of land development schemes). In addition to the parents of secondary school pupils, my most valuable Maori informants included Maori Welfare Officers, tribal elders, clergymen, teachers, wardens, and members of tribal committees and executives.

The range of topics covered by interviews was very wide and necessarily varied from one type of informant to another. Among the more frequently discussed topics were attitudes towards and issues relating to work, vocational achievement, child rearing, school, government assistance, "urban drift", boy-girl relations, delinquency, truancy, thrift, and Maori cultural survival. A careful distinction was made in all instances between informants' opinions or attitudes, on the one hand, and knowledge based on their own first-hand experience, on the other. No credence was given to hearsay evidence, and wherever possible, data furnished by one informant were cross-checked against corresponding data furnished by another.

Numerous occasions for participant observation were found in the home, *pa,* and school environments, and in the course of attending such community functions as *huis, tangis,* weddings, birthday celebrations, youth club concerts, sports events, and tribal committee and executive meetings. It was possible, for example, to make observations on such matters as housing, sanitation, community morale, hospitality, leadership, parent-child relationships, infant care, child rearing practices, teenage activities, drinking and spending behaviour, etc.

Because of its crucial significance for the academic and vocational achievement of Maori youth, special attention was paid to the problem of race relations. The racial attitudes of a broad sample of both Maori and pakeha adults in a large variety of North Island districts were ascertained by informal interview; and information about various inter-racial practices (e.g., apprenticeship, employment, housing, hotel accommodation) was obtained by interviewing pakeha landlords, employers, teachers, hotel proprietors, and shopkeepers. The authenticity of the latter information was checked against local data on Maori apprenticeships, employment, housing, and membership in civic and fraternal organisations. Numerous opportunities for observing Maori-pakeha interaction also existed in the school setting and in bars, restaurants, dance halls, cinemas, parks, and other public places.

Pakeha informants married to Maoris, proved to be unusually good sources of information about race relations, since they were in an exceptionally strategic position to observe anti-Maori attitudes and practices, Maori attitudes towards pakehas, and Maori reactions to colour prejudice.

Reporting of Material. Descriptive material and evaluative statements based on informal interview and participant observation are reported in general terms. Specific anecdotes and verbatim accounts of conversations are not provided, and no reference whatsoever is made to the behaviour, attitudes or opinions of particular individuals. Such generalisations as are made reflect unambiguous or overwhelming trends in the direction of the evidence.

Two principal reasons underlie this reporting policy. First, it is absolutely essential to protect the identity of my informants and to offer no clues, no matter how trivial or indirect, that might make them recognisable. Secondly, since these data are primarily meant to supplement and serve as interpretive background for the more quantitative evidence, the use of considerable space for the selective citation of specific anecdotal and interview material hardly seems defensible. It should also be borne in mind that although such material has considerable didactic value and undoubtedly enhances readability, it *illustrates* rather than proves the generalisations to which it refers.

The reader can easily distinguish in the text between those descriptive or evaluative statements based on participant observation and informal interview, on the one hand, and comparable statements based on the administration of personality tests and structured interviews to pupils, on the other. In addition to such differentiating factors as the age of subjects and the nature of the data (e.g., race relations, employment practices and community morale as against pupils' vocational aspirations, achievement motivation and scholastic competitiveness), the latter statements typically refer to the quantitative instruments used, and are further qualified in the Appendices by tests of statistical significance. Where data other than the author's original research material are utilised, i.e., census data, official Government documents, historical and ethnological evidence from the literature, the source is always acknowledged. Both the use of these supplementary materials and, in certain instances (e.g., race relations), the extension of the participant observation and informal interview methods to other North Island areas than the one urban and one rural district intensively studied in this investigation, add national and historical perspective to the data.

Validity. To what extent do the participant observation and informal interview materials accurately mirror prevailing attitudes and behaviour in the communities under investigation? Obviously, limitations regarding validity stemming from such methodological shortcomings as variability in content and sequence of interview questions, absence of any check on observer reliability, and difficulty in subjecting largely non-quantitative data to the usual kinds of statistical treatment, cannot be ignored. My informants, furthermore, who were explicitly chosen on the basis of accessibility, articulateness, and knowledge of the local setting, can hardly be considered a representative sample of even the particular Maori communities I was studying. In terms of the *kinds* of information desired, however, more structured, representative and quantifiable data (e.g., of the Gallup Poll variety) would have yielded much less valid albeit statistically more impressive findings.* It was also possible, as already pointed out, to enhance the validity of the data somewhat by cross-checking informants both against each other and against actual observations, by rejecting all second-hand or hearsay evidence, and by avoiding generalisations in instances where the evidence was ambiguous or contradictory. Nevertheless, I would still have hesitated to employ participant observation and informal interview methods as the sole sources of evidence in studying various aspects of Maori adolescent development. In the present study these methods were primarily used to supplement and interpret more rigorous data of a quantitative nature.

---

* It would be possible, of course, to use the methods of participant observation and informal interview, and still control adequately such factors as observer reliability, representativeness of sample, and statistical treatment of data, if one had a large team of investigators at one's disposal over a period of years, and were prepared to subject all observation and interview records to exhaustive content analysis.

CHAPTER TWO

The Local Settings

BECAUSE SO MUCH REGIONAL VARIABILITY PREVAILS IN THE pattern of Maori acculturation—in accordance with the particular kinds of historical, social, economic, and community factors that are operative in a given local district—it is incumbent upon any investigator to delineate the distinctive characteristics of the locality in which his study is conducted. But since this investigation does not purport to be either an intensive or global ethnographic study of a particular community, only a brief description of the more salient of these characteristics relevant to the problem of adolescent academic and vocational aspirations will be attempted.

In selecting urban and rural samples, there was, of course, in theory a very large number of communities from which appropriate choices could be made. Actually, however, the chief methodological requirement of the study—the availability in each setting of at least fifty Maori secondary school boys and a matched pakeha group, all attending the same school—restricted the choices to a virtual handful of possibilities. The urban sample had to be selected from a large provincial centre, since in one of the principal urban centres of the North Island (Wellington-Hutt) there were relatively few adolescent Maoris of school age, whereas in the other principal centre (Auckland) the population of adolescent Maori pupils was scattered among many different schools. In rural areas, on the other hand, the difficulty was in finding a secondary school with a sufficiently large number of Maori pupils that also (unlike the private, church sponsored Maori secondary schools or the Maori district high schools) enrolled appreciable numbers of pakeha pupils.

THE URBAN SETTING

The city, a major North Island urban centre, is situated on the west coast of the Wellington Provincial District astride one of

New Zealand's principal navigable rivers. Surrounding the city are considerable tracts of pastoral land, but the river valley itself, to the northeast, is narrow and heavily forested. It is an important mercantile, shopping and transportation centre for the regional countryside, and also contains a large number of industrial establishments (meat freezing works, woollen mills, steel and pipe works, fertilizer works, railway workshops) as well as numerous regional offices of various Government departments.

For a long time the city was New Zealand's fifth largest centre, but more recently it has failed to keep pace with such rapidly growing urban areas as Hamilton and Palmerston North. Its population of roughly thirty-two thousand has been relatively stable over the past 30 years.[15] Expansion has been hampered by its proximity to the capital city and by the lack of a broad fertile outlying area. During the depression of the middle 1930s the population actually decreased, and the city suffered a serious decline in commercial and industrial activity which was first halted by World War II.

The Maori population of the city, currently about eleven hundred (or 3.3 per cent of the total) has increased markedly since the pre-war period, but the percentage rate of increase between 1951 and 1956 has been less than half as great as during the preceding intercensal period of 1945 to 1951.[13] The general pattern of Maori population change in this area has been a gradual movement from the surrounding countryside and river valley into the city, the natural increase being absorbed locally with very "little migration out of or into the district".[13]

Residence of Pupils

Of the 48 Maori pupils in our urban secondary school sample, 19 were drawn from the city proper, eight lived in dispersed dwellings in the surrounding rural area, and 21 resided in nucleated Maori settlements *(pas)* within a radius of 12 miles from the city. The latter number included three boys from a *pa* at the outskirts of the city; ten boys from a *pa* 12 miles south of the city; two boys each from two settlements seven and ten miles northwest of the city respectively; and two boys each from two settlements in the river valley.

Thirty two of the 48 pakeha subjects were residents of the city and 16 lived in the outlying rural area. Thus, although all of the subjects, both Maori and pakeha, attended the same urban secondary school and lived in close proximity to the city, a greater percentage of the pakeha boys resided directly within the urban environment.

Occupations of Pupils' Fathers

The occupations of pupils' fathers in our urban and rural samples are shown in Table II. It must be remembered, however,

TABLE II

OCCUPATIONS OF SUBJECTS' FATHERS IN URBAN AND RURAL SAMPLES

Occupation					Urban Sample	Rural Sample
Professional	----	----	----	----	----	0	1
White Collar, Commercial		----	----	----	3	0
Skilled Trades	----	----	----	----	----	7	4
Shop Foremen	----	----	----	----	----	2	1
Unskilled Labour (total)		----	----	----	(16)	(17)
Railway	----	----	----	----	----	6	0
Public Works	----	----	----	----	----	2	3
Freezing Works	----	----	----	----	4	0
Truck Driver	----	----	----	----	----	2	5
Mill Hand	----	----	----	----	----	0	2
Wharf	----	----	----	----	----	0	2
Miscellaneous	----	----	----	----	----	2	5
Agricultural (total)	----	----	----	----	(20)	(27)
Farmer	----	----	----	----	----	10	21
Agricultural Contractor		----	----	----	3	3
Farm Labourer	----	----	----	----	7	1
Drover	----	----	----	----	----	0	2
TOTAL	----	----	----	----	----	48	50

Note: *The figures shown for each sample apply to both Maori and pakeha groups within the sample.*

that since paternal occupation was one of the criteria for matching Maori and pakeha subjects, this distribution of fathers' occupations (deliberately held constant for Maori and pakeha subjects in each of our settings) is *not* representative of the actual distribution of occupations of either cultural group in either locality. In both of these districts, as is true of the national vocational scene generally, Maoris (compared to pakehas) are over-represented in unskilled manual and agricultural labouring occupations, particularly of a seasonal nature, and are under-represented in professional, commercial, clerical and managerial occupations, in the skilled trades, and in farm ownership.

Urban-rural differences for our sample shown in Table II—the greater number of urban fathers engaged in white collar occupations, farm labour and the skilled trades, and the greater number of rural fathers operating their own farms—are approximately reflective of actual urban-rural differences prevailing in these two districts.

Tribal Organisation and Social Life

The Maori tribes in this district customarily use a collective tribal name in referring to themselves, and are also known and referred to by Maoris in other parts of New Zealand under the name of the river and river valley in which they dwell. They trace their ancestry both to pre-Fleet Polynesian settlers and to the crews of the Fleet canoes of *Aotea* and *Kurahaupo*. For the most part they were content in pre-pakeha days to remain within the river valley, to protect their rich resources of fish and fowl from inland tribes, and to prevent the latter from using the river to reach the Tasman Sea. Thus, having little contact and practising little intermarriage with other Maori tribes, they remained relatively circumscribed both in territory and outlook. This parochial, isolationist and backward attitude is still quite evident today among the people who reside in the river valley.

With the advent of the pakeha, the area became one of the earliest foci of missionary activity in New Zealand and one of the first sites selected for permanent European settlement. Incompetent negotiation on the part of the agent of the New Zealand Company coupled with resistance on the part of the Maoris to parting with their land, however, led to chronic inter-racial conflict, punctuated by occasional armed skirmishes, during the first decade of Maori-pakeha contact.[29] The city was garrisoned for many years by British troops. In the Taranaki phase of the so-called Maori Wars, the local Maoris joined forces with pakeha troops in order to settle an old score with their traditional Taranaki foes. Hence, although huge tracts of Taranaki land were confiscated following the war, none of the Maori land in the district met a similar fate.

Apart from some family visiting, Maoris living within the city proper practise little or none of the traditional Maori community life. Even the *tangi* is fast dying out. In the *pas,* an attentuated form of Maori social life is still current, but it is only a pale shadow of the intensive community activity formerly centred around the *marae*. In addition to church affairs and occasional meetings at which tribal matters are discussed, most social life consists of informal gatherings and parties quite indistinguishable from their pakeha counterparts. A Maori youth club is active in

the old, well-established *pa* on the outskirts of the city and gives
frequent concerts featuring the *haka, poi,* and other action songs
in traditional Maori attire (*piupiu, taniko* bodice, and headband).
A great deal of heavy drinking among both men and women goes
on at the local pubs and in private homes.

Another distinctive feature of this area—in addition to the
relative backwardness and isolationist outlook of the Maoris living
in the river valley and more recently migrating to the city—is the
presence of a *pa* inhabited by the adherents of one of the modern
Maori churches, twelve miles to the south of the city. The people
originally came from all parts of New Zealand, disposing of their
homes and property in order to live in proximity to the founder of
the Church and among their fellow-believers. In the beginning,
the community was held together by common bonds of strong
cultist faith and by the dynamic personality of the founder. With
the death of the latter about twenty years ago, and the consequent
decline in the strength of the movement, the community has undergone progressive social demoralisation. Lacking ties of tribal
kinship, the only thing the people have in common is a rapidly
dying faith in the esoteric doctrines of the Church and a strong
interest in national Maori politics. It is a community almost totally
devoid of cohesiveness, social morale, effective leadership and
willingness to help itself. An atmosphere of apathy, purposelessness
and hedonistic irresponsibility prevails. Alcoholism, sexual promiscuity and "bodgieism" (adolescent cultism) are rife. Community projects are invariably doomed to failure because of
constant bickering, petty intrigue and inter-tribal rivalries. The
people are uninterested in progress, unwilling to assume any res-
ponsibilty for civic betterment, resistive to constructive suggestion
and generally suspicious of pakeha motives and institutions.

Religious Affiliations

As in most other areas of New Zealand, the Maoris in this district tend to be neither very doctrinaire nor very intolerant about
religious matters. According to local tradition, when the first
missionaries arrived on the scene, the chiefs, having decided to
embrace Christianity, and perceiving little difference between the
Anglican and Roman Catholic faiths, simply queued up the people
and assigned them alternately to one of the two Churches.
Approximately 40 years ago a modern Maori church entered the
field; and more recently the Mormon Church has, with indifferent

success, made a bid for local Maori membership. Although church functions are ordinarily supported by most Maoris irrespective of religious affiliation, Catholics and Anglicans typically exhibit greater tolerance towards each other than towards members of either of the two newer churches. The religious affiliations of pupils in our urban sample are shown in Table III. Maori affiliation exceeds pakeha in the Catholic, Mormon and Maori Churches,

TABLE III

*RELIGIOUS AFFILIATIONS OF SUBJECTS
IN URBAN AND RURAL SAMPLES*

	Urban Sample		Rural Sample	
Religion	Maori	Pakeha	Maori	Pakeha
Anglican	15	12	21	14
Roman Catholic	8	1	12	11
Presbyterian	2	20	4	17
Methodist	1	4	0	6
Baptist	0	2	0	0
Mormon	3	0	0	0
Minor Protestant Sects	1	6	0	2
Ratana	17	0	0	0
Ringatu	0	0	12	0
(Doesn't know)	0	2	1	0
TOTAL	47	47	50	50

whereas the reverse is true of all the other Protestant sects with the exception of the Anglican.

The founder of the Maori church gathered about him many Maoris who experienced difficulties of one kind or another in adjusting to pakeha culture. Unlike the Young Maori Party,* he recruited his followers from among the rank-and-file of the people, particularly among those with relatively little education. He stressed the importance of preserving the identity of the Maori people and sought to unite them under a supra-tribal banner, but inveighed against such traditional aspects of Maori culture as *tapu, tohungaism,* and the veneration of ancient heirlooms. His teachings were permeated by a strong undercurrent of suspicion of pakeha education, medicine and sanitation. At first he only practised faith healing, prophecy and revelation, but later founded his own church, superimposing on the doctrine of the Trinity the

---

* A group of young Maori intellectuals who achieved political prominence and considerable social reform during the first half of the twentieth century.

dogma of "a band of faithful angels" and the "Mouthpiece of God" (namely, himself). The Maori church exhibits many cultist features such as a nondescript mosque-like "temple" built by voluntary labour and covered with various esoteric astronomical symbols; various orders of clergy attired in brightly hued robes; a brass band; and two special days commemorating respectively the founder's birthday and his divine investiture with healing powers. The service is conducted in Maori but hardly anyone pays attention to it or assumes a reverent attitude; the droning monotone of the minister can scarcely be heard above the crying of infants, the brawling of older children, and the loud conversation and occasional snores of the adult worshippers. Recently many of the devout have reported seeing "visions" of the founder sitting in his great chair on the pulpit.

Housing

The overall standard of Maori housing in the district is comparable to the general standard of Maori housing in New Zealand. Only relatively few families—those fortunate enough to have obtained a Maori Affairs Department housing loan—live in homes that could be described as reasonably satisfactory or on a par with homes occupied by Europeans in similar economic circumstances. Maoris living in the city find it virtually impossible, because of strong pakeha prejudice, to rent a desirable house in a good neighbourhood, and are thus confined to more or less dilapidated structures, badly in need of painting and repairs, in the slummiest parts of town. Because families tend to be large, even the better homes are dreadfully overcrowded.

In the *pas,* however, housing conditions are considerably worse since roads, toilets and inside washing facilities are frequently lacking. Apart from the new State-financed houses, most dwellings are little better than tumble-down shacks or hovels, unhygienic, poorly lit and ventilated, and inadequately furnished. It is, therefore, hardly surprising under these circumstances that sporadic outbreaks of dysentery are not uncommon, and that many children suffer from impetigo, pediculosis (lice), scabies, upper respiratory ailments and middle ear infections.

Race Relations

Another distinctive feature of the area is that race relations tend, on the whole, to be less satisfactory than in most districts of New Zealand with the possible exception of Northland, the Waikato, Pukekohe, and parts of metropolitan Auckland. In the course of ordinary conversation, one hears an astonishing volume of undisguisedly anti-Maori comment, including, on occasion, such expressions as, "The only good Maori is a dead Maori". This attitude stems in part from the generally closed social structure of the city. Social life is organised and dominated by small, tightly knit cliques that are only open to members of the "best families" or to the descendants of the original settlers of the region. Most doors are firmly closed to strangers and out-group members. When to this pakeha social orientation is added the strong under-current of anti-pakeha sentiment among members of the local Maori church and the long-standing tradition of backwardness and isolationism on the part of the indigenous Maori residents of the river valley, coupled with rigid opposition to social intercourse and intermarriage with Europeans, the prospects for enlightened inter-racial attitudes and practices are obviously not very propitious. Race relations have, I suspect, steadily deteriorated over the past twenty years, largely as a result of the increased tensions and vastly expanded occasions for intercultural contact attending the gradual migration of Maoris from the river valley into the urban area.

The practically universal stereotype of the Maori held by many pakehas in the district is that of a lazy, shiftless, unreliable, improvident, happy-go-lucky individual with no other ambition than to booze, sit in the sun and sponge off the Government. These traits are perceived as inherently Polynesian and as part of the general pattern of moral and intellectual inferiority inherited by members of coloured races. Maoris are believed to be fit for road work, tractor driving, shearing, fencing and freezing; any other work involving sustained effort, initiative or intellectual ability is thought to be beyond their capacity. It is frequently asserted that money spent on Maori education or housing is shamefully wasted since Maoris "invariably go back to the mat". Hence, despite the frequently reiterated claim that "any Maori who behaves as a European is treated as one", this negative stereotype is so deeply ingrained that Maoris are actually prejudged on the basis of their racial membership rather than judged on the basis of individual merit, and the unfavourable characteristics of the individual Maori are indiscriminately generalised to the entire race.

Informal social interaction between the two peoples is virtually non-existent. Maoris and pakehas rarely greet or stop to talk to each other on the street. Some workingmen believe that it is socially acceptable to say, "Hello", to a Maori acquaintance or to have a beer with him in the pub, but draw the line at taking him home and introducing him to the family. Maoris, with rare exceptions, are not members of local civic and fraternal organisations. Relatively few pakehas accept them as social equals. Middle-aged and older persons typically refer to them as "just Maoris"; the more tolerant say that Maoris are all right as long as they "keep their place" (i.e., remain in the *pa* and aspire to menial jobs), and don't attempt to mix with Europeans. Maoris, in turn, understandably react to such attitudes with aloofness, unfriendliness, inhospitality, and anti-pakeha attitudes. Hence, inter-racial home visiting rarely occurs, and intermarriage is severely condemned by members of both cultural groups. Dating between Maori boys and pakeha girls is a new phenomenon in the district, takes place on a very limited scale, and meets with harsh disapproval from pakeha parents and relatives and with offensive insinuations from neighbours and peers.

Discriminatory practices against Maoris are commonly encountered in the city. Most hotels will not knowingly book Maoris as guests, and Maoris do not feel welcome in and hence do not patronise certain pubs and restaurants. Private offices, shops, and banks do not employ Maoris, and relatively few firms hire Maori tradesmen or take on Maori apprentices. Most shops do not extend credit to Maori customers. Discriminatory practices with respect to housing have already been mentioned.

The School Environment

Our sample was drawn from an established and well-known technical high school founded approximately forty-five years ago. It is a coeducational school enrolling about one thousand pupils, three-quarters male, 7.5 per cent of whom are Maori.* Like most technical schools it has little snob value and does not enjoy

---

* Pupils are classified as Maoris in the official school census if their Maori ancestry is 50 per cent or greater. In practice, however, no genealogical analysis is attempted; pupils are simply asked how they wish to be listed on the school rolls. This social rather than biological criterion of cultural membership was eminently suitable for our research purposes, since in a psychoethnological study a Maori may be most realistically defined as a person who considers himself a member of the Maori cultural group.

the social prestige of either the older public secondary schools or the private boarding schools. Nevertheless, it has a good reputation for passes on the School Certificate Examination, and it has produced a fair number of graduates who subsequently made their mark in academic, professional, and public life. It offers three principal kinds of courses for boys: (1) academic (professional and general); (2) technical (woodwork and engineering); and (3) agricultural. In our sample the percentages of boys enrolled in these three courses were 25, 62.5 and 12.5 respectively. Entering pupils are also streamed in ability groups on the basis of IQ and placement tests.

Few Maori pupils have much background in Maori language or culture. Only three of the 48 Maori boys in our sample were able to carry on a conversation in Maori. The majority were only familiar with a bare handful of the more common colloquial expressions. Most of them stared blankly when the investigator asked them in Maori if they were able to speak the Maori language.

Race relations are incomparably better in the school than in the community at large. Nevertheless there are many obvious signs of racial cleavage. Maori pupils tend predominantly but not exclusively to associate with each other. This tendency, however, is probably as much a matter of shyness and preference on their part as of any social barrier (explicit or implicit) imposed by pakeha pupils. The latter regard them as excessively "clannish". Little or no indications of overt racial friction (name-calling, taunting, scapegoating, brawling) are evident, and Maori boys do not perceive themselves as socially victimised by the pakeha majority.

Although most of the teachers subscribe to the same negative stereotype of the Maori that is current in the community, and are vigorous exponents of the inherent racial inferiority and "back to the mat" theories of Maori acculturational difficulties, none has the reputation of being overtly anti-Maori or discriminatory in their classroom dealings with Maori pupils. Their sentiments, however, are reflected in the fact that they offer the latter very little encouragement to remain in school beyond the minimal leaving age.

THE RURAL SETTING

The area from which the rural sample was drawn is a prosperous pastoral, dairying, and market gardening county in the Eastern

Bay of Plenty. The commercial and administrative centre of the county (and also the seat of the high school) is a borough situated between two rivers and bounded on the north by the Bay of Plenty. It is on the main highway between Rotorua to the west and Gisborne to the southeast. In addition to local body offices and district offices of various Government departments, it contains an important dairy factory servicing the county and much of the area towards East Cape, a bacon factory, a clothing factory operated by Maori workers, and numerous shops, banks, mercantile establishments and trucking firms.

The population of the county[15] is roughly 5,200 (57 per cent Maori) and the population of the borough*[15] is approximately 2,500 (22.5 per cent Maori). The Maori population of the county has remained relatively constant over the past ten years, but the Maori population of the borough has increased greatly during the same interval, i.e., 43 per cent between 1951 and 1956 and 36 per cent between 1945 and 1951.[13] The flow of Maori population is from the county and neighbouring counties to the borough, and, to some extent, from both county and borough to the larger urban centres and to other parts of the Bay of Plenty where more extensive rural development has taken place.

Residence of Pupils

Fourteen of the 50 Maori pupils in our rural secondary school sample resided within the borough and seven lived in dispersed dwellings in the surrounding rural area. The remaining 29 boys were drawn from nucleated rural settlements *(pas)* as follows: one, five, one, and eleven boys respectively from four settlements 10, 12, 14, and 16 miles east of the borough; one boy from a *pa* five miles south of the borough; and three, four and three boys respectively from three settlements four, ten, and 20 miles west and southwest of the borough.

Thirty-one of the pakeha pupils were residents of the borough and 19 lived in outlying rural areas. Hence, just as in our urban sample, the home environment of the Maori boys was more rural than the corresponding environment of the pakeha boys.

---

* The county population does *not* include the borough population.

Occupations of pupils' fathers (see Table II) has already been discussed above.

Tribal Organisation and Social Life

Three separate tribes are represented in the Maori pupil population of the secondary school. The principal tribe in the district (contributing 70 per cent of the pupils in our sample) resides within the borough and in those parts of the county most adjacent to it. It claims descent from the *Mataatua* canoe, and is organised in eight *hapus* living in seven settlements within a radius of 14 miles from the borough and within the borough itself. Twenty-two per cent of the boys in our sample were members of a small tribe, originally from the west coast, living in a settlement 16 miles east of the borough. Eight per cent of the boys in the sample were drawn from the eastern branch of a large tribe inhabiting the Urewera Country, and also claiming descent from the *Mataatua* canoe. They resided in a settlement twenty miles southwest of the borough.

During the Maori Wars the area was the scene of sporadic *Hau Hau* activity, including the brutal murder and mutilation of an Anglican missionary.[1] Because of actual and alleged local Maori support of both this activity and of the later guerilla campaigns of Te Kooti, the Government confiscated large tracts of land belonging to the three Maori tribes in the district.[1] Maori resentment over the confiscations, which has still not completely abated today, led to much inter-racial friction and occasional outbreaks of violence even 15 years after the nominal termination of hostilities in 1872. A claim for compensation from the Government arising from the confiscations is still pending and constitutes one of the chief grievances of the local people. Other outstanding grievances include the alleged usurpation by pakehas of their ancestral sea-food rights in the harbour; the slow progress of land development, land title consolidation and housing schemes in the area; and the Act of 1953 making possible the alienation of neglected, unused, or uneconomic units of Maori land. The Tribal Executive has also been agitating for the teaching of the Maori language in the high school, for a hostel to accommodate pupils from outlying areas, for tar sealing of the highway east of the borough, and for the granting of more extensive police powers to Maori wardens. Residual evidence of Te Kooti's great influence in this region is found in the large Maori membership in the religious sect that he fathered.

Community life centred about the *marae* is much more co-hesive, integrated and vigorous than in the urban area, and is conducted along more traditional lines. Kinship, *hapu* and tribal bonds are also stronger and mutually reinforce each other. Meeting houses and associated dining-social halls on the various *marae* of the tribe are used frequently for Tribal Committee, Tribal Execu-tive and Women's League meetings, and for concerts, *huis,* weddings, birthday parties and informal gatherings. Meetings of the Tribal Committees and of the Tribal Executive are conducted in an orderly manner and in strict accordance with parliamentary procedure; by pakeha standards, however, they appear unduly prolonged. Standing committees of the Tribal Executive concern themselves with such matters as education, sanitation, hospitals, road safety, and the activity of Maori wardens. Alcoholism, sexual promiscuity, and bodgieism are less serious problems than in the urban district. The Tribal Executive, nevertheless, has repeatedly expressed its concern over the excessive drinking that is practised in some homes, but is powerless to prevent it.

Religious Affiliations

The religious affiliations of pupils in our rural sample are shown in Table II. More pakeha pupils were affiliated with the Presbyterian and Methodist Churches, whereas more Maori pupils were members of the Anglican Church. The other principal inter-cultural difference was the relatively large Maori membership in the Church founded by Te Kooti. The pupils whose families belonged to the latter church tended, on the whole, to speak Maori more fluently and to be more familiar than other pupils with traditional aspects of Maori life. They were somewhat embarrassed and reluctant, however, about acknowledging their religious affiliations.

Since religious loyalties are easily overshadowed by kinship and tribal loyalties, doctrinal differences do not have a decisive effect on local Maori community life.

Housing

Within the borough proper, Maori homes are generally of a good standard, are well cared for, and except for overcrowding, are not particularly distinguishable from pakeha homes. In the outlying *pas,* however, Maori housing, for the most part, conforms to the description given above of prevailing standards in the nucleated settlements of the urban area.

Race Relations

Although race relations got off to a very inauspicious beginning about a century ago, wide agreement exists among residents of this district that relations between Maori and pakeha have materially improved over the past 20 years. As the bitterness referable to the war and the confiscations began to recede, and as the Maoris became more accustomed to European ways of life, education, agriculture, and technology, the gulf between the two people gradually narrowed. This Europeanisation of the Maori, furthermore, was not accompanied by an abrupt increase in inter-racial contact, undue economic competition or sudden detribalisation. Most Maoris in the district are still independent and relatively prosperous farmers physically separated from their pakeha neighbours; and the Maoris residing in the borough enjoy good housing conditions and high morale. They have also retained more of their traditional social organisation and self-respect than the Maoris in our urban sample. In addition, quite unlike the situation characterising the urban area, pakeha social life is open and friendly, and the traditional courtesy, graciousness, and hospitality of the Maori people are nowhere more evident.

Even casual observation reveals that race relations in this district are incomparably superior to those described above for the urban centre. Maoris and pakehas commonly greet each other and stop to exchange pleasantries when they meet publicly. Not only is there no segragated Maori housing in the borough but also no noticeable discrimination in hotels, bars, and restaurants. Maoris are more highly represented on local bodies and civic organisations, and the two people interact more frequently in such formal social situations as church and sports.

On the other hand, closer observation reveals that the same negative stereotype of the Maori and the same notions regarding his allegedly inherent intellectual and motivational inferiority prevail as in most other parts of New Zealand. The stereotype, however, is less highly crystallised and less rigidly applied than in these other areas. There is less tendency to prejudge the individual Maori on the basis of racial stereotype and greater disposition to judge him on his merits as a person. Another encouraging feature of race relations in the district is that local

pakehas are more forthright than the general run of their countrymen in admitting the existence of racial prejudice and discrimination.

The fact that each cultural community mostly leads its own
separate social life is not necessarily undesirable. This type of
social segregation is largely *self*-imposed by the Maori community
both because many Maoris do not feel comfortable in intimate
social situations with pakehas, and because pakeha society cannot
possibly provide the traditional aspects of Maori social life (e.g.,
huis, hangis, tangis, hakas, action songs) which they desire. Part
of the lack of informal social intercourse and family visiting
between the two peoples, however, is a reflection of pakeha
prejudice. Maoris are not explicitly excluded from pakeha gatherings, but are either not invited, are given "rhetorical" invitations,
or are not always made to feel genuinely welcome when they do
attend. Many pakeha families refuse on principle to mix socially
with Maoris—even if they are next door neighbours; in some
instances this policy is an attempt to "live down" the small amount
of Maori blood in their own veins. Remarkably few pakehas are
knowledgeable about or show any interest in the Maori language,
in Maori customs, or even in the history and organisation of the
local Maori tribes.

Although discriminatory practices with respect to employment
are much less stringent than in the urban area, some firms, particularly banks, and various retail shops, private offices, garages,
and building contractors, will not employ Maori workers or
apprentices. Most limitations in vocational opportunity, however,
inhere in the narrow range of occupations, the few facilities for
advanced training, and the restricted possibilities for promotion
that characterise any small town in a remote country district, and
apply with almost equal force both to Maori and pakeha youth.

The School Environment

Prior to 1953 the school was a district high school. It is now
a full multilateral, coeducational secondary school with an enrolment of 325 pupils (46 per cent boys) of whom 47 per cent are
Maori. It offers professional (academic), technical (woodwork
and metalwork), and agricultural options to boys, and has an
excellent new physical plant, first-rate shop facilities, and attractive
playing fields. Pupils are streamed on the basis of I.Q., entering
examinations, and (in the case of upper-form pupils) prior

academic performance.

Maori pupils in this school have a much better background in Maori language and culture than Maori pupils in the urban centre. Twelve of the 50 Maori boys in our rural sample spoke the language fluently, and an additional five boys spoke sufficiently well to carry on an ordinary conversation. Thirty-one of the pupils were able to understand the gist of a conversation, and of these 22 could also speak a few words and phrases. Only two of the boys in our rural Maori sample disclaimed any comprehension of the language.

Race relations within the school were generally similar to the picture described above for the urban sample, except for evidence of greater inter-racial mixing and stronger inter-racial friendships. It was not uncommon, for example, to see Maori and pakeha girls strolling about the school grounds with their arms entwined around each other; and more often than I observed in most other parts of New Zealand, such friendships tended to survive the adolescent period. On the whole, however, Maori pupils preferred to associate with each other rather than with pakeha classmates. Several pakeha boys who had the reputation of coming from violently anti-Maori families, sporadically became involved in fisticuffs with the more assertive and nationalistic Maori pupils who quite understandably resented their chauvinistic and racially offensive remarks.

In general, the racial attitudes of the teachers were also more enlightened than those of their urban colleagues. In several instances, however, they were tainted by varying degrees of anti-Maori prejudice. Snide remarks about Maoris were frequently passed in the staff room and usually went unchallenged. One teacher particularly enjoyed the reputation of harbouring ill-feeling towards Maoris, and was perceived by his colleagues as constantly picking on Maori pupils. Although the latter did not feel generally discriminated against within the school environment, they complained about the tendency on the part of teachers automatically to attribute all thefts in and about the school to the Maori segment of the population. They felt, in other words, that they were presumed to be guilty until proven innocent.

ORGANISATION OF REMAINING CHAPTERS

In order to make this report more readable for those persons who are not concerned with the detailed and systematic statistical treatment of the data, the latter material has been placed in the Appendix. Interpretation of the major findings and their implications for the vocational and educational adjustment of Maori adolescents are discussed in Chapters III, IV, and V. Practical recommendations based on this discussion are considered in Chapter VI.

Appendix II is devoted to a presentation of Maori-pakeha uniformities and differences in both urban and rural samples, and Appendix III is devoted to a presentation of urban-rural uniformities and differences in both Maori and pakeha samples. The relative magnitude and direction of Maori-pakeha and urban-rural differences are also compared in Appendix III. All of these comparisons are made in terms of the eleven categories of variables delineated in Appendix I. Some readers may prefer to read the Appendices before proceeding to Chapter III.

CHAPTER THREE

Implications for Vocational Achievement

IN THIS AND THE FOLLOWING CHAPTER, I PROPOSE TO INTERPRET the major findings of this study in terms of their implications for the vocational and educational achievement of Maori youth. Wherever relevant in connection with this task, I will draw on data derived from participant observation and informal interviews with parents and community leaders, as well as on census and other data applying to Maori youth as a whole. Because the rural and urban samples used in this study are not representative of the general population of adolescent Maori males, implications from findings can only be regarded as suggestive or tentative in nature, and must in any case be qualified by the distinctive characteristics of the samples in question.

After consideration of some general findings that apply to both educational and vocational achievement, the remainder of this chapter will be devoted to factors influencing vocational achievement. Factors affecting the educational attainment of Maori youth will be discussed in Chapter IV.

MAORI-PAKEHA UNIFORMITIES AND DIFFERENCES

Perhaps the major finding of this study was the overall degree of similarity between Maori and pakeha secondary school boys in academic and vocational aspirations, underlying motivations for achievement, supportive traits, and perceptions of both prevailing opportunities and family and peer group pressures for achievement. This finding substantiated the impression that many of the traits commonly regarded as typically Maori are in fact largely reflective of low occupational and social class status, predominantly rural residence, and environmentally stunted verbal intelligence. When these variables are controlled by appropriate matching techniques, much of the expected intercultural difference simply vanishes.

We cannot completely discount the possibility, of course, that some intercultural differences were partly obscured either because the measuring instruments were not sufficiently sensitive to detect existing differences between the two cultural groups, or because they were so transparent that the subjects merely supplied the responses they believed the investigator ˌwished to receive. Several considerations, however, detract from the credibility of this interpretation. In the first place, an adequate range of intra-group variability was obtained for most of the instruments. Secondly, much intercultural uniformity was found in relation to instruments (e.g., teachers' ratings, achievement imagery, and responsiveness to prestige incentives) where transparency to pupils was either not at issue or highly improbable. Thirdly (see p. 183-184), the interview situation was so constructed as to discourage insincere responses.

It can also be argued with justice that unavoidable discrepancies in the matching procedure as well as various distinctive aspects of our sample exaggerated rather than reduced actual differences between Maori and pakeha groups. In both urban and rural samples, for example, pakeha pupils lived in a more urban environment, enjoyed better housing and the benefits of higher per capita income, and had slightly higher I.Q.'s. Furthermore, the greater than average membership in the Maori churches in both our rural and urban districts, and the isolationist history of the Maori tribe in the urban centre favoured a more traditional approach to problems of social and economic adaptation than is typical of most Maori communities.

A second major finding was the fact that Maori-pakeha uniformities were more striking at the level of expressed educational and vocational aspirations than with respect to underlying needs and motivations for achievement, supportive traits, and perceived pressures and opportunities for academic and occupational success. The aspirations of Maori pupils, in other words, were approximately equivalent to those of their pakeha classmates; but in terms of the drives, supportive traits and environmental pressures necessary for the implementation of these aspirations, they were in a much less favourable position than the latter. This is not to imply that the stated aspirations of Maori youth were insincere or purely verbal expressions unmatched by corresponding intentions within the individuals in question. Such is undoubtedly the case among many Maori adolescents in remote and backward districts with poor community morale and an anti-pakeha orientation (see p. 23). In our particular sample, however, there was no evidence to indicate that the expressed aspirations of Maori pupils were either insincere or were superficial mouthings intended both to satisfy and mislead the investigator.

A more credible explanation of the discrepancy between the level of aspiration of Maori pupils, on the one hand, and their motivations, supportive traits and perceived pressures for achievement, on the other hand, is that their aspirations, while genuine, were neither firmly internalised nor stood much chance of realisation because of the absence of suitable family, cultural and peer group pressures. The actual pressures that were operative—as inferred from participant observation and informal discussion with parents, elders and peers—were even less coercive than those perceived and reported by Maori pupils. Because of inadequate communication between Maori parents and children, the latter tended to perceive parent attitudes regarding achievement that were consonant with their own (i.e., the pupils') aspirations rather than attitudes that parents actually manifested.

Also accounting in part for the incongruously ambitious aspirations of Maori pupils is the fact that high and unrealistic expressed aspirations tend to be characteristic of many physically handicapped, minority and socially underprivileged groups. (See Ausubel,[4] p. 311, for a review of studies in this area). Even though all of the ingredients necessary for the implementation of high aspirations for achievement may be absent, mere nurturance of such aspirations tends to provide ego enhancement and compensate for the ego deflation associated with physical deformity or social discrimination. This tendency is especially evident in relation to remote goals distantly removed from current reality considerations. Although Maori pupils, for example, were quite restrained about the marks they hoped to receive by the end of the year and about improving their current class standing, they were relatively expansive (i.e., either equalled or surpassed pakeha ambitions) with respect to School Certificate, university degrees, occupational choice, and tenacity of striving for a hypothetical vocational goal.

Thus, despite impressive evidence of aspirational uniformities among Maori and pakeha youth, it is patently clear that significant intercultural differences prevail between the two groups with respect to factors affecting the implementation of aspirations, i.e., underlying needs and motivations for achievement, supportive traits, and perceived opportunities and pressures for achievement. These differences (generally in the hypothesised direction) still remain, and are of the same order of magnitude as urban-rural differences among Maori pupils, even after Maori and pakeha samples are matched on the basis of paternal occupation, urban or rural location of the school, form, course, and ability group. It is also clear, for the reason indicated above, that *actual* intercultural differences in vocational opportunity and in cultural, family, and peer group pressures for achievement are greater than those perceived and reported by the Maori and pakeha pupils in our sample. Hence it seems probable that insofar as some of the basic motivational aspects of his character structure are concerned, the Maori will be more than simply a coloured pakeha for at least another generation.

The greater prominance of Maori-pakeha differences in our urban than in our rural sample highlights the proposition that the Maori population still has a long way to go before it fully assimilates the urban pattern of pakeha achievement. This, of course, is largely a function of the recency of Maori migration to the cities. In addition to the fact that the rural pattern of life is much closer than the urban to his indigenous pre-pakeha culture, the Maori has had at least a hundred years more time in accustoming himself to it.

URBAN-RURAL UNIFORMITIES AND DIFFERENCES

As the urban segment of the Maori population progressively increases, urban-rural differences among the Maori people are becoming increasingly more important. Since 1926, the number of Maoris living in cities, boroughs and independent towns has increased six-fold, and since 1936 it has doubled.[15, 32] The average rate of growth in the urban Maori population between 1951 and 1956 was 35 per cent or more than three times that of the population at large.[15] Between 1945 and 1956 the percentage of urban Maoris (including those residing in small towns) increased from 19.7 to 27.9 per cent of the total Maori population, and in absolute figures their numbers doubled.[13] In some districts (Taranaki,

Hawkes Bay, Manawatu), the flow of Maori population has been from country to town areas within the same district, whereas in other districts (Northland, East Coast) the flow of population has been out of the district into more distant urban centres.[13] Several rural areas (Bay of Plenty, Rotorua-Taupo, and parts of the King Country) have increased in population as a result of the development of new timber, paper, and hydro-electric industries.[13]

Reasons for the Urban Drift of Maori Population

The Maori migration to the cities, which began during World War II with the opening up of many attractive industrial jobs, must inevitably continue. Much of the reason for this movement inheres in Maori population trends. A phenomenally high birth rate coupled with a spectacular decrease in mortality rates* have resulted in an unusually high annual rate of increase of 3.4 per cent—more than double that of the pakeha.[15] Furthermore, since the Maori population is more heavily concentrated in the younger age groups than is the pakeha population, relatively more jobs in the future will have to be found for Maori than for pakeha workers. Forty-six per cent of the Maori as compared to 31 per cent of the pakeha population are under 15 years of age;[32] and although six out of every hundred New Zealanders are Maoris, the latter consitute only 4.5 per cent of the population over 15 but nine per cent of the population under 15.[32]

When the pressure of a rapidly expanding population is considered in relation to the limited amount of Maori-owned land, it is clear that the Maoris have little alternative but to migrate to the cities for employment. As long ago as 1939, when the Maori population was only 88,000 (about 60 per cent of the current figure), it was authoritatively estimated by a leading economist that even if all of the Maori land were fully developed it would still adequately provide for only one-quarter of the Maori people.[11] Rural jobs for the landless are available, but are limited in scope and tend to be seasonal and uncertain;[25,26,27] and although rural development schemes and the decentralisation of industry can and already have opened up new channels of employment, they obviously cannot absorb all of the surplus Maori working population. In Ruatahuna, a small backblock Urewera community, for

---

* Except for infant mortality, Maori and pakeha mortality rates are practically identical.

example, at most 40 to 50 jobs can be expected to become available for the 131 boys who will be leaving school within the next 15 years.[24] Maori adolescents who remain in such areas can only look forward to casual and temporary employment interspersed with long periods of idleness and aimless drifting. Such experience obviously does not promote sound attitudes towards, and satisfactory habits of, work.

Even apart from these coercive demographic and economic considerations, many other factors have combined to render the continuing Maori drift to the cities an irreversible process. With progressive Europeanisation, increase in educational level and emergence from self-imposed isolation has come a demand for better paid, more highly skilled, and more prestigeful pakeha-type jobs. Young Maoris have also been attracted by high wages, by the plentifulness and variability of urban employment and by the freedom, pleasures, excitement and novelty of city life.

Although most Maoris of the older generation are reconciled to the economic necessity of urban migration, some of the old people remain stubbornly and unalterably opposed. They stress the importance of holding fast to the tribal lands and traditional values of their forefathers, and they warn against the loss of *Maoritanga* and the deterioration of moral discipline that allegedly result when young people are separated from their local *maraes* and removed from the control of their village elders. Not without reason they also fear the decline of their hereditary status and power as the young folk move away and come under the influence of pakeha egalitarianism.[25] But even they realise that they are fighting a losing battle and that the tide of acculturation has already advanced much too far to be reversed.

General Trends in Urban-Rural Differences

In view of the relative recency of Maori migration to the city it is hardly surprising that urban-rural uniformities among the Maori pupils in our sample were more conspicuous than urban-rural differences. For reasons already specified (see p. 25-26), it also came as no surprise that urbanisation had roughly the same effects on the aspirational pattern of rural adolescent boys (both Maori and pakeha) as a shift from Maori to pakeha cultural environment. These effects were most marked with respect to expressed educational and vocational aspirations, prestige motivation, desire for occupational success, and supportive traits. But particularly in the Maori group, consistent urban-rural differences were not found in relation to task-oriented and group welfare motivation, and perceived opportunities and family and peer group pressures for achievement.

It appears, therefore, that at least in smaller urban centres less distantly removed from indigenous tribal lands, urban surroundings may induce pakeha aspirations, motivations, and supportive traits without correspondingly attentuating Maori motivations. Also since Maori parents are only recent arrivals in the city, they apparently do not play an important role in transmitting pakeha achievement patterns to their children; they are not perceived by the latter as demanding higher educational or vocational achievement than the parents of rural Maori adolescents. In fact they are perceived as reacting with *less* anger to the school failure of their sons than are the parents of rural pupils. The relatives and friends of rural pupils are also perceived as being more disappointed than urban relatives and friends when they (the pupils) do poorly in school. This probably does not indicate that rural families and peer groups value educational achievements differentially more highly than their urban counterparts do, but that since collateral family and peer group ties are weaker in the city, relatives and friends of urban adolescents are generally less concerned with the latter's well-being than is the case in rural districts.

Interview data from pupils did not adequately reflect the very definite impression gained from participant observation and informal interviews with parents and community leaders (a) that rural parents were generally more authoritarian than urban parents and played a more important role in determining their children's vocations, and (b) that urban parents had less control over their children and enjoyed less contact with them. The only indication of this trend in pupils' responses was the greater measure of perceived agreement between urban parents and children regarding the latter's choice of career. Quite significantly, although urban Maori pupils were more optimistic than their rural contemporaries about achieving vocational success, they were also in a much more advantageous position realistically to perceive the obstacles lying in the path of such success.

Contrary to our hypothesis, urban-rural differences were slightly greater in the Maori than in the pakeha sample. The original prediction was based on the assumption that because of relative recency of urban residence, the Maori population would have assimilated the urban pattern of achievement less completely than their pakeha countrymen. Although this factor was undoubtedly operative (as shown by the greater prominence of Maori-pakeha differences in the urban than in the rural group), it was apparently more than offset by the fact that movement to the city constituted a much greater change, and hence had more of an impact on a Maori than on a pakeha population. For the same reason, although urban-rural differences were less pronounced in the pakeha than in the Maori group, they were nevertheless more consistent as well as more frequently in the hypothesised direction.

MAORI-PAKEHA VERSUS URBAN-RURAL DIFFERENCES

With the progressive advance of Maori acculturation and migration to urban centres, the increasing importance of urban-rural differences among the Maori people has been paralleled by a corresponding decrease in the magnitude of Maori-pakeha differences. A credible hypothesis supported by our data would be that Maori acculturation with respect to aspirational patterns has proceeded to the point where Maori and pakeha rural youth are more similar to each other than are urban and rural Maori adolescents. In the city, however, Maori youth are, relatively speaking, not quite as far along on the acculturation continuum: Maori and pakeha pupils are still more different from each other than are matched urban and rural pupils within a Maori population.

FACTORS AFFECTING MAORI VOCATIONAL ACHIEVEMENT
Expressed Vocational Aspirations

The stated vocational aspirations of Maori and pakeha pupils in our sample (see Table IV) show fewer intercultural differences in the prestige and the pattern of occupational choice than are indicated by national statistics of "probable destination of pupils leaving public post-primary schools in 1956".[13] According to the latter figures higher percentages of pakeha boys were bound for professional, commercial, and clerical occupations and for the skilled trades with private employers, whereas higher percentages of Maori boys were bound for farming, factory work and the armed forces. These statistics are in agreement with our findings only insofar as clerical and commercial occupations are concerned; "factory work" and "armed forces" were chosen by too small a percentage in each case to make comparison possible. The main discrepancies, therefore, are in farming, professional occupations and the skilled trades.

Despite the small size of our sample, however, there are good reasons for believing that Table IV more accurately reflects the actual state of affairs with respect to pupils' vocational aspirations than the above-mentioned statistics reported by the Department of Education. In the first place, the information collected by the Department often represents an informed guess by headmaster or teachers regarding a pupil's ultimate destination rather than a genuine expression of vocational aspiration; in any case it is seldom obtained in the course of an extended personal interview in which careful attention is paid to matters of rapport. Secondly, the Department's figures of 18 per cent for "other occupations" and 11 per cent for "not known" are not only disproportionately high in relation to our data, thereby rendering the percentages attributed to more specific categories less accurate, but also reflect the cursoriness of the inquiry. Thirdly, the Department does not distinguish between farm ownership and agricultural labour; and although farm ownership was less common among the Maori than among the pakeha families in our sample, this situation is not unrepresentative of the general position, except perhaps on the East Coast. Fourthly, the vocational aspirations of Maori parents for their children in Ruatahuna, a smaller and more isolated Maori community than our rural area, parallels more closely the distribution shown in Table IV than that reported by the Department. Forty per cent of the parents preferred one of the skilled trades, 29 per cent favoured a professional career, and only 23 per cent wanted their sons to go into farming.[24]

In short, therefore, we would postulate that on a national basis a higher percentage of pakeha than Maori pupils aspire to farm ownership and to clerical and commercial occupations, that a higher percentage of Maori than pakeha pupils aspire to the skilled trades and to agricultural labour, and that the percentage of Maori and pakeha pupils aspiring to the professions is approximately the same.

It is frequently asserted by Government and Education Department officials in New Zealand that as a racial group Maoris are inherently "good with their hands", but show little aptitude for mathematics, shopkeeping or supervisory work. Such statements, of course, confuse hereditary endowment with phenotypic development of capacity. In terms of genetic potentialities, Maoris have precisely the same range of occupational interests and abilities as pakehas, but as the result of differential cultural experience, values and opportunities, their interests and abilities have developed more along mechanical than along abstract, intellectual, mathematical and commercial lines (see pp. 91-92). Maoris, for example, tend to make poor shopkeepers because they are more highly disposed than pakehas to grant credit to indigent friends and kinsmen and are less concerned with amassing wealth. They similarly tend to value good comradeship with their fellows much too highly to make effective foremen in the pakeha sense of the term. Much of their alleged superiority to pakehas in mechanical skills is also more apparent than real; their ability to handle tools tends inordinately to impress teachers because, relatively speaking, it is more highly developed than their intellectual skills. In any case this type of thinking serves no useful purpose, and is potentially dangerous. It is not only reflective of scientifically discredited racist doctrines, but also leads to an undersirable stereotyping of racial interests and abilities which ignores individual differences within racial and cultural groups.

That the expressed vocational aspirations of Maori and pakeha youth are so nearly alike—despite the greater likelihood that the aspirations of the latter will be more highly internalised and implemented—is a datum of tremendous cultural and psychological significance. It reflects the accomplishment of an important first step in the assimilation of pakeha achievement patterns, and is indicative of a degree of acculturation that undoubtedly was not present and could not have been predicted a generation ago. At that time, pakeha channels of vocational achievement were negatively sanctioned in the Maori culture to an extent that precluded the assimilation of European occupational aspirations in all but a handful of Maori youth.

It is true, of course, as Ritchie's and Mulligan's data suggest (see p. 23), that in certain more isolated and tradition-bound Maori communities, pakeha achievement patterns still receive insufficient social approval to support the development of *genuine* pakeha-like vocational aspirations in Maori adolescents. It is also probably true that in *most* Maori communities today, pakeha achievement motives do not command enough cultural sanction to provide for the adequate internalisation and implementation of European occupational ambitions. Neither of these considerations, however, detracts from the fact that (if the findings rep this study are shown to be representative of Maori you whole),* Maori acculturation has proceeded to the point wi can sustain the generation—if not the implementation—of pa ...ia vocational aspirations. The development of these aspirations during late childhood and early adolescence is facilitated, of course, by the relatively poor communication of Maori children and young adolescents with their parents and adults generally (see p. 24). As this communication improves, the aspirations in question not only fall short of realisation, but are also attenuated in their expression.

Parental Influences

Many factors in the Maori home environment contribute to the less favourable outlook for the realisation of Maori than of pakeha pupil's vocational aspirations. The most important of these factors will be discussed below.

Lack of Vocational Sophistication. Maori parents are less capable than their pakeha counterparts of helping their children with appropriate vocational advice, information and guidance. They are generally less sophisticated than pakeha parents about the prevailing range of occupational choices, about the current availability of various kinds of jobs, and about the requirements and procedures for entering a given field of employment. The larger size and lower per capita income of Maori families also make Maori parents more reluctant about committing themselves to plans involving long-term vocational preparation (i.e., prolonged schooling or apprenticeship) for their children. It is true that Government bursaries and tribal trust funds are often available for these purposes, but most Maori parents are hopelessly confused about the procedures involved in applying for such assistance.

A related problem is found in the tendency for Maori parents to start too late in placing their children in suitable jobs. They typically wait until the end of the school year, by which time all of the vacancies are filled by pakeha youths.

Inadequate Parent-Child Communication. Another serious difficulty standing in the way of adequate home guidance for

---

* As pointed out above, both Maori parents and the adult community take a greater interest in youth during middle and late adolescence.

Maori youth is the fact that lines of communication between parents and children seem to be less open in Maori than in pakeha families during late childhood and early adolescence.* Maori pupils are more deeply immersed in the world of their peers, and not only rarely exchange views with their parents, but also enjoy relatively little physical contact with them. Hence, parents are less able to pass on to their children helpful insights and advice gleaned from their own life experience.

One striking illustration of this lack of communication is the remarkable degree of naiveté exhibited by Maori pupils regarding anti-Maori discrimination in such fields of employment as banks, shops, offices, and the skilled trades. Although the evidence for this type of discrimination is blatantly obvious to their parents, only one-quarter of the Maori pupils in our sample were aware of the situation. It is evident, therefore, that quite unlike minority group parents in the United States, Maori parents fail to transmit such information to their children. And the latter, in consequence, nurture very vague and unrealistic notions about the kinds of obstacles they are up against in many kinds of jobs and how best to avoid and surmount them.

Better parent-child communication in the pakeha group did not affect the relative extent to which Maori and pakeha pupils in our sample perceived themselves as influenced by parents in the choice of a career. As a matter of fact, in the rural area Maori pupils perceived more parental influence than did pakeha pupils. Apparently, therefore, the influence that Maori parents lose through inadequate communication is more than compensated for by their greater tendency to be authoritarian in matters of vocational choice, and, at least in rural districts, to get away with it. The more democratic approach of pakeha than of Maori parents in these matters, particularly in urban centres, is indicated by the suggestive tendency for more pakeha than Maori boys spontaneously to solicit their parents' advice, and for more pakeha parents both to approve and not to interfere in their sons' choice of career.

Permissiveness and Neglect. Maori parents more frequently than their pakeha counterparts tend to adopt a passive, disinterested, and *laissez-faire* attitude towards their children's vocational

---

* To avoid awkward repetition of this qualification, this phrase will not be repeated but will be implicit in the statement of all further implications arising from this study.

careers. They are more willing to let an adolescent son drift and find his own way as best he can without help, guidance or encouragement. If the latter, for example, suddenly decides to abandon his apprenticeship and take a job in the freezing works, they interpose fewer objections and apply fewer coercive pressures than would the parents of a pakeha boy under comparable circumstances; as a matter of fact, they frequently don't find out about it until weeks or months after the decision is made. It is small wonder, therefore, that Maori apprentices, upper form pupils, and university students are less able to resist the lure of making "big money" immediately in unskilled occupations. Thus, although no reason exists to question the current sincerity of the Maori pupils in our rural sample when they profess greater tenacity than pakeha pupils in adhering to *hypothetical* long-term vocational goals in the face of serious obstacles, when the latter situation *actually* arises they exhibit strikingly less goal tenacity.

This attitude of parents is part of a more general pattern of Maori child rearing that is lax and overly permissive, often to the point of outright neglectfulness. By pakeha standards, Maori children receive inadequate care, attention, and supervision. Even making due allowance for depressed housing and economic circumstances, standards of health, cleanliness, and dress among Maori children are discouragingly low. Often coupled capriciously with parental laxness and indifference are attitudes of abruptness and harshness as well as immoderate use of corporal punishment. One occasionally encounters shocking instances of unscrupulous Maori adults who make a practice of "collecting" orphans and the children of indigent relatives for the Family and Child Welfare Benefits involved, overworking, beating, and otherwise mistreating them, and even exploiting them for sexual purposes. Child Welfare and Maori Welfare officers commonly complain that Maori parents are grossly negligent in protecting their adolescent children from alcohol and gambling, from undesirable companions, and even from physical and sexual assault. The widespread Maori practice of permitting children to live with and be brought up by grandparents and other relatives, although frequently inspired by altruistic motives, leads to a lack of continuity in upbringing that makes consistent home guidance impossible.

Some of these attitudes and practices are simply reflective of lower social class status aggravated in many instances by the especially deplorable sanitary and housing conditions, rampant alcoholism, and extreme social demoralisation characterising large segments of many Maori communities. The large size of most Maori families also sharply limits the amount of both money and parental time and energy available for each child. Compounding these difficulties are the frequent loss of parental control over Maori adolescents in urban centres, and the genuine confusion experienced by parents caught between two cultures regarding the proper relationship that should prevail between parent and child. In interpreting the long-term significance of these conditions, however, it is important to point out that teachers and other persons who have had prolonged and intimate contact with Maori communities report a growing concern on the part of Maori parents (particularly mothers) with the education and vocational careers of their children.

Parent Values and Example. The actual values regarding vocational achievement held by Maori parents and the example they set their children in occupational matters tend to discourage the latter from implementing their own vocational aspirations. Maori parents have high occupational ambitions for their children (see p. 61), but place much less stress on the importance of occupational success than pakeha parents do, incline more towards the short-term view in vocational planning, and are less insistent on the internalisation of supportive traits consistent with long-term striving and the deferment of immediate hedonistic gratifications. Maori pupils perceive correctly the vocational aspirations their parents cherish for them; but they do not perceive until much later (when parent-child communication improves) the somewhat more subtle fact that actual parental values and demands regarding vocational achievement are not consistent with these aspirations. The only indication of insight into the situation they do show is less feeling than that reported by pakeha pupils that their parents would be greatly disappointed by their (the pupils') vocational failure (see p. 197). More so than their pakeha classmates, however, Maori pupils perceive their parents as reacting to the vocational failure situation with anger, loss of love, and loss or respect (see p. 197), but this difference more probably reflects a cultural difference in emotional expression (i.e., in abruptness, volatility, and immediate violence of response) than greater Maori concern with occupational success.

Ambivalence about Children Leaving Home. Although largely resigned to the necessity of their adolescent children leaving home in order to pursue various occupational careers, rural Maori parents tend to be very ambivalent about the prospect. On the one hand, they fear the loss of *Maoritanga* and the greater likelihood of involvement in delinquency, and, on the other hand, they are apprehensive that their children will not be able to compete successfully with more sophisticated pakeha youth in the city. Such feelings on the part of parents undoubtedly influence some Maori teenagers to remain at home rather than seek more desirable vocational opportunities in urban centres.

Peer Group Influences

It is also apparent from participant observation that Maori boys generally receive less encouragement from their peers than pakeha boys do to strive for vocational achievement. Not only is occupational success less highly valued in the more cohesive Maori peer culture, but the greater availability of derived status based solely on conformity to group standards removes much of the incentive for seeking vocational achievement. In those Maori communities suffering from poor social morale (e.g., one of the *pas* in our urban centre and several rural *pas* observed by the investigator but not included in the rural sample) vocational achievement tends to be negatively sanctioned in the peer group. If any individual exhibits occupational ambition, his fellows actively strive to pull him down to their own level.

In these latter communities also, adolescent cultism (bodgieism) is extremely prevalent. Teddy boy types with gaudy dress, long hair and sideburns, flashy leather jackets, and motorcycles are much in evidence. Gangster films, horror comics, rock-'n'-roll music are in great vogue as well as slick talk, affected behaviour, inordinately late hours, brash drinking habits, sexual promiscuity, and sporadic hooliganism and delinquency. Many of these boys have no real interest in work and exhibit an apathetic and "couldn't care less" attitude towards life and hostile, defiant attitudes towards authority. This situation is largely a product of social demoralisation within the local Maori community, unfamiliarity with urban life, removal from the control of parents and village elders, parental indifference and irresponsibility, and traumatic experience in secondary schools with unsympathetic,

authoritarian   teachers   and   an   inappropriate   and   frustrating
curriculum.

Maori Cultural Factors

Paralleling   and   supplementing   parental   and   peer   group
influences on the implementation of Maori vocational aspirations
are factors stemming from the culture at large of which the
former influences are idiosyncratic expressions. They include
cultural values and other personality traits affecting achievement,
Maori attitudes towards work, the current vocational status of
the Maori people, and personal and social morale. Cultural handicaps such as language retardation, which affect vocational
achievement indirectly by influencing University work and performance on the School Certificate and University Entrance Examinations, will be considered in Chapter IV.

Cultural Values Regarding Achievement. The great emphasis
Maori culture places on derived status (i.e., status and self-esteem
derived from group psychological support and from membership
in and acceptance by the group) creates less need for personal
achievement than is characteristic of modern Western civilisation.
If simply by virtue of his membership in a kinship or tribal group,
participation in group activities, fulfilment of his obligations
towards the group, and conformity to group norms he is accepted
and intrinsically valued as a person, irrespective of his capabilities
and accomplishments, a Maori obviously feels less need than a
pakeha to demonstrate his worth through meritorious performance.
The present-day stress on derived status is both a residual reflection of its original importance in pre-pakeha days as well as a
compensation for the declining importance of primary status in
post-pakeha Maori culture (see p. 23).

The self-aggrandising features of primary status (i.e., personal
ambition, success, prestige, and power) have always been less
prominent in Maori than in pakeha culture, particularly since the
active rejection of European values following the Maori Wars.
This intercultural difference was especially marked in our urban
sample. Pakeha pupils had higher occupational prestige needs than
Maori pupils, rated prestige, wealth, and advancement as more
important reasons for seeking vocational achievement, and considered occupational success a more important life goal. Within
the Maori sample the urban group had higher occupational prestige

needs than the rural group, valued vocational success more highly, and made higher scores on the Achievement Imagery Test.

Our data likewise gave some support to the hypothesis that task-oriented motives—pride in craftsmanship, personal satisfaction in mastery of skills—are more important spurs to achievement in Maori than in pakeha culture. In our urban sample, Maori pupils considered "liking the job" a significantly more important reason for desiring vocational success than did their pakeha classmates.

The more significant role of group welfare motivation (i.e., regard for kinship obligations, co-operative sharing of economic burdens, emphasis on social goals in economic enterprises, enhancement of group prestige, concern for the common good) in Maori than in pakeha achievement patterns was also reflected in our data. Maori pupils gave a higher rating to "helping others" both as a factor in vocational choice and as a reason for seeking occupational success.

Other Personality Traits. Consistent with its relatively low valuation of primary status and prestigeful individual achievement, Maori culture places less emphasis than pakeha culture on personality traits important for implementing achievement goals. Less concerned with achieving occupational prestige, the Maori is less willing than the pakeha to practise initiative, foresight, self-denial, and self-discipline, to persevere in the face of adversity, or to defer immediate hedonistic gratification in favour of remote vocational goals. Secondary school teachers, university lecturers, and land development supervisors frequently complain about the Maori's lack of determination to carry forward a long-term objective to a successful conclusion. He starts off full of enthusiasm, but then allegedly becomes discouraged, abruptly terminates his studies when they are only half completed, or permits his farm to revert to gorse and blackberry. Valuing personal relationships, derived status and kinship ties above material possessions and vocational success, it is small wonder that in his eyes helpfulness, generosity, hospitality, sociability, and conformity to group standards count for more than punctuality, thrift and methodicalness. In our urban sample teachers rated pakeha pupils more highly than Maori pupils on persistence, conscientiousness, planning capacity, and initiation of activity.

Lack of concern with prestigeful vocational achievement tends to make the Maori preoccupied with the present and with the short-term view. He is reluctant to theorise, to experiment with anything outside his own past experience, or to consider the advantages of more distant goals when such tangible and immediate benefits as high wages are available. Except for day to day decisions of a practical nature he tends to adopt a dilatory, evasive, and "let's wait and see" *(taihoa)* attitude.* The underlying hope, of course, is that if a decision can be postponed long enough the problem itself will disappear.

Largely because of these traits Maoris impress pakehas as being lazy, shiftless, and improvident, and as having a casual, happy-go-lucky, and "couldn't care less" approach to life. Although this uncharitable and ethnocentric interpretation of Maori personality obviously applies to only some Maoris, and also characterises many pakehas, sufficient intercultural difference does exist in these respects to provide a kernel of truth for the widespread stereotype of the Maori.

Maori Attitudes towards Work. Many Maori attitudes towards work, stemming both from his indigenous and current value system as well as from his pre-pakeha organisation of economic life, impede his vocational adjustment. In the first place he is less accustomed than the pakeha to regular and steady employment. The rhythm of his prior economic activity was more seasonal and spasmodic, marked by periods of intense work load alternating with periods of relative idleness. Secondly, in former times his work was more diversified and less specialised than it is today. Hence, he finds dull, monotonous labour less congenial than the pakeha does. Thirdly, it is only recently that he has shifted from a subsistence to a money economy. The concept of thrift for vocational or economic purposes was foreign to him. He amassed wealth solely to implement his lavish hospitality. Even today he entertains visitors on a scale that by pakeha standards is far out of proportion to his meagre resources. Fourthly, his ties of kinship and sentiment to the locality where he is born are greater than those of the pakeha, and he is, therefore, less eager to migrate to other districts in order to take advantage of more attractive vocational opportunities. Simply by virtue of his predominantly

---

* Historically, the policy of *taihoa* arose as a defensive manoeuvre to counter the Maori's earlier tendency unthinkingly to trade his patrimony for ready cash.

rural residence the Maori, relative to the pakeha, is at a vocational disadvantage.

Fifthly, unlike the pakeha he does not value work as an end in itself, as a badge of respectability or as a means of getting on in the world. He works primarily to supply the necessities of life; and hence when his immediately foreseeable needs are satisfied and a small surplus is accumulated, he sees nothing immoral in taking a prolonged respite from his labours. In the light of this attitude, monetary reward is a much more important reason than occupational prestige for choosing a career, and possible loss of job is fraught with less threatening ego, moral and social implications for him than it is for the pakeha. Thus it is not unusual for him to stay away from work because he is bored or put out with his employer; and if he is fired he feels that he can always revert to a subsistence economy or fall back on Social Security benefits and the hospitality of relatives.

Lastly, the Maori is more dependent than the pakeha on the psychological support of an intimate group in his work environment. He dislikes solitary labour or working among strangers in unfamiliar surroundings. Thus he prefers out of door gang work (e.g., shearing, Public Works) with fellow Maoris to working in an office with pakehas. Army life also appeals to him because of its community aspects. As already pointed out, it is not uncommon for a highly qualified Maori to abandon a promising professional or Public Service career and seek employment as a labourer in order to obtain the type of job companionship he desires. Because he takes his kinship and community responsibilities more seriously than the pakeha does, he often feels obligated to attend *tangis,* weddings, and *huis* even if they interfere with his job. His irate employer, however, rarely appreciates the problem of conflicting cultural values involved and tends to regard such behaviour as the epitome of irresponsibility.

Present Occupational Status and Morale. The extent to which the vocational aspirations of the youth of any ethnic group can be implemented is obviously influenced in part by the current occupational status and morale of their elders. The vocational achievements of the latter create precedent and tradition and set a standard for the younger generation to emulate. Practical considerations are also involved. If his parents are successful in a given career, their experience, guidance and financial backing are invaluable assets to any ambitious youth with long-term occupational aspirations.

In all of these respects pakeha secondary school pupils have the advantage over their Maori classmates in as much as Maori adults are under-represented in professional, clerical, and commercial occupations, in farm ownership, and in the skilled trades, and are over-represented in agricultural and unskilled labour.[32] The mean annual income of the Maori is only three-quarters that of the pakeha, and relatively fewer Maoris than pakehas are in the moderate and upper income brackets.[32] In 1951 the percentage of pakehas earning incomes over £500 was four times as great as that of Maoris.[32] On a per capita basis the Maori is at an even greater disadvantage since his smaller income must be spread over more than twice as many children per family. His average per capita income in 1951 was only £54 as compared to £123 for the European.[32] It is hardly surprising, therefore, that the prospect of immediate high wages for unskilled labour should have such great appeal to a vocationally unsophisticated and underprivileged people with relatively little tradition of professional achievement and long-term occupational planning. This is especially true in a country with an undifferentiated wage scale and a long history of full employment (see below).

It must also be appreciated that there are relatively few Maori farmers who are prosperous in the pakeha sense of the term. Most Maoris in rural areas are agricultural labourers or own small farms that are barely large enough to be workable and support their families at subsistence level. Many Maori farmers are negligent about ploughing, fertilising, and regrassing their fields, about milking their herds regularly, about keeping their fences in repair, and about maintaining their vehicles properly. Even on the East Coast and in Hawkes Bay, where there were no confiscations and where vigorously implemented land development schemes have resulted in better than average Maori holdings, many Maori farms are depressingly shabby and relatively few are as well cared for or are operated as efficiently as pakeha farms. In other areas, considerable Maori-owned land exists that is improvable and could be put into profitable production if the owners had sufficient enterprise and vision, and were willing to accept reduced immediate remuneration in return for more adequate incomes in the future. Yet the land remains idle because, on the one hand, they refuse to sell it and, on the other hand, they are unwilling to work it or pay rates.

Such conditions undoubtedly reflect differences in cultural values, unfamiliarity with or incomplete assimilation of pakeha standards, and inevitable difficulties in adapting to an alien economic system. It is, therefore, manifestly unfair to consider them outside their cultural context or to invoke discredited explanatory principles predicated on allegedly inherent racial inadequacies. Nevertheless, regardless of their explanation, their very existence is prejudicial to the implementation of the aspirations of Maori youth.

Social Demoralisation. Compounding the conditions of low vocational morale under which Maori adolescents are frequently raised is the social demoralisation characteristic of not a few Maori communities. An atmosphere of wretched housing and sanitary conditions, uncontrolled drinking, improvident spending, and gross neglect of children are hardly propitious for the implementation of youthful vocational ambitions. Under these circumstances adolescents and adults alike tend to become demoralised, apathetic, and unwilling to take even the simplest steps to improve their lot, e.g., to apply for a State housing loan or to assign their wages for house payments. Unfortunately also, this pattern of demoralisation is intensified rather than ameliorated when Government assistance programmes (housing, land development, consolidation of land titles) fail to meet their objectives because of inefficiency, red tape, excessive delay, and lack of finance. As the matter was vividly expressed to me: people tend to become discouraged after waiting five years in vain for a State housing loan, after filing countless applications for clarification of title with the Maori Affairs Department that are never acted upon, or after writing numerous letters to the same Department the receipt of which is not even acknowledged.

Between the ages of 15 and 25, many Maori youths in rural areas are aimless and unsettled with respect to employment. They shift about frequently from one temporary job to another and are often idle for long periods of time. After the age of 25 they appear more anxious to settle down and obtain permanent employment; in most instances, however, migration to an urban centre is necessary.

In contrast to this picture among Maori boys, Maori girls seem to be vocationally much more stable, mature, and ambitious. This is consistent with the fact that Maori women generally constitute a more cohesive and responsible influence than Maori men in family and community life. The same phenomenon has been noted among the American Negro.[3, 4] In times of rapid cultural transition, the burden of keeping the family intact apparently falls more heavily on women than on men because of their stronger emotional ties to home and children.

General Factors in New Zealand Culture

In addition to the aforementioned aspects of Maori culture that hamper the implementation of Maori vocational aspirations, several current features of the larger New Zealand culture in which it is embedded contribute to the difficulties confronting Maori youth in this regard. First, because of the relatively specialised nature of post-primary and undergraduate courses of study in New Zealand, vocational choices must be made quite early in the game —before young people are really mature enough to know their true interests and abilities, as well as the actual nature, requirements and opportunities of the various jobs that appeal to them. This problem is less serious in the United States, because the longer period of general education in American secondary schools and universities provides more time for genuine occupational interests to crystallise before definite commitment is necessary. A related difficulty is the non-availability in New Zealand of many technical and industrial jobs in which adolescents are strongly interested (e.g., automobile, aviation, television, electronics, chemical, metallurgical, nuclear energy). Unless a young person with these interests is prepared to emigrate or redirect his aspirations along other channels, he may flounder aimlessly for a long time before making a satisfactory vocational adjustment.

A second major problem is the relatively casual, "She'll be right" attitude, characteristic of many New Zealand teenagers in contemplating their vocational careers. Fully confident that the future will take care of itself, they exhibit a surprising reluctance to look ahead and make definite plans for a career. This attitude is in part a reflection of the relatively casual and lackadaisical (by American standards) approach to vocational matters currently prevailing in New Zealand. Less cultural emphasis is placed on occupational achievement than in the United States, and adult workers do not set as high a standard for youth regarding the degree of ambition, enterprise and efficiency they display in their jobs. New Zealand parents do not expect and demand as much in the way of vocational accomplishment from their children as their American counterparts do, and the children of professional and middle-class persons are under less family and social class pressure to aspire to professional and managerial careers.[5] Higher education is also used less commonly as a vehicle for rising in social class status, and parents feel less obligated to help their children financially in securing professional and trades qualifications.

Most important of all, however, is the fact that insufficient incentive exists in New Zealand for a young person to acquire a trade or profession—to exhibit the necessary persistence and self-discipline required to complete a prolonged, arduous, and often discouraging period of education and training. Until quite recently many good jobs were available to individuals who lacked the customary educational qualifications. Furthermore, because of the relatively undifferentiated wage scale in New Zealand, unskilled labour is often just as or even more remunerative than jobs requiring considerable schooling or advanced training. Thus, it takes much strength of character for a youth to remain in school or complete his apprenticeship when his friends are making big money in the freezing works. The argument about greater security in the long run fails to impress him when he knows that there has been no scarcity of labouring jobs since World War II.

Racial Prejudice and Discrimination

Reference has already been made to prejudiced attitudes and discriminatory practices in the two local districts in which this study was conducted (see pp. 42-44 and 49-50). A lack of sympathetic understanding (see pp. 45 and 51) and an attitude of sufferance on the part of some teachers ("What's the use of bothering with them—they only go back to the mat?") obviously do not encourage Maori pupils to remain in school or go on to the university in order to obtain the educational qualifications required for various professional and semi-professional occupations. Among the pakeha population at large, prejudice in employing Maoris stems from strong colour bias, from the popular stereotype of the Maori as lazy, happy-go-lucky, undependable, and capable of only rough manual labour, and from unfavourable experience with one or more individuals that is uncritically generalised to the entire race.

Thus, apart from unskilled labour and Public Service jobs, Maoris encounter considerable prejudice in most fields of employment, particularly in banks, shops and offices. Hostile reactions from other employees, may also tend to bar them from managerial and supervisory positions. Generally speaking, with the exceptions noted above, pakeha employers only consider a Maori job applicant if no European is available. It is true, of course, that since World War II, the job market has been generally favourable for Maoris as a result of the underemployment situation. Nevertheless, it is perfectly clear that in many instances they were hired with great reluctance—simply because employers had no other choice— and that they will be the first employees to be laid off in the event of an economic recession.

The apprenticeship situation is especially important in view of the large percentage of Maori boys aspiring to the skilled trades. In small towns, where relatively few apprenticeships are available, Maori boys have virtually no chance at all—partly because of strong anti-Maori prejudice, and partly because pakeha lads are preferred for the few openings that do exist. Hence, Maori boys who are keen on entering a skilled trade must be willing to migrate to the principal centres. It has been easier in recent years to obtain apprenticeships for these boys in Auckland and Wellington; but with the number of vacancies decreasing and the large crop of pakeha war babies now reaching apprenticeship age, the situation is becoming tighter.

A serious problem faced by Maori apprentices (as well as university students) is the great difficulty they experience in obtaining board and lodging in the principal centres because of colour bias. Unless they can find accommodation in special hostels their position is quite hopeless. If they board with Maori families in slum areas, they frequently become distracted by the pleasures and attractions of city life, perhaps become involved in criminal activity, or find themselves unable to resist the lure of immediate high wages in unskilled occupations.

As already pointed out, only one-quarter of the Maori pupils in our sample were aware of the discriminatory practices standing in the way of their vocational aspirations, and the overwhelming majority (90 per cent) were confident that they would ultimately enter and remain in their occupation of choice. They were less confident, however, about achieving vocational success and saw more obstacles of a general nature in their path. Another indication that Maori pupils have some insight into the problem of discrimination in employment is that unlike their pakeha classmates they more frequently aspire to clerical and trades positions with Government and local bodies than with private employers.[31]

Of all the factors impeding the implementation of Maori vocational aspirations, the problem of colour prejudice and discrimination is the most serious and potentially the most dangerous. Difficulties originating in the home, the peer group and the Maori cultural pattern will gradually vanish as acculturation progresses, and as each succeeding generation of Maori parents receives more education. Colour bias, however, is extremely deep-seated in the pakeha population as a whole; and, as the experience of other countries suggests, it will most likely increase as Maoris continue to grow rapidly in numbers, migrate to the cities, contribute disproportionately to the crime and delinquency rates, control the balance of power in Parliament, compete with pakehas for jobs, and interact more intimately with them under inauspicious circumstances in urban slums.

Unfortunately, however, one of the least hopeful aspects of this situation, almost wholly precluding the adoption of effective preventive and remedial measures at the present time, is the unwarrantedly sanguine and self-congratulatory attitude on the part of the New Zealand Government and people—despite all of the evidence to the contrary—that the country is uniquely and completely free of any racial prejudice or discrimination. Unless a more forthright and realistic approach to this problem is soon taken, the unchecked denial of equal vocational opportunity to Maori youth will increasingly foster those social conditions retarding Maori vocational adjustment, i.e., inadequate housing and sanitation, unemployment, segregation in slum areas, delinquency, alcoholism, broken homes, and community demoralisation. This development would not only tend to perpetuate a vicious and well nigh unbreakable circle of vocational and social maladjustment, but would also tend to perpetuate many of the factors underlying colour prejudice as well as incite ugly racial tensions not unlike those in the United States and the Union of South Africa.

CHAPTER FOUR

Factors Affecting Maori Educational Achievement

EXPRESSED ACADEMIC ASPIRATIONS

THE EXPRESSED ACADEMIC ASPIRATIONS OF MAORI AND PAKEHA pupils were remarkably similar in both our urban and rural samples. Urban pupils in each cultural group aspired mostly to "top" and "well above average" marks, whereas rural pupils in each cultural group aspired to "well above average" and "slightly above average" marks. In the urban area, both Maori and pakeha pupils were hopeful of improving their current class standing about five places; but in the rural area, pakeha pupils were significantly more optimistic than their Maori classmates in this respect. Teachers in the urban area also rated pakeha pupils as having higher academic aspirations than Maori pupils.

The expansiveness of Maori pupils showed up particularly in connection with long-term educational aspirations unconstrained by current reality considerations. Approximately 87 per cent of the urban pupils in each cultural group expected to remain in school after the minimal leaving age of 15. The corresponding figure for the rural sample was 90 per cent. There was a suggestive tendency in both urban and rural samples for more Maori than pakeha pupils to aspire to the School Certificate, and in the urban sample for a greater number of Maori pupils to aspire to university education. All of the Maori and pakeha boys who contemplated university studies were hopeful of obtaining degrees.

Examination of the relative educational *attainments* of pakeha and Maori pupils, on the other hand, shows that the aspirations of the latter are less realistic and less likely to be realised. In the urban school the percentage of Maori boys leaving school at the age of 15 was more than four times as high as the corresponding pakeha figure; above the age of 15, the percentage of Maori school leavers in forms III, IV and V, was twice as high as the percentage of pakeha school leavers. In the rural school, the percentage of Maori passes on the School Certificate Examination over the past four years was only 17 per cent as compared to 56 per cent for the pakeha group. Similar figures were reported by a public post-primary school in Hawkes Bay that also has a Maori enrolment of approximately 50 per cent.

National statistics tell much the same story. Although the percentage of Maori primary school leavers who enter post-primary school has increased spectacularly from 30 per cent in 1941 to 85 per cent at the end of 1956,[21] it is still below the 95 per cent level reported for pakeha pupils. [21] The percentage of Maori boys who leave school after completing form III (35 per cent) is almost three times as great as the corresponding figure (13 per cent) for pakeha boys [31] ; in part, however, this difference must be qualified by the fact that Maori boys in form III are on the average seven months older than their pakeha classmates,[31] and hence are more likely to reach their fifteenth birthdays before the end of the school year. By the beginning of the fifth form, 59 per cent of the pakeha boys but only 40 per cent of the Maori boys are still in school.[31] Reflecting the intercultural difference in School Certificate passes, 22 per cent of the pakeha boys and only 4.5 per cent of the Maori boys who enter post-primary school go on to form VI;[31] and whereas 3.5 per cent of the original group of pakeha third-formers go on to the university, only 0.2 per cent of the corresponding group of Maori third-formers do likewise.[20] It is true that the number of Maori students in the universities is much greater today than it was a generation ago. The rate of increase, however, has not been nearly as great as in the post-primary schools and in the teachers' training colleges. In general also, relatively few Maori students complete their university studies or, in the opinion of most lecturers queried by this investigator, make as good academic records as other non-European students from Asiatic and Pacific countries attending New Zealand universities. The latter, however, tend to be much more highly selected for their intellectual ability.

It is clear, therefore, that

the Maori people are not making full use of the opportunities for education that exist. If the loss continues at this rate it will raise in the future serious issues in matters affecting racial relationships. Social integration will best be achieved when points of contact are multiplied so that members of both races meet freely at work and play at all levels. Our aim, therefore, should be to ensure that Maoris enter the the whole range of occupations available to Europeans in approximately the same proportions as do Europeans. This aim cannot be achieved if Maoris are permitted to leave school in large numbers, equipped for nothing but unskilled work.[20]

We shall endeavour to identify in the following sections some of the principal reasons why Maori pupils fail to implement their educational aspirations. In any case, however, as was similarly true of vocational achievement, the root of the difficulty obviously does not lie in low aspirations. It is indeed a highly significant cultural datum that the educational aspirations of Maori pupils are so high in spite of the fact that they are not adequately internalised and will not be appreciably implemented, and despite the existence in the community at large of a pattern of values and behaviour favouring low academic achievement. As already pointed out, this constitutes an important first step, in the assimilation of the pakeha achievement pattern (see p.62).

HOME INFLUENCES

Education as a Value. From discussions with parents and community leaders it is easily apparent that Maori parents do not place as high a value on the social and economic importance of education as pakeha parents do. The current attitudes of Maori parents towards education are roughly comparable to those exhibited by pakeha parents two generations ago. Many Maori parents have had little schooling themselves and hence are unable to appreciate its value or see much point in it.

On the other hand, the position today is incomparably better than it was even a decade ago. Where Maori parents have had some education, they tend to perceive its value and relevance to the vocational adjustment of youth, and usually expect and demand that their children complete more years of schooling than they themselves did; and since the general level of Maori educational attainment is improving each year, we may reasonably anticipate progressive improvement in the attitudes of Maori parents with each succeeding generation. Eighty-five per cent of the next generation of Maori parents, for example, i.e., the boys and girls now attending post-primary school, will have had some taste of secondary school instruction.

Parental Demands and Expectations. It would be fair to say, therefore, that the vast majority of Maori parents today—even those living in remote backblock areas such as Ruatahuna,[24] which has no secondary school facilities—accept the proposition that post-primary schooling is essential for youth. But while they are reconciled to the necessity for such schooling, they have not yet been able in the main to provide the active and wholehearted support that is necessary if their children are to succeed in school and reach the higher rungs of the educational ladder. Pakeha pupils in both urban and rural samples perceived their parents as demanding higher school marks than Maori pupils did, and in the rural sample rated "parent approval" as a more important reason for seeking school success. Paralleling the intercultural difference in pupils' expressed aspirations, Maori parents were perceived as more concerned with School Certificate attainment. As suggested above (see p. 66), however, Maori pupils were probably unable, because of relatively poor parent-child communication to perceive that their parents' aspirations for them in this regard were somewhat nebulous and were not supported by unequivocal demands and expectations. In actual practice, as was evident from everyday observation, Maori parents were much more permissive than their pakeha counterparts about homework, school marks, regular school attendance, and sitting the School Certificate Examination. Maori pupils in our rural area reported less prodding from parents about homework than pakeha pupils did; and in the urban area this greater permissiveness was compounded by a significant loss in parental control over adolescent children.

With increasing age and improved parent-child communication, it becomes progressively more evident to Maori pupils that their parents are, on the whole, not vitally concerned with educational achievement. Hence they tend increasingly to emulate the latter's pattern of hedonistic self-indulgence, procrastination, and lack of long-term striving. This situation, of course, is not improved when responsibility for children's upbringing is divided, as is frequently the case in Maori families, because of the widespread practice of adoption, and because marital arrangements are more casually undertaken and dissolved than in pakeha society.

Thus, experienced teachers of Maori pupils commonly observe —with considerable justice—that the latter seem to lead two almost entirely discrete lives—one at home and in the *pa,* and the other in school. In each situation the pupils speak and act differently. There is relatively little carry-over from school to home, but probably much more in the reverse direction. In school they conform reasonably well to pakeha standards, particularly with respect to the sports programme and the prefect system, and partly in academic matters. At home, however, they tend to relapse to the casual, lackadaisical, and unpunctual ways that prevail in their cultural environment.

This conflict between home and school standards persists until middle adolescence, and is resolved by the aforementioned dichotomization of behaviour that is compatible with high educational and vocational aspirations, on the one hand, and with a more easy-going, self-indulgent orientation to life, on the other. In some instances Maori pupils make quite impressive records in primary school and in forms III and IV. After middle adolescence, however, parental values reinforced by increased contact with the Maori adult community tend to predominate over influences exerted by school and the wider pakeha culture. Existing aspirations weaken and fail to become internalised; and only a bare handful of the youths who had earlier shown promise of conspicuous achievement continue to do well in school and go on to the upper forms and university.

Apart from the lesser value they place on academic achievement, Maori parents are also handicapped in guiding and helping their children in school because of their own lack of attainment and sophistication in these matters and because of their extremely large families. Even if they wanted to help, most of them would not be able or have the time to do so. In both of our samples, particularly the urban, pakeha parents helped their sons more than Maori parents did with their lessons. Maori parents are also more handicapped, by virtue of more frequent residence in outlying areas, both in getting acquainted with and in consulting their children's teachers and headmaster. This is a far different situation from the generally close parent-teacher contact that is maintained in the Maori primary school and in some rural Board schools.[20] For much the same reason, few Maori parents in rural areas participate in Home and School Association activities.

The depressed economic circumstances of the Maori home are also a significant factor militating against high educational achievement. Keeping a youth in secondary school is an expensive proposition and is particularly apt to constitute a burden to Maori parents in view of their large families. Quite apart from the loss of wages, the cost of books, stationery, uniforms, laboratory, and sports fees may run as high as £30 to £40 yearly,* and in some cases room and board are also necessary. In many instances too, parents are either ignorant or totally confused about the availibility and procedures of applying for Government and tribal trust fund scholarships.

Many Maori children are required to perform various household, gardening, or dairying chores, both before and after school, and hence have insufficient time and energy left for their lessons. Even more disruptive to schooling is the widespread practice of Maori parents moving to other districts during the shearing season and taking their children with them. An adolescent boy can be quite helpful in the shearing shed, and more often than not he does not attend school during this period when he is helping his parents.

Squalid housing conditions and overcrowding also adversely affect the quality of Maori school work. Maori pupils rarely have a quiet place in which to do their lessons, and must sometimes study by candle light or kerosene lamp. Frequently, because of late adult entertainment in the home, tribal social functions, or excessive visits to the cinema, they do not get sufficient sleep to be attentive the next day in school. Serious malnutrition and the various maladies associated with unsatisfactory housing (see p. 42) are also common distracting influences. Much of the petty thievery that goes on in some Maori schools stems directly from the fact that many Maori pupils receive an unwholesome and inadequate diet at home (i.e., largely *kumara,* bread, butter, *puha,* and potatoes).

PEER GROUP INFLUENCES

What has been said about the effects of the Maori peer group on vocational achievement (see p. 67-68) is equally true of its influence on the educational attainments of Maori youth. Academic success is a less important value and determinant of individual status in the Maori than in the pakeha peer group, partly as indicated above, because of the more important role of derived status in Maori group structure. Largely for this reason, pakeha teachers often have great difficulty in understanding on what basis certain

---

* The new Government policy of providing textbook grants should materially ease this situation.

Maori pupils seem to enjoy so much *mana* among their age-mates.

Another reason for the relative unimportance of school success as a criterion of status in the Maori peer group is that the latter group (particularly after middle adolescence) increasingly tends to reflect the values of adult Maori culture. These values are more at variance with the ideals of the secondary school than are those of the pakeha peer group and of the adult pakeha culture it mirrors. The fact that more Maori than pakeha pupils in our rural sample perceived their friends and relatives as reacting with disappointment if they (the pupils) failed in school, probably points to the greater cohesiveness of Maori than of pakeha family and peer group structure, rather than to any greater value that Maori friends and relatives attach to school success as such. Under these circumstances Maori pupils would tend to perceive significant persons in their peer and kinship groups as being *generally* more concerned with their welfare than would correspondingly be true in the case of pakeha pupils.

The negative effects of the peer group on educational achievement are greatly enhanced under conditions of social demoralisation, especially when bodgieism and juvenile delinquency flourish. In some such communities, particularly where teachers adopt an ultra-authoritarian and punitive approach, Maori boys are either sullen, defiant, and unruly in school or else adopt a completely apathetic attitude. Racial pride among these pupils has a somewhat chauvinistic and anti-pakeha flavour. They make little effort to better themselves, to reflect credit on their ethnic group, or to acquire a working knowledge of the Maori language or a genuine understanding of Maori culture, but are just fiercely and militantly proud of being Maoris and not pakehas.

MAORI CULTURAL FACTORS

Cultural Attitudes towards Education. A positive cultural factor influen:ing Maori educational achievement is a tradition of veneration of learning stemming from pre-pakeha times. Relatively few peoples with a comparable Stone Age material culture have achieved as high an intellectual standard in religion, mythology, folklore, philosophy, genealogy, and oratory. The former Maori *whare wananga* or house of learning, with its extended courses of formal studies, has few parallels among so-called primitive cultures.

It is true, however, that such studies were reserved for the *rangatira* class.

Much more important is the fact that only tiny remnants of this tradition are still functional today among the Maori people. Prolonged contact with the pakeha, especially with lower-class elements, has resulted in a gradual erosion of the Maori intellectual tradition and traditional respect for learning—a loss that has not yet been compensated for by a corresponding acquisition of European intellectual pursuits. The modern Maori, like so many of his fellow lower-class New Zealanders, tends to be distrustful and somewhat disdainful of book learning and higher education, as well as intensely suspicious of intellectuals.

Disenchantment with pakeha education was also one of the more conspicuous features of the withdrawal of the Maori people following the Maori Wars. In addition to their general disillusionment with all facets of pakeha culture, the people felt especially bitter towards the educated pakeha classes—Government officials, lawyers, ministers of religion—who had lulled them into a false sense of security with high-sounding phrases while other pakehas alienated their land. In some districts, Maoris strenuously resisted early attempts on the part of the Government to establish schools under the Native Schools Act of 1867;[25] and Te Kooti is widely believed to have placed a ban on any Urewera Maori attending the university.

Older Maoris, nevertheless, were quite resistant to the introduction of trade and homecraft subjects into the curriculum of the Maori district high schools when they were first established on the East Coast in 1941. Impressed by prevailing pakeha standards as well as by the enormous prestige of the Maori denominational colleges, they felt that any departure from the strictly academic curriculum of the post-primary school represented a reversion to an inferior type of education and the loss of one assured route to success and a good job. Their resistance first subsided when these subjects were included as options in the School Certificate Examination.

The relatively low existing level of educational attainment among the Maori people obviously limits the potential achievement level of current and succeeding generations of Maori pupils. The latter are not only handicapped by the absence of a strong tradition of academic success among their elders, but also lack the support, guidance, and encouragement of visible emulatory models in their immediate environment. As already pointed out, a higher percentage of Maori than pakeha pupils lives in remote areas where there are only district high schools or no post-primary facilities whatsoever, relatively fewer Maori than pakeha primary school leavers enter secondary school, and a much smaller percentage remain for the upper forms or go on to the university. In some Maori district high schools, difficult staffing problems and/or the lack of positive support of the school's objectives from parents and community have resulted in a serious lowering of academic standards.

The general situation, however, is improving all the time. Even today the older infant mistresses in the Maori schools perceive a vast difference for the better in the learning and deportment of the current generation of Maori youngsters as compared with that of their parents whom they had also taught as children. Inevitably, therefore, the cultural level of the Maori home, the degree of intellectual stimulation it offers Maori children, and the standard of English spoken by Maori parents must progressively improve until they approach or equal pakeha standards.

Cultural Values Regarding Achievement. We have already noted that Maori culture places greater emphasis than pakeha society on derived status, and less stress on the prestige than on the task-oriented and group welfare aspects of primary status (see pp. 68-69). These cultural values affect the educational as well as the vocational accomplishments of Maori youth; but since Maori acculturational progress has been greater in the educational than in the vocational sphere—in terms of the cultural gap currently separating the two peoples—our sample yielded fewer intercultural differences in the former than in the latter motivational area. Motivations for educational achievement, being referable to the less remote future, were also less influenced by the values of the peer group and of the adult Maori community. Pakeha pupils in our urban sample rated "importance for career" more highly than Maori pupils did as a reason for seeking school success; and in our rural sample Maori pupils rated "interest in studies" correspondingly more highly than did pakeha pupils. Within the Maori sample the latter consideration was also more important to rural than to urban pupils as a reason for desiring high marks in school.

One wholly unanticipated finding was the greater responsiveness of Maori than of pakeha urban pupils to immediate prestige incentives in the context of an academic speech contest. But since Maoris customarily respond with great vigour to competition in sports, this datum probably has little or no implications for responsiveness to more *long-term* prestige incentives. It should also be pointed out that in culturally mixed groups, the competition (although nominally among individual pupils) unintentionally assumed some of the characteristics of a contest between two racial *groups*. Another unexpected finding was the higher mean rating urban teachers gave to pakeha than to Maori boys for "co-operativeness in group enterprises". This too, however, was partly understandable in the light of the relatively poor morale and the sullen or apathetic attitude of many Maori pupils in this school, and in view of the fact that the ratings were based on behaviour within a *pakeha* setting.

Maori-pakeha differences with respect to behaviour important for implementing educational aspirations (i.e., amount of time reportedly spent on homework and "swotting" for examinations; worry about examination results) were also relatively minor. The only significant intercultural difference was the greater mean time expended by pakeha pupils in the rural sample in preparing for examinations. Within the Maori sample, however, urban pupils reportedly spent more time both on daily homework and in studying for end of the year examinations.

DIFFICULTIES IN ADAPTING TO SECONDARY SCHOOL

Because they generally come from smaller rural primary schools and country districts, Maori pupils have a more difficult time than their pakeha classmates in adapting to the new secondary school environment.

> In many cases they have come from schools where they were in the majority and where their contacts with Europeans were limited. They knew all their fellow pupils. They had come to know their teachers well. Frequently they had been taught by the same person for the previous three or four years. By far the greatest number of these Maori pupils have now enrolled at fairly large post-primary schools or at large district high schools where they no longer form majority groups.[20]

From my own observations, however, there is a world of difference between the unduly subdued Maori third-former in February, who is as shy and frightened as a rabbit, and the same boy who by

November is relatively poised, self-confident, and out-going.

But at least for the first few months of school, Maori pupils
are likely . . . to be overwhelmed by the large numbers of
new pupils and teachers with whom they come in contact
and to experience an undue feeling of personal inadequacy
. . . They find themselves for the first time mixing with
large numbers of pupils most of whom are strangers and
. . . members of another race. They meet many new
teachers, and instead of having one teacher whom they look
upon as their own, they have several teachers each day. . . .
Methods of teaching will almost certainly be different, and
in their new studies these third-formers will be expected to
rely much more than they have so far had to do on their own
resources. In many cases transport arrangements will debar
them fully from entering into the corporate life of the school.
   For those pupils who have come from Maori schools the
changes are even more marked. For years they have looked
upon their school as their own. They have cleaned it every
day and have cut the lawns and maintained the gardens. . . .
They have felt themselves to be members of a community.
. . . Their teachers have been interested in their health, their
cleanliness, their clothing, and have been quick to investigate
reasons for absences. The pupils have come to interpret these
outward signs as indicative of the measure in which their
teacher is interested in them as persons. Their curriculum
has been planned around their immediate interests and needs.
Significant aspects of their Maoritanga have been emphasised.
Much of the work in the classroom has been oral, to help
them to achieve confidence and competence in the use of
English. Furthermore because of the very nature of the community in which they live, their teachers know their parents,
their homes, their families; they tend to know quickly too of
out-of-school misdemeanours and of erratic and anti-social
behaviour. The pupils have come to look upon their teachers
almost as second parents: they know their house, their car,
their children; they feel that teachers are real people. . . .
In the post-primary schools . . . their teachers frequently
seem impersonal. . . . They know little of their homes, their
family-things in which Maori children are intensely
interested.[20]

Generally speaking also, Maori pupils are less well prepared by
their primary school training for secondary school studies than
their pakeha classmates are. They have been less well grounded
in the academic subjects (see p. 91), and their language handicap

becomes much more disabling (particularly in written work) in dealing with the more difficult subject matter of the post-primary curriculum. In view of the undue stigma attached to poor academic performance and the unaccounted authoritarian and distant attitudes of many post-primary teachers, it is hardly surprising, therefore, that some of the duller Maori pupils become sullen and apathetic, acquire bodgie or anti-social tendencies, or simply mark time until their fifteenth birthdays.

RACIAL PREJUDICE

The various ways in which racial prejudice, especially on the part of some post-primary teachers, affects the educational achievement of Maori pupils have already been discussed in Chapter II (see pp. 45 and 51) and Chapter III (see p. 75). Hence it is only necessary at this point to consider the special difficulties confronting Maori university students. Constituting a very small minority, they are still quite a rarity at the universities and are not easily or naturally accepted by the pakeha student population. Patronising attitudes are very prevalent: Maori students are not uncommonly responded to as if they were simple-minded or incapable of understanding words over two syllables. Many are socially ostracised or given the "silent treatment" by their fellow students. The virtual impossibility of obtaining board and lodging with pakeha families also comes as a shock to some of the more unsophisticated students from rural areas.

In discussing the scholastic proficiency of Maori students with university lecturers, I was unpleasantly surprised to find many of them invoking the "back to the mat" theory in explaining why the latter do not achieve as highly or exhibit the same goal tenacity as other Asiatic or Pacific non-European students in their classes. Few of them appeared to take into account sampling differences as well as relevant cultural, home, intellectual, peer group and situational factors contributing to the relatively poor academic achievement of Maori university students. Unsympathetic attitudes such as these on the part of many of their instructors, coupled with a lack of positive encouragement, obviously do not strengthen the determination of Maori students to persist at and succeed in their studies.

STUNTING OF VERBAL INTELLIGENCE

Maori pupils in primary and post-primary schools, as well as Maori students in the university, are undoubtedly handicapped in academic achievement by a lower average of intellectual functioning than is characteristic of comparable pakeha groups. The mean Otis I.Q. of *all* entering third-formers in our rural school was 83 as compared to a pakeha mean of 96. In our particular rural sample, however, using matched groups, the difference was less marked (Maori mean: 84.9; pakeha mean: 92.8), but was still statistically significant beyond the one per cent level of confidence. Ritchie reported similar findings for his Rakau sample.[35]

In our urban sample the mean Otis I.Q. of Maori pupils was 90.3 or exactly 4 points less than that of pakeha pupils. This intercultural difference was considerably smaller than in the rural sample but was still significant at the five per cent level of confidence. That the latter Maori-pakeha difference may not be representative of all urban environments, however, is suggested by the fact that Leone Smith, using the General Ability Test of the Australian Council for Educational Research, did not obtain a significant intercultural difference in Auckland City for her sample of 11 to 13 year-old pupils.

Marked retardation in English usage and in ability to handle abstract concepts was evident both in the oral expression and in the written composition of the pupils in our Maori sample. Their stories on the Achievement Imagery Test (see p. 185) were inordinately meagre and matter-of-fact in content. Beaglehole and Ritchie,[9] in interpreting their Rakau Rorschach data, have also commented on "the extreme limitation of the role of imagination and fantasy in Maori cognitive organisation". Some Maori children in rural areas have a tendency to use Maori word order in speaking English, e.g., to place the predicate before the subject; to express the interrogative by concluding a declarative sentence with a rising inflection of voice followed by "eh". They also sometimes carry over Maori prepositional usage to English (e.g., arrive *to* a place; go for a ride *on* a car). In some aspects of the language arts, however, Maori pupils are superior to their pakeha classmates. They generally have a more legible handwriting and are less apt to convert simple vowels into diphthongs. In our urban sample also, pakeha pupils mis-spelled words more than twice as frequently as Maori pupils did on the Achievement Imagery Test.

Retardation in language and intellectual development among Maori children is reflected in markedly inferior levels of attainment in the basic school subjects when they enter post-primary school. In our rural sample, Maori third-formers made significantly lower scores than pakeha pupils on both English and arithmetic entrance tests. Comparable findings have been reported by the Hawkes Bay high school mentioned above (see p. 79) where Maori pupils have consistently gained less than ten per cent of the places in the top third form and more than 90 per cent of the places in the lowest of the six third forms. On the 1958 School Certificate Examination, Maori pupils in our rural school made an average score of 31 on the English test as compared to an average score of 47 made by the pakeha pupils.

Causes of Maori Intellectual Retardation. Intellectual retardation among Maori children is attributable to two main factors: (a) the status of the Maori people as a generally underprivileged and rural lower-class minority group with unusually large families, and (b) special disabilities associated with problems of acculturation. Abundant research in the United States and elsewhere has unequivocally demonstrated that the mean I.Q. of rural and lower-class children is lower than that of urban and middle-class children respectively.* The presence of many children in the family also tends to reduce the amount of cognitive stimulation available to each child. "The per capita expenditure on education, recreation, housing, medical care, etc., is ordinarily lower when there are many siblings in the family; and even more important in terms of language development, the extent of parent-child contact is restricted."[4] The importance of social class and urban-rural residence in determining the level of intelligence among Maori pupils in our sample is pointed up by the fact (a) that the overall intercultural difference in I.Q. was significantly lower when Maori and pakeha boys in our sample were matched on the basis of paternal occupation (see p. 90); (b) that in both Maori and pakeha samples, the mean I.Q. of urban pupils was significantly higher than that of rural pupils (see Table I); and (c) that the Maori-pakeha difference in I.Q. was significantly higher in the rural than in the urban area (see p. 90).

But why do pakeha pupils still make higher scores than Maori

---

* See D. P. Ausubel,[4] Chapter 18, for a summary of evidence on the relationship between measured intelligence, on the one hand, and social class, urban-rural residence, and family size, on the other hand.

pupils on intelligence tests when social class and urban-rural residence are held constant for both groups? One plausible possibility suggested by Ritchie[35] is that Maori children lack self-confidence and hence do not strive as hard during the latter stages of the test as the tasks become progressively more difficult. Probably more important, however, is the extreme intellectual impoverishment of the Maori home over and above its rural or lower social class status. The Maori has largely lost the intellectual stimulation of his indigenous culture but has not yet learned to replace it with appropriate intellectual stimulation from pakeha sources. Thus, the Maori child is exposed to a very poor standard of both Maori and English in the home. Books and magazines are seldom available, comics constituting the chief literary fare of most Maori children. Their parents do not ordinarily read to them or tell them stories; and conversation between parents and children tends to be minimal—even at the dinner table. Compounding all of these factors is the generally larger size of Maori than of pakeha families.

Supporting this interpretation of Maori-pakeha differences in I.Q. is the fact that as the level of intellectual stimulation in the Maori environment increases, the intercultural difference correspondingly decreases. Not only is the Maori-pakeha difference less in urban than in rural areas, but urban Maori pupils also make significantly higher intelligence test scores than rural Maori pupils do [see L. M. Smith[40]]. In the face of these data, the frequently advanced argument that Maoris are *inherently* inferior in intellectual endowment is obviously not very tenable. It is equally futile, on the other hand, to argue that because of language retardation or insufficient environmental stimulation, a Maori pupil's *true* intelligence is *really* higher than his score on an intelligence test indicates. An intelligence test does not purport to measure an individual's hereditary intellectual potential but his *current level of intellectual functioning* as influenced by *both* genetic and environmental factors. If he does not score as high as he might have, had he been reared in a more favourable environment, we may properly decry the lamentable waste of human resources; but this in no way detracts from the validity of the score as a true indication of his level of intellectual functioning. The same inability to handle verbal concepts that leads to a low intelligence test score—irrespective of whether it is genetic or environmental in origin—also renders the individual less competent to handle verbal materials in educational and vocational situations.

BILINGUALISM

It is widely believed, by both Maori and pakeha alike, that bilingualism is one of the major factors responsible for the language and intellectual retardation of the Maori pupil and for his relatively poor performance in school. Knowledge of the Maori language, it is asserted, confuses word-idea relationships in his mind, and thus detracts from his capacity for learning English as rapidly as the pakeha child. This view is supported in part by overseas research on the effects of bilingualism on language development and verbal intelligence. Even when bilingual and monolingual children are matched for social class, urban-rural residence, and non-verbal intelligence test scores, the latter still surpass the former on verbal tests of intelligence.*

These studies, however, do not take into account such important factors as (a) the special intellectual impoverishment characterising the home and community environments of an acculturating ethnic group (see p. 92), (b) the social stigma commonly attached to speaking a minority language, and (c) whether children are exposed to the second language before the first one is thoroughly consolidated. Although more definitive research in this area is urgently required, there are good reasons (see below) for believing that the retardation of Maori pupils in the English language can be largely attributed to the poor level of English spoken by their parents, to the absence of suitable reading materials in the home, and to the generally impoverished intellectual environment in Maori rural areas. The socially inferior status of the Maori language, and the frequent practice of exposing Maori children to both languages simultaneously in early childhood, before they acquire a functional knowledge of either, may also be contributory factors.

The Maori child who speaks little or no English is obviously handicapped when he first enters primary school, but if all other cultural factors were equal he would undoubtedly soon overcome this handicap. In addition to the evidence cited above on the relationship between I.Q. and environmental stimulation (see p. 92), examination of records in our two-post primary schools did not show that school marks generally or passes in School

---

* See D. P. Ausubel,[4] pp. 530-531, for a summary of research evidence in this area.

Certificate English were any higher among Maori boys who
scarcely knew a word of the Maori language than among those
who spoke it fluently. It is also noteworthy in this connection
that pupils from Samoa, Fiji, and the Cook Islands (although
undoubtedly selected on the basis of superior academic ability)
generally do quite well in New Zealand universities and secondary
schools, despite the fact that they tend to be fluent in their native
tongues.

<h2 style="text-align:center">ABSENTEEISM</h2>

A final negative factor affecting the educational achievement of
Maori pupils is greater irregularity of attendance than is typical
of their pakeha classmates. When added to their later average age
of beginning and their earlier average age of leaving school, it
materially increases the existing difference between the two peoples
in actual number of years of schooling completed. The mean rate
of absenteeism for the Maori pupils in our urban sample was 10.1
per cent as compared to 5.9 per cent for pakeha pupils.

Four principal patterns of absenteeism were distinguishable
among the Maori pupils in our urban centre. The first type was
due to illness or inadequate sleep, the latter sometimes resulting
from excessive participation in late dances, picture shows, or social
functions at the *pa*. A second type was practised clandestinely
by some Maori boys who took the bus to school in the morning,
but then wandered off into town to purchase or pilfer sweets and
attend an early matinee at the cinema, returning home on the same
bus in the later afternoon. The third type tended to be seasonal.
Some 14 year-old Maori pupils simply stopped attending school
in November at end-of-the-year examination time or when the
freezing works became especially busy. In applying for employment
they either lied brazenly about their age, produced an older
brother's birth certificate, or relied on absent or loosely kept birth
records. In many instances they were aided by the fact that
reaching pubescence at an earlier average age than pakeha boys,
they looked older than their years. Nomadic practices among
Maori parents during the shearing season accounted for the fourth
type of absenteeism. The latter either took their adolescent sons
along to help out in the shearing sheds, or left them at home to
perform the farm chores in their absence.

The high rate of absenteeism among Maori pupils in this urban

district was attributable in part to undue laxness on the part of
Maori parents, school authorities, and other Government officials.
In the first place, many parents did not know (or were not sufficiently interested in their children's education to make it their
business to find out) whether they were attending school regularly.
But even when irregularities were brought to their attention, they
often did not care enough or lacked sufficient control over their
children to remedy the situation. Secondly, school authorities were
much too lackadaisical about investigating reasons for absences,
about promptly notifying visiting teachers regarding serious cases
of truancy, and about initiating the necessary steps leading to the
prosecution of the parents of truant pupils.* Since pakeha pupils
did not ordinarily get away with such flagrant instances of truancy,
one could not help feeling that this permissiveness was in part a
reflection of the prevailing "What difference does it make anyway?
—they only go back to the mat" attitude among pakeha teachers
and educational authorities (see p. 45).

---

* In the few instances where Maori parents have been prosecuted for the
truancy of their children, the fines have been much too lenient (often no
more than a day's wages in the freezing works) to serve as a deterrent
to others.

CHAPTER FIVE

Acculturational History and Personality Development

IN THE PRECEDING CHAPTERS, I HAVE INTERPRETED THE educational and vocational aspirations of Maori youth, their motivations for achievement, and other related traits in terms of family, peer group, and cultural factors affecting the implementation of their aspirations. Still unanswered, of course, is the question of the origin of current Maori values regarding educational and vocational achievement. Hence, after a brief historical survey of the various stages in Maori acculturation, I shall attempt the somewhat more ambitious theoretical task of interpreting the development and transmission of the foregoing cultural values in the light of Maori acculturational history. In the final section I shall hazard some predictions about the future course of Maori acculturation.

STAGES IN MAORI ACCULTURATION*

The following brief survey of stages in Maori acculturational history does not purport to be a definitive account of Maori history in post-pakeha times based on primary source materials. The latter task, although urgently required, would be a monumental undertaking far beyond the scope of the present study. I can only hope to sketch schematically those aspects of acculturational history essential for an understanding of Maori personality development.

Pre-Colonisation (1769-1839)

The first stage of Maori-pakeha interaction was characterised by the exchange of a limited number of specialised goods and

* This section is largely based on the following sources: J. C. Andersen and G. C. Petersen;[1] R. Firth,[17] Chapter 14; H. Holst;[21] J. Miller;[29] K. Sinclair;[39] and I. L. G. Sutherland (Ed.), *The Maori People Today*,[42] Chapters 3 (H. Miller), 5 (A. T. Ngata), 9 (A. T. Ngata), and 10 (A. T. Ngata and I. L. G. Sutherland).

services without any fundamental changes in Maori social or economic organisation. Following Cook's rediscovery of New Zealand in 1769, explorers, whalers, traders, and missionaries came into increasingly greater contact with tribes inhabiting the coastal areas, but the extent of their influence was limited by the absence of large-scale settlement. The Maori quickly perceived the greater efficiency of such European metal tools as axes, hoes, hammers, nails, and fishhooks over his own stone implements, as well as the utility of European blankets, clothing, and weapons. He also saw the advantage of growing potatoes, maize, and cabbage and of raising pigs and cows. In return for these articles he gave the pakeha dressed flax, kauri spars, *kumara,* preserved heads, and land. Other early factors in addition to trade that promoted Maori acculturation included intermarriage and informal sexual liaisons between Maori women and pakeha whalers, the establishment of missionary schools, the association of Maori and pakeha children, mutual learning of each other's language, and the employment of Maori seamen on British ships.[17]

Despite its somewhat sporadic nature, this early contact between Maori and European had some far-reaching effects on Maori culture. The introduction of musket, ball, and powder, for example, greatly intensified the frequency and destructiveness of inter-tribal warfare, leading to the wholesale slaughter of the inhabitants of entire villages and the large-scale migration and displacement of many tribes from their traditional lands. Newly introduced European diseases had no less deadly an impact on the Maori population. In order to obtain the prized musket, various tribes devoted a disproportionate amount of time to the production of dressed flax, moved their villages to swamp areas, and neglected their other cultivations and economic pursuits; malnutrition, starvation, unsanitary living conditions and pulmonary disease were some of the inevitable consequences of this practice. Contact with European material accessories stimulated new economic perspectives, desires, values and ambitions;[17] and as the influence of the missionaries grew, the institutions of inter-tribal warfare, cannibalism, slavery and polygamy were proscribed with consequent loss in the *mana* of the chiefs and in their power to exercise economic leadership. Nevertheless, goods

> were still produced by ordinary native methods, and the
> organisation of activity was carried out on the usual lines.
> The family or *hapu* worked under the leadership of their

head man, the *tohunga* or priestly expert had his place to
fill, native technical processes were largely retained, among
themselves the former Maori system of exchange and distribution of goods, of ownership and acquisition of property
remained practically unaffected.[17]

Colonisation (1840-1859)

The beginning of permanent colonisation in 1840 under the
Wakefield immigration scheme, coupled with the assumption of
British sovereignty over New Zealand, inaugurated a new phase
of Maori acculturation. Colonisation represented a serious and
permanent threat to the cultural autonomy of the Maori and to the
integrity of his indigenous social and economic institutions. An
element of coercion was added to his previous voluntary acceptance of certain selected aspects of pakeha culture. This coercive
threat was implicit in the rapid growth of the pakeha population
and of the size and number of the European settlements; in the
acknowledgement of Queen Victoria's sovereignty; in the presence
of British troops and Government officials; and in the acceptance
of the Queen's law and control over his land.

During this phase the Maori people not only continued to adopt
an ever increasing variety of European goods but also took over
many pakeha technical methods and processes of production. They
learned to grow wheat with the aid of ploughs, horses, and
bullocks, and built barns for storing and threshing it and mills to
grind it to flour. They constructed timber mills, raised maize,
potatoes, vegetables, fruit, and pigs for the market, and acquired
and operated coastal vessels to transport their produce to distant
markets. Many Maoris—children and adults alike—attended
school, where in addition to reading, writing, arithmetic, and
scripture, they learned agriculture, carpentry, sewing, and other
practical arts. European clothing almost completely supplanted the
blanket and native garments.

These material innovations also wrought some significant
changes in the Maori economic system. The people began to produce surpluses for purposes of barter and profit, learned the use
of money as a medium of exchange, and acquired habits of thrift
and the technique of driving a hard bargain. To some extent also,
employment, economic responsibility and the expenditure of wages
and profits were individualised. For the most part, however, the
new methods of production and exchange were simply incorporated
into the existing social and economic organisation of Maori

village life. Capital goods such as flour mills and coastal vessels remained the property of the tribe, and groups of kinsmen laboured co-operatively under the direction of their chiefs and shared in the distribution of the produce. The chief retained his position as economic organiser, entrepreneur, and trustee of the interests of the people, and hospitality and reciprocal feasting were practised as before. In short, the Maori sought to gain all of the benefits of European technology, but to retain as far as possible his land, his customs, his social institutions, and his distinctive way of life.

But in accepting colonisation and British sovereignty, the Maori failed to reckon with the political and economic realities of the European system of colonisation—forces that were only dimly apparent in early Victorian New Zealand but which had everywhere else where Europeans settled in force resulted in the subjugation of native peoples, in the alienation of their land, and in the destruction of their autonomous cultures. It is true that in 1840 humanitarian missionary influences were dominant in the British Colonial Office, and that the Imperial Government was motivated in part by humanitarian considerations in extending its sovereignty over New Zealand. The Treaty of Waitangi was in fact designed to protect the Maori people from the predatory designs of the New Zealand Company, and to guarantee them the possession of their lands and the privileges of British citizenship. The colonists, however, had no understanding of or sympathy for the rights, welfare, and aspirations of the Maori, regarding him contemptuously as an inherently inferior and ignorant savage presumptuously standing in the way of their immediate possession of all the desirable land in New Zealand. They were outspokenly impatient with the British Government's policy of safeguarding the interests of the Maori people and with the latter's reluctance to part with their land, and did everything in their power to subvert the Treaty of Waitangi and wrest control of Maori Affairs from the British Colonial Office. Maoris were denied representation in the General Assembly, and huge tracts of Maori land were alienated by sharp practices and by questionable, coercive, or frankly illegal means. The Maori people responded to this pressure by refusing in organised fashion to sell their land, ownership of which was not only the essential basis of their economy but was also a matter of deep tribal sentiment and an important symbol of resistance to further pakeha encroachment. When in 1860 the Atiawa tribe refused to surrender land at Waitara that had been illegally purchased, the colonists forced war upon the Maori people and subsequently confiscated much of the best land in Taranaki, the Waikato and the Bay of Plenty.

War (1860-1872)

Active Maori opposition to European domination in New Zealand had actually broken out long before 1860. Many chiefs, in fact, were vigorously opposed to signing the Treaty of Waitangi; and as early as 1843 Hone Heke rebelled against the British flag at the Bay of Islands. Similar sporadic resistance to pakeha settlement by Te Rauparaha and his followers led to fighting at Wairau in 1843 and in the Hutt Valley in 1846; and the settlement at Wanganui was attacked in 1847 following many long-standing disputes over land purchases and the accidental shooting of a Maori. All of these skirmishes, however, were relatively circumscribed and unorganised, and did not command the support of wide sections of the Maori people. Resistance to the sale of land was largely an intra-tribal affair; and even within a particular tribe, sentiment was often divided and fluctuated rapidly between selling and holding.

During the next decade various inter-tribal conferences laid the basis of more effective national resistance to European encroachment, culminating in the election of the celebrated Waikato chief, Te Wherowhero, as Maori King in 1858. The Maori King movement combined organised resistance to the further sale of land with supra-tribal nationalism, a striving towards *kotahitanga* (i.e., unity), and an insistent demand for some measure of autonomous self-government under the Queen. Thus by 1860, when the fighting erupted in Taranaki, most of the Maoris "south of Auckland and outside the settlements were supporters, if not of the King, at least of the anti-land-selling principles of the movement".[39]

The Taranaki War that began at Waitara soon spread to the Waikato, the Bay of Plenty and the East Coast, and eventually involved on one side or the other most of the principal tribes of the North Island except those in Northland and in parts of the southern portion of Wellington Province. The most violent phase of the war was over in 1864, but intermittent guerilla fighting continued in Taranaki, the Bay of Plenty and the Urewera until 1872.

Withdrawal (1872-1927)

The war and the confiscations left bitterness, disillusionment, and resentment in the Maori camp. In addition to the grievous loss of life and land, houses, cultivations, capital goods, mills, farm implements, and coastal vessels were destroyed; and although he had acquitted himself bravely against the pakeha's overwhelming military superiority, the Maori's *mana* was broken. He felt himself a humbled stranger in the land of his forefathers, betrayed by the greed and cunning of the white man. He lost confidence both in himself and in the pakeha. Throughout the length and breadth of Maoridom a wave of revulsion arose against European values, customs, education, and religion. Even the everyday motives of the pakeha became suspect. For the most part, the Maori withdrew from contact with the European, retiring into large reservation-like areas like the King Country and the Urewera or into his backblock villages. The general mood was one of apathy and despondency. He lost interest in work and grew careless and heedless of the future. Economic stagnation set in, and as the Maori population continued to decline in numbers the rapid disappearance of the Maori race was freely predicted in many quarters.

Some improvement in the Maori's psychological attitude occurred in the eighties. The voluntary opening up of the King Country to pakeha settlement reflected some softening in his uncompromising withdrawal and a gradual rapprochement with the European colonists. The Maori population, however, continued to decline, reaching an all-time low of 42,000 in 1896.[15] At this critical juncture in Maori history the Maori will to survive was buttressed by a small group of Europeanised, educated, and dedicated young men (including A. T. Ngata, P. H. Buck, and M. Pomare) members of the Te Aute College Students' Association, who in 1897 organised a movement, later known as the Young Maori Party, for uplifting the condition of the Maori people through a programme of education, sanitation, sobriety, industry, and economic rehabilitation. Although they stressed the importance of preserving Maori cultural identity and racial pride, they recognised that the "economic future of the race lay in the conscious adoption of European methods and culture, of taking over as far as possible all that could be learned of European techniques and processes".[17] Their efforts bore some fruit but they could hardly be expected to remake the face of Maori society. For one thing the party had little rank-and-file basis; its members were "sports" with an aspirational level several generations ahead of their time. They left the great mass of the people far behind. Even today, 60 years later, a Maori leader approaching their stature is nowhere in sight.

Much more in keeping with the mood of the people were a large number of "adjustment cults" that flourished during the period of withdrawal. Some were largely religious and messianic in character, others were more secular, political, and nationalistic in orientation; but they all stemmed from a deep-seated urge to resist pakeha encroachment and to perpetuate Maori cultural identity. In one form or another they emphasised various traditional themes in Maori culture, embellishing them with some of the more spectacular features of European religion and government.

Four of these movements—the King movement, Hau Hauism, the Ringatu Church and Te Whitism—had their origins in the conditions preceding and accompanying the Maori Wars. The aims and status of the King movement (see p. 100) have changed remarkably little over the past century. The parochial basis of its membership and loyalties, and its preoccupation with certain moribund and ceremonial aspects of Maori life (except during the "regency" of Princess Te Puea) have prevented it from uniting the people under a supra-tribal banner and from playing a truly progressive role in Maori acculturation. The fanatical Hau Hau cult, originating out of the desperation of the Taranaki War, combined the elements of magic, ritualism, revelation, religious ecstasy, blood lust, and messianic deliverance. It also inspired some of the symbolism (including the name) of Te Kooti's Ringatu Church. The latter movement, however, placed greater emphasis on prophecy, faith healing, the Jehovah concept of the Old Testament, and Te Kooti's betrayal and martyrdom. Te Whiti's movement was largely predicated on deep-seated Maori grievances associated with the Taranaki confiscations. It featured prophecy, the *haka* and the *poi* dance, and passive resistance to such European institutions as roads, public health, and education.

In addition to these major religious movements, almost every district had (and still has to this very day) its own local *tohunga* who practised a form of folk medicine based on residual Maori beliefs in *tapu, atua,* and *makutu.* In professing to cure the *mate Maori,* the *tohunga* relied on his personal *mana* or "power" (often acquired from his preceptor) and on a combination of scripture, prayer, faith healing, and superstitious ritual.

Among the more modern adjustment cults may be counted the militant and nationalistic *Kotahitanga* movement in Northland with its aspirations for national unity, and the Ratana movement which originally started as a form of faith healing and later developed into a separate Maori church with its own esoteric theology and orders of clergy. It too contains elements of supra-tribal nationalism and strong reactionary undercurrents reminiscent of Te Whiti's teachings. As a religious and social movement it is rapidly dying out. The main factor accounting for its survival to date is its tremendous influence in Maori Labour politics.

On the economic front, the large-scale communal enterprises in agriculture and commerce that flourished prior to the wars were largely replaced by an individualised type of subsistence farming. Each family tended its own *kumara* and potato patch, and some families raised a few pigs, grew some maize and vegetables or kept a few cows. In coastal areas and along rivers the people supplemented their diet with fish; and in the forest wild pigs, deer, and pigeons were often available. Cash for clothes and groceries was obtained by working seasonally for European farmers and by helping the pakeha clear the bush, develop his land, and build roads and railways. For the most part each family assumed individual responsibility for its own economic activities, worked alone, and kept the fruits of its own labour. The old communal system of common- ownership, co-operative labour organised under the direction of chief and *tohunga,* and sharing of the harvest among the kinship group was largely abandoned. In some activities (i.e., large-scale net fishing, ploughing, shearing, road work), however, co-operative work on a *whanau* or *hapu* basis was common. In any case, a Maori in need could always count on the help and support of his kinsmen. Mutual assistance, co-operative sharing of the economic burdens and vicissitudes of life, lavish hospitality, and recognition of kinship responsibilities remained central values in Maori village culture.

Social life in the village—*huis,* tribal politics, concerts, oratory, *tangis,* the welcoming of visitors—was centred on the *marae* and meeting house. The chiefly families retained their social and political status to some extent, took the lead in village and tribal matters and on ceremonial occasions, but largely relinquished their role as economic organisers and entrepreneurs. The people continued to wear European clothing and gradually adopted European style houses. In general they accepted the principles of a money economy, of individual ownership of land and (except for

marriage) of pakeha law.[17] A growing percentage of Maori children attended primary school but few went on to secondary school
and university or entered the skilled trades. The Maori electorate
was divided into four districts and granted four seats in Parliament.
Most of the established European churches in the Maori field
organised Maori mission boards and kept their members despite
some defection to the Ratana and Ringatu Churches and more
recently to the Church of the Latter Day Saints (Mormon Church).
Generally speaking, although Maoris were not unwelcome in
pakeha churches, they preferred to worship among themselves.

About the turn of the century, some Maoris turned to European-
type pastoral and dairy farming. Relatively few, however, were
successful in this endeavour. They were hampered by lack of clear,
permanent, and individual title to the land, by progressive atomi-
sation of communal land titles, by lack of capital, by ignorance
of modern agricultural techniques, and by the general spirit of
apathy, slipshodness and demoralisation that prevailed in the
villages. The alienation of Maori land continued apace, and most
of the Maori-owned land that was not sold outright was rented
to pakeha farmers or left idle rather than worked by Maori owners.

Later, largely through the efforts of Sir Apirana Ngata, the
title position was improved by resorting to such devices as incorporation, consolidation of fractional interests, and the vesting of
title in statutory bodies. In the late twenties capital for land
improvement became available from Maori Land Boards and the
Native Trustee, and in 1930 the Department of Maori Affairs
established its own land development scheme which also provided
the important elements of instruction and supervision in addition
to capital advances. Some Maori communities, particularly on
the East Coast, established their own dairy companies. As already
pointed out, however, most Maori dwellers in rural areas either
did not attempt modern pastoral or dairy farming, or (with certain
outstanding exceptions on the East Coast and in Hawkes Bay)
became marginal producers (see p. 72).

During the late thirties the economic position of the Maori
people was greatly ameliorated by the inauguration of Social
Security. Renewed interest was also shown in the cultural, artistic,
and ceremonial aspects of Maori life. This latter movement was
encouraged by a shift in 1931 from a purely academic curriculum
in the Maori schools, based on a policy of rapid assimilation, to a
curriculum that included more practical instruction as well as

Maori folk-lore, history, songs, dances, games, and arts and crafts.[21]

Underlying Bases of Maori "Resistive Acculturation". We might very well raise at this point the question of why Maori culture was able to withstand the inroads of pakeha influence and preserve its value system and basic patterns of social organisation largely intact despite the disorganisation of its economic system and the adoption of European material culture. What factors prevented the assimilation of Polynesian by European culture as, for example, occurred almost completely in Hawaii and partially in American Samoa? The answer to this question undoubtedly hinges (a) on the nature of the indigenous culture prior to European contact, and (b) on the nature of the contact. With respect to the first variable, it is reasonable to suppose that the resistance of Maori culture to European assimilation was related in part to the vigorousness of its own adaptive mechanisms. Adaptiveness was forced on the Maori by virtue of their migration from a semi-tropical to a temperate climate only four centuries prior to European contact. They alone of all the Polynesian peoples were obliged to devise drastically new solutions to the fundamental problems of food, clothing, and shelter. In the process of adapting to a new physical enviroment, they not only enhanced their resistance to cultural extinction but also evolved new techniques of warfare and elaborated distinctive forms of art, technology, religion, and social organisation. Furthermore, they found these cultural forms efficient, congenial, and psychologically satisfying, and hence were understandably more reluctant to scrap them for a strange and untried set of values and customs than if they had been unhappy and disgruntled with their lot.

Secondly, when this vigorous, stable, and psychologically congenial culture felt itself seriously threatened by the predatory designs of aggressive colonists from an alien civilisation, it reacted violently—first in sporadic armed resistance and in forming a supra-tribal nationalistic movement aimed at preserving Maori land holdings, and then in defending its territory fiercely when forced into war. The bitterness and resentment provoked by aggression, war, and confiscation led both to profound disillusionment with and rejection of European culture and to a conscious and organised effort to emphasise as far as possible the central values of the indigenous culture. In some instances, as a result of desperation, disorganisation, and demoralisation, the people turned to such unadaptive but adjustive devices as magical and messianic cults, emphasis on moribund and ceremonial features of the culture as ends in themselves, and arbitrary rejection of progressive material aspects and techniques of the new culture. If we contrast this sequence of events with an acculturational situation in which the new culture is introduced gradually and insidiously (e.g., solely through missionaries, traders, and their descendants) without mass colonisation or violent head-on collision between the two cultures, it is not difficult to understand why assimilation of the indigenous culture is a very likely possibility, particularly if it lacks vigour and stability or is productive of anxiety and dissatisfaction.

Once the motivation for perpetuating the distinctive features of the indigenous culture and for resisting absorption by the introduced (European) culture exists—on the basis of either the satisfying and adaptive features of the original culture or the violent nature of the contact, or both—perpetuative mechanisms are necessary. As Freed[18] points out, the existence of such "boundary maintaining mechanisms" as language and ritual is not enough; all cultures have such mechanisms. Hence, "if their presence alone were sufficient to preserve a group's key values there would be fewer disintegrating native cultures today than there are".[18] The most obvious type of perpetuative mechanism (yet, strangely enough, completely overlooked by Freed), especially under circumstances of catastrophic defeat following violent conflict, is complete or semi-complete physical, social, and psychological withdrawal into reservations or reservation-like areas, and the practising of an attenuated form of the indigenous culture combined with partial adoption of European material accessories and techniques and a subsistence economy. This solution—forced on and adopted by both the Maori and the American Indian under quite comparable circumstances—allows for the preservation of the central values of the indigenous culture and of the basic features of its social organisation. Withdrawal implements the determination of the indigenous people to preserve their cultural identity and to resist assimilation, by providing a protected socio-economic environment in which the principal themes and values of the original but shattered culture can be practised and transmitted to the younger generation without much possibility of exposure to and "contamination" by European civilisation. Hence, over the course of several generations, a tradition and a *modus operandi* of *resistive acculturation* are evolved, consisting of (a) a hard core of indigenous values, customs, and forms of social organisation, (b) affectively charged repudiation of European values, and (c) such modifications of the original culture as are conditioned or necessitated by apathy and demoralisation, by the breakdown of certain traditional social institutions and modes of leadership and economic organisation, and by the adoption of some European cultural forms (see p. 103).

Complete assimilation and resistive acculturation represent the extremes in culture contact situations. The first outcome results when a primitive culture lacking vigour and stability, and failing to provide adequately for basic psychological satisfactions, is insidiously superseded by a more efficient and attractive introduced culture without any violent clash between them. The second outcome results when precisely the opposite set of circumstances exists, providing that defeat stops short of virtual annihilation, and that relatively complete withdrawal into physically and socially isolated areas is both possible and acceptable.* Under less extreme conditions, e.g., Fiji, Western Samoa, and New Zealand in the pre-colonisation phase of acculturation (see p. 96), where the indigenous culture is adequately vigorous and productive of psychological satisfactions, and where Europeans either do not attempt an overly aggressive policy of subjugation, colonisation, and alienation of land, or as a matter of policy seek to preserve native institutions, various forms of both non-assimilative and non-resistive acculturation take place, i.e., adaptation, blending, syncretism, and alternative manifestation of antithetical traits (each in its appropriate cultural setting). Ample motivation exists for perpetuating the existing culture, but (unlike the situation in resistive acculturation) *not* for emphasising indigenous symbolic elements and rejecting European values and techniques as ends in themselves apart from their inherent merits in particular circumstances. European cultural elements are voluntarily incorporated with more or less modification into the existing cultural pattern on the basis of their inherent compatibility with the "sum total of custom, belief, technique, and material apparatus by which the people regulate their lives".[17] The structure of tradi-

---

* The same objectives accomplished by withdrawal have been attempted on a more coercive basis in South Africa, New Guinea, and southern United States through the creation of a caste or colour bar system. When caste lines are rigidly enforced by means of violence, terror or restrictive legislation, however, nationalistic resistance to segregation *per se* often overshadows the rejection of alien values.

tional, social, and economic institutions remains essentially intact without any demoralisation or breakdown in leadership. Physical, social, and psychological withdrawal is unnecessary for the preservation of indigenous social structure, and the people have no motivation to withdraw on the basis of their acculturational experience. But the danger of gradual erosion of traditional values and social organisation—simply by virtue of continuous contact with or envelopment by a dominant European culture—still exists. Mechanisms for preserving the integrity of the basic social structure are therefore necessary, for should disintegration occur the problem of maintaining the key values of the culture is rendered incomparably more complicated and difficult.

Using the Old Order Amish of Pennsylvania and the former *shtetl* society of Eastern European Jews as examples, Freed describes two perpetuative mechanisms that operate to prevent the erosion of traditional social organisation in this type of *adaptive acculturation,* and then goes on to use these two examples as the basis of a typology of indigenous cultures that are successful in resisting assimilation.

The *shtetl* and the Amish represent different types of solution to the problem of preserving traditional cultural values in the face of external pressures to change. The *shtetl-*type features a class system with the upper classes being most concerned with the cultural focus. Correlated with this is a rather wide range of permitted social behaviour and the infrequent use of extreme forms of social control. Characteristic of the Amish-type is the lack of a class system, and this is correlated with strong mechanisms of social control which are readily invoked and which result in the frequent expulsion of deviant individuals. If there are enough deviants they may form a "progressive" faction and then split off as a schismatic group. Both societies readily accept innovation in peripheral areas of culture.[18]

Although the above mechanisms are undoubtedly applicable to the cultures described and perhaps to other examples of adaptive as well as resistive acculturation,* they obviously do not constitute in themselves a complete typology of non-assimilative culture contact. Freed's theoretical structure neither takes into account

---

* Both types of mechanisms are operative in contemporary Maori society which is currently in a post-withdrawal phase of acculturation (see pp. 109-111). The burden of perpetuating the traditional aspects of Maori culture (i.e., knowledge of tribal genealogy and history, leadership in tribal affairs, formal Maori oratory on the *marae*) still falls primarily on middle-

the role of motivation in perpetuating cultural identity, nor the different kinds of motivation that are operative in coercive (resistive) and non-coercive (assimilative and adaptive) acculturational situations. It also ignores completely the very common perpetuative mechanism of withdrawal in resistive acculturation and the ways in which it differs from non-withdrawal mechanisms in adaptive acculturation. Finally, it fails to make clear that most effective perpetuative mechanisms operate to preserve the traditional values of a culture "in the face of external pressures to change" by helping to keep intact its indigenous pattern of social organisation.

Post-Withdrawal (1940-   )

As long as physical, psychological, and social withdrawal made possible the preservation of Maori village life and social organisation, a hard core of Maori values survived and was easily transmitted from one generation to the next. But the cumulative impact of several factors favouring emergence from withdrawal had already been operating for some time, and only required the catalytic influence of World War II to effect this outcome. In the first place, the Maoris were psychologically ready for emergence from their self-imposed isolation. Over the course of three generations the motivations that sustained the desire for withdrawal (i.e., bitterness and resentment related to the Maori Wars and the confiscations; suspicion of the pakeha, distrust of his motives, and disillusionment with and repudiation of his way of life) had been gradually attenuated with the passing of the old people and the institution of a generally benevolent Government policy towards the Maori population. The young generation was better educated, more highly Europeanised, more desirous of obtaining better paid, pakeha-type jobs, and less disposed automatically to reject pakeha values simply because of their origin. Secondly, an expanding network of new highways and the introduction of electricity, the telephone, the wireless, and the automobile into Maori cultural life had insidiously reduced the physical as well as the psychological isolation of the backwater village. Thirdly, the

---

aged and old males in the tribe, especially on those elders (*kaumatua*) descended from chiefly families (the *shtetl*-type mechanism) as it always has in Maori history. The Amish-type mechanism is exemplified by some older adolescent peer groups, particularly in demoralised Maori communities, which impose severe sanctions for any expression of achievement motivation among their members (see p. 67).

rapid growth of the Maori population, coupled with the steady diminution of Maori land resources, had created a serious problem of unemployment in rural areas. Hence, when World War II broke out and thousands of good jobs became available in urban centres, Maori young people were quite prepared to migrate to the cities, to sample the pleasures and novelty of urban life and to enter into closer contact with the pakeha. The military experience of thousands of young Maori soldiers, as well as various civilian aspects of the war effort, also helped to catapult the Maori people out of their backblock isolation into the mainstream of New Zealand life.

The disintegration of the withdrawal mechanism, however, did not mean that the Maori people were suddenly placed in the same acculturational position as those indigenous peoples who had *never* practised withdrawal in adaptive culture contact situations. First, from the very beginning, traditional social structure was much more disorganised in resistive withdrawal than in adaptive, non-withdrawal acculturational situations; and with the large-scale urban migration and disruption of village life characteristic of the post-withdrawal phase, this discrepancy became even greater. Secondly, the abrupt resumption of contact in the post-withdrawal stage made for a more traumatic, conflictful, and anxiety producing adjustment process than in situations where the contact had been gradual and continuous over a long period of time. As a result of this precipitous reintroduction to contact, particularly in urban situations, and of the rapid breakdown of traditional social organisation and village controls, it was reasonable to suppose that much more "generation conflict", crime, juvenile delinquency, adolescent cultism, and alienation of youth from indigenous cultural practices and values could be anticipated in the former than in the latter situation.

Finally, neither the process of emergence from withdrawal nor the reversal of 70 years experience in actively resisting pakeha culture were phenomena that could be accomplished overnight. The Maori population was and still is predominantly rural; and although village social structure and tribal loyalties have been palpably weakening, they are still factors to be reckoned with today, almost twenty years after the onset of this phase of Maori acculturational history. A strong residuum of traditional values, of ingrained mechanisms of resistance to acculturation, and of deep-seated tendencies indiscriminately to reject pakeha values is still current among the Maori people—even in urban areas. This is particularly true of the middle and older generations of Maori adults who intellectually accept the desirability of young people acquiring European educational and vocational skills, but are emotionally ambivalent about the situation and actually do very little to help them realise these objectives. Hence, even though young Maori adolescents satisfactorily assimilate the pakeha pattern of educational and vocational aspiration they still fail to internalise and implement it adequately—largely because of in-sufficient support (i.e., expectations, demands, example) from their parents, older sibling and peers, and from the adult Maori community. It is hardly surprising, therefore, that in comparison with their counterparts from the Cook Islands, Fiji and Western Samoa, Maori pupils appear to be lacking in achievement motiva-tion, persistence, self-discipline, and long-term determination to succeed.

The emergence-from-withdrawal phase of Maori acculturation has been characterised by the following major developments stem-ming from the re-establishment of contact with the pakeha: (a) very gradual disintegration of Maori village life and social organi-sation; (b) the growth of a youthful urban proletariat and of various youth and social problems associated with excessively abrupt urban acculturation; (c) the revival of latent anti-Maori racial prejudice in the pakeha population; (d) the growth of Maori racial nationalism; (e) notable advancement along many social and economic fronts; and (f) the establishment of self-government at a community level.

Disruption of Maori Village Life. The primary cause of the gradual disintegration of Maori village life has been the slow but consistent erosion of those physical and psychological mechanisms that isolated it from the main-stream of New Zealand society and gave it a semi-autonomous cultural status not unlike that of the Cook Islands or of an American Indian reservation. As a result of the operation of these erosive forces (see pp. 109-110), the major psychological orientation of youth has been de-flected from the tribe and village towards the wider pakeha world both in New Zealand and overseas. As the young people migrated to the towns and cities, and to other country districts undergoing more extensive rural development, leaving the old people at home, the population balance between the generations was upset and the authority of the tribal elders was undermined. Hereditary status counted for little when there was no one to guide, instruct, advise, and lead; when youth looked elsewhere for direction, status, and approbation; when the power of the chief to influence the lives of his people diminished; and when his prestige and authority were largely restricted to ceremonial functions and occasions.

All of these factors plus the influence of pakeha egalitarianism have altered the traditional pattern of village leadership. Hereditary rank and knowledge of tribal lore have become less important criteria for exercising leadership, and executive competence and sophistication in the economic and political aspects of European life have correspondingly gained in importance. Autocratic techniques and authoritarian methods have decreased in favour; and women have assumed an increasingly more active and influential role in community affairs, partly as a consequence of pakeha example, partly because their role in home and community is generally a more cohesive and responsible one than that of men, and partly because the Maori Women's Welfare League is currently the only dominion-wide Maori organisation. The establishment of some local self-government at the community level through the institution of tribal committees and executives under the Maori Social and Economic Advancement Act of 1945 has also provided new channels for the assumption of leadership.

The extent to which these changes in village life have occurred varies considerably from one district to another. In some areas community life has been almost completely disorganised, and many once flourishing and orderly *pas* have been turned into "ghost" villages or into rural slums beset by lawlessness, juvenile delinquency, alcoholism, slothfulness, and neglect of basic interpersonal responsibilities. In other districts traditional community life is still vigorous, but patterns of leadership have changed and the old spirit of isolation from European culture has vanished.

Growth of a Youthful Urban Proletariat.* The past generation has witnessed, for reasons enumerated above (see p. 57-58), the remarkably rapid growth of an urban Maori working class. Within a four-mile radius of the Central Post Office of Auckland City there are today some 14,000 Maoris, whereas in 1936 there were less than 1,800, and in 1945 less than 5,000.[13, 26] Equally significant is the disproportionate concentration of young Maori adults and small children in urban centres.

In the city, especially among the psychologically more flexible

---

* This section is based on Metge's Auckland material[26, 27] and on data from my own urban sample.

and impressionable young people, the pace of acculturation obviously quickens. For lack of opportunity and proper atmosphere and because of pakeha amusement or derision, many specific traditional practices—language, *hongi, tangi, hui,* open-handed hospitality—are either abandoned or greatly attenuated. Children and youth are more exposed to pakeha ways of life, have less chance to absorb traditional Maori values, and are largely released from the control of parents, elders, and Maori community opinion. And, as we have already seen, in their educational and vocational aspirations and in their desires for occupational prestige and success, they approximate the urban European pattern much more closely than their rural cousins do (see p. 58).

Yet, although *Maoritanga* is altered and diluted in urban settings, it is not completely destroyed. The Maori are still very much of an identifiable ethnic and racial minority in the city; and despite the fact that their interests, activities, and ideology are increasingly dominated by the wider pakeha world, in their immediate personal orbits they primarily identify and associate with their own people. In their attitudes towards primary and derived status, work, money, achievement, success, marriage, children, sex, and kinship obligations, in their vocational and educational aspirations, in their needs for community living and group psychological support, urban Maoris are still much further removed from urban pakehas than their rural counterparts are from rural pakehas (see p. 56). Some urban Maoris, especially the bright and aspiring young men in professional and public service careers, succeed in adopting the pakeha way of life; but the vast majority fail in the attempt—partly because pakehas do not really accept them as they do their own people, and partly because of their own deeply ingrained needs for Maori group fellowship and derived status.

One outstanding symptom of urban acculturational stress is the unusually high rate of Maori crime and juvenile delinquency, which is three to four times as high as the pakeha rate in terms of such indices as number of arrests, convictions, and Borstal and prison inmates.* Compounding the acculturational tensions stemming from the abruptness of exposure to pakeha ways are such factors as inexperience in coping with the temptations of urban life,

---

* Summary of statement by Mr S. T. Barnett, Secretary of Justice, in the annual report of the Justice Department, as quoted by the *Auckland Star,* 6th August, 1958.

feelings of loneliness and homesickness in the city, the earlier Maori age of leaving school, segregation in urban slum areas, and racial prejudice and discrimination. In connection with the latter factor it is noteworthy that Maori crime rates are highest in those urban areas where race relations are poorest, i.e., Northland, Auckland City, and the Waikato. Other probably contributory causes include intense "generation conflict"; the loss of parental control; excessive permissiveness and neglect on the part of many Maori parents; lack of explicit and consistent ethical training in the home because of parental confusion regarding reasonable standards of discipline; and release from the restraining influence of village elders and community opinion. Having less plausibility and totally unsupported by my observations are the frequently voiced suggestions (a) that delinquency is a Maori behavioural equivalent of pakeha neurosis (thereby accounting for the relatively low rate of Maori mental disorder), and (b) that Maori elders are tolerant of anti-social conduct directed against the pakeha community.

The Revival of Colour Prejudice in New Zealand. The British colonists who settled in New Zealand during the colonisation phase of Maori acculturation (1840-1859) shared the generally held contemporary European view about white supremacy and the inherent inferiority of coloured races.[39] Their feeling towards the Maori people were also hardly rendered more favourable when they discovered to their dismay that the British Colonial Office had decided, at least in theory, to protect the Maori's legal rights to his land holdings, and that the latter steadfastly stood on his Treaty rights in refusing to sell more land when he felt that pakeha penetration had proceeded far enough. These were especially bitter pills to swallow in view of the highly extravagant promises which the New Zealand Company in London held out to them before they decided to emigrate more than halfway around the world.[29]

After the Maori Wars and the confiscations, however, when the greater bulk of the Maori landed estate* passed into his hands, and the Maoris became a small and rapidly diminishing minority, safely withdrawn into their *pas,* the pakeha's sentiments towards them gradually mellowed. Goaded perhaps by a troubled conscience he could easily afford to adopt a magnanimous, senti-

---

* The Maori people had lost all but 11 of their original 66 million acres by 1891, and all but four million acres by 1939.[11]

mental, and paternalistic attitude towards his erstwhile foes. From a respectable distance he even perceived the Maori as quite an admirable fellow, as a truly "noble, brave, and intelligent native race of whom New Zealand might well be proud". Race relations were excellent, as they certainly should have been, since inter-racial contact was virtually non-existent. The pakeha congratulated himself profusely on his tolerance and humanity, proudly proclaimed to the world that no colour bar existed in New Zealand, and scathingly condemned racial bigots in America and South Africa for their treatment of the Negro. But he seldom stopped to reflect that there was also no American Indian problem in the United States as long as the latter remained on his reservation.

When the Maori emerged from his withdrawal, however, race relations consistently took a turn for the worse. All of the strong colour prejudices of the pakeha that had remained latent during the phase of withdrawal and self-congratulation gradually rose to the surface. Racial tolerance was quite a different matter now that the Maori was no longer a sentimentalised abstraction on a remote *pa*, but was his fellow-townsman and fellow-employee at the mill, flocked into the bar, requested accommodation at the hotel, waited his turn in the hairdressing saloon, and sent his children to school with dripping noses and impetigo sores.

"It stands to reason that when two ethnic groups with different traditions and behavioural standards are brought into more intimate relationship . . . the occasions for friction between them necessarily increase."[5] That increased Maori-pakeha contact during the post-withdrawal phase of acculturation has led to anti-Maori racial prejudice and extra-legal discriminatory practices not unlike those directed against Negroes in the United States has been amply documented by the writer both in Chapters II, III, and IV and in another volume.[5] In fact, it would be fair to say that the Maoris are currently as much of a racial as an ethnic minority group, and that the problem of Maori-pakeha relations is as much a matter of race and colour as of cultural differences.

Growth of Maori Racial Nationalism. Concomitantly with their emergence from withdrawal, the weakening of their tribal loyalties, and the attenuation of traditional Maori practices, the Maori people have increasingly developed a supra-tribal or national self-consciousness based on racial rather than on cultural identification. The Maori today expresses his *Maoritanga* more as pride of race and feeling of brotherhood with *all other* Maoris (on the grounds of common ancestral origins) than as positive interest in or practice of traditional cultural traits as ends in themselves.[27] Much of this racial nationalism, of course, is also a reaction against pakeha racial prejudice and discrimination.

Despite the frequently heard claim of a so-called renaissance in traditional aspects of Maori life (meeting houses, carving, language, arts and crafts), the overall, long-range trend in this aspect of culture has been one of gradual decline. Maori youth are generally not only ignorant of, but also do not identify themselves emotionally with, Maori cultural history and products. Members of Maori youth clubs, for example, have very little intrinsic interest in traditional Maori practices; the importance of the latter largely inheres in the fact that they have become significant overt symbols of racial and supra-tribal nationalism. One expression of this nationalism is the pride that the Maori people feel in the exploits of the Maori Battalion and the Maori All Blacks; in their distinguished political and professional leaders, i.e., Sir James Carroll, Sir Maui Pomare, Sir Apirana Ngata, and Sir Peter Buck; in individual sports heroes such as Nepia, Walsh, Davis, and Miss Ruia Morrison; and in the famous Maori opera singer, Inia Te Wiata.

Prior to World War II, many educated Maoris—teachers, professionals, civil servants—tried to become assimilated as rapidly as possible, live as pakehas, marry pakeha women, work in European surroundings, and even deny their birth and cultural affiliations. Now, Maoris in comparable positions (even those of quarter, eighth, and sixteenth blood) are eager to assert their Maoriness and affirm their identification with the Maori people. Educated Maoris are seeking careers in the Maori Affairs Department, and Maori teachers are more desirous of teaching in Maori than in Board schools. Intermarriage is becoming less common, and half-castes are tending to marry full-caste Maoris rather than pakehas.*

Social and Economic Advancement. The post-withdrawal phase of Maori acculturation has been marked by significant advancement along many social and economic fronts. Along with the rest

---

* Between 1945 and 1951 the rate of increase of persons with full Maori blood was almost four times as great as that of persons with part Maori blood. Full-blooded Maoris constituted two-thirds of the entire Maori population in 1951 (*New Zealand Population Census, 1951,* Vol. VI— *Maori Census.* Wellington: Government Printer, 1954).

of the New Zealand population the Maori has benefited from Social Security and from the general prosperity and under-employment situation following World War II. His income and living standards have risen, but as already pointed out, his mean annual income (especially on a per capita basis) is still much below pakeha standards (see p. 72). The Maori Housing Act of 1935, and the amendments of 1938 and 1944, have improved housing conditions for some families, but in general the Government programme has been pitifully inadequate in relation to the actual need. The number of new dwelling units constructed[13] has barely kept pace with the growth in population, and hence has not touched all the huge backlog of dilapidated, sub-standard homes that existed prior to the inauguration of the programme. No sooner does one family move out of a tumbledown shack and into a new State house than another family moves into the vacated premises. Making matters worse in urban areas is the virtual impossibility of Maori families renting decent flats and houses because of discriminatory practices on the part of pakeha landlords.

The general acceptance of pakeha preventive and therapeutic medical techniques, and their extension to the Maori village, have brought about tremendous improvement in the health of the Maori people. Maori mortality rates are now comparable to pakeha rates except in infant mortality and in deaths from tuberculosis;[32] and even here the advancement in recent years has been heartening. Further improvement in such areas as tuberculosis, typhoid fever, dysentery, respiratory diseases, impetigo, scabies, and pediculosis must await the amelioration of the housing situation and the provision of additional personnel for a dedicated but hopelessly understaffed public health nursing service.

The percentage of Maori primary school leavers going on to secondary school has increased greatly during this period (see p. 79), and beginning in 1941 post-primary education has been brought to many previously inaccessible areas through the establishment of 13 Maori district high schools. Thousands of Maoris have entered urban factory work for the first time; and although they are generally not entering the skilled trades and professions anywhere in proportion to their numbers, a spectacular increase has occurred in the number of Maoris who have qualified in such vocational fields as teaching, nursing, the building and engineering trades and the public service. The Maori Affairs Department has

in fact become the primary channel through which ambitious and
career-minded young Maoris can achieve middle-class status in
New Zealand society. Lastly, special mention must be made of
the work of the Maori Welfare Officer who has played a significant
role in the social education of his people and in facilitating their
adjustment to pakeha culture in such areas as housing, health,
education, vocational placement, recreation, and community self-
government.

Sources of Maori-Pakeha Differences in Aspirational and Motivational Traits

In this section I propose to identify the sources or determinants
of aspirational, motivational, and supportive traits in the Maori
adolescent. The crucial question here is how and in what ways do
cultural values regarding status and achievement constitute the
raw materials from which aspirations, motivations and other
related psychological traits in the *individual carriers* of the culture
are created? How, in other words, "is variability in cultural values,
customs, and institutions related to significant intercultural variability in [these aspects of] personality structure"?[4] This is a
related but somewhat different issue from the problem of identifying the mechanisms whereby such traits are *transmitted* from one
generation to the next in the process of enculturation so that "the
child eventually becomes a reasonable facsimile of the modal
adult in his culture."[4] The latter problem will be considered in the
following section.

Our position here is that the principal values of a culture with
respect to achievement are reflected in rather self-evident ways—
via transmitting mechanisms—in the needs and drives that individual members of the culture interiorise for particular kinds and
degrees of status. Thus, intercultural differences in the *content* of
these values determine (a) corresponding intercultural differences
in the indoctrination and role models to which developing individuals are exposed, and (b) differential institutionalisation of the
actual interpersonal experience of children and adults in the course
of growing up. In so far as the kinds of parent attitudes, role
models, and childhood and adolescent experience a given culture
institutionalises are simply derived from its achievement ideology,
they merely constitute mechanisms of transmitting cultural traits.
In some respects, however, they are partially independent of the

latter ideology, and hence may be regarded as subsidiary sources of motivational traits.

The following sources of Maori-pakeha differences in aspirational and motivational traits, therefore, need to be considered: (a) the achievement ideology of both pre- and post-pakeha Maori culture; (b) childhood and adolescent experience; and (c) social-class and I.Q. variables.

Pre-Pakeha Maori Achievement Ideology

From the standpoint of the theoretical orientation employed thus far in this chapter, the ultimate source of Maori-pakeha differences in adolescent personality development may be attributed to two core aspects of traditional Maori value structure dealing with the basis of self-esteem: (a) greater emphasis on derived status throughout the entire post-infantile life cycle of the individual (see pp. 22-23); and (b) less emphasis on the self-aggrandising aspects of primary status and greater emphasis on task- and group-oriented aspects of primary status. Responsiveness to leadership and emulation of group example were always powerful motives in Maori work psychology.[17]

The socio-economic organisation of pre-European Maori society, its history of successful adaptation to the material and economic demands of an unfamiliar temperate climate,[14, 17] and its vigorous and progressive response to initial contact with the radically different pakeha economy[17, 28] support the view (a) that primary status was highly valued by the Maori as a proper source of self-esteem, and (b) that achievement motivation was fostered by the encouragement of appropriate supportive traits. Highly differentiated channels for the acquisition of primary status were available in various economic enterprises, in arts and crafts, in warfare and political leadership, and in specialised knowledge of religious and magical lore, mythology, and tribal history.[14, 17] Expertness, craftsmanship, and executive ability were highly prized, and in the pursuance of these goals, great stress was placed on industry, perseverance, goal tenacity, ability to postone immediate hedonistic gratification, initiative, responsibility, foresight, self-discipline, and methodicalness.[17]

The self-aggrandising features of primary status, however, (i.e., personal ambition, hierarchical distinction, and their supportive correlates of individualism, competitiveness, hoarding of wealth, compulsive need to work, and a relentless anxiety-driven need to succeed and "get ahead" at all costs) although not unknown, were not as highly emphasised as in pakeha society. Greater stress was laid on mastery of skills for its socio-economic importance and as an end in itself, on pride of craftsmanship, and on the personal satisfactions of meritorious accomplishment; on kinship obligations, on enhancement of group welfare and prestige, on the personal-social values of co-operative effort towards a common goal, and on inter-tribal competition; and on the satisfactions associated with working together in an intimate, personal context of reciprocal psychological support.[17]

These characteristics of primary status and the continued importance of derived status engendered and made valuable in turn traits of mutual helpfulness and co-operative effort in bearing economic burdens, generosity, hospitality, and concern for the welfare of fellow group members. Less vocational specialisation, greater seasonal fluctuations in work load, a lower standard of material comfort, and the continual demands of a variety of ceremonial social activities led to somewhat less regularity in work habits than is typical of pakeha culture.[17] In the light of the prevailing system of reciprocal obligation, thrift was also both a less necessary and a less possible virtue.

Post-Pakeha Maori Achievement Ideology

Although the Maori economic organisation worked well enough in a subsistence economy requiring little technology, capital, and specialisation of labour, it was not suited to the more specialised, individualistic, mass production, money economy of the pakeha. The pakeha economic system demanded specialisation of labour within a single type of enterprise rather than diversified craftsmanship, greater regularity of labour, the production of surpluses and the accumulation of capital, utilisation of labour-saving machinery, habituation to dreary, monotonous work, and ability to work in a more impersonal context. Hence, the skills, activities, and techniques of the traditional Maori economy, as well as the associated social organisation and leadership devices, were no longer completely compatible with the dominant new economic system; and since traditional channels for implementing the traditional pattern of primary status were no longer wholly functional, modification of the latter was clearly inevitable.

During the early colonisation phases of acculturation (see pp. 98-99), when the Maori still hoped to assimilate the desirable features of pakeha technology while retaining his cultural autonomy, he made an earnest and truly remarkable effort to modify his economic system in accordance with the demands of European material culture. He accepted the principle of producing surplus commodities for the market, of accumulating capital goods, and of using money as a medium of exchange, and was able to incorporate these features successfully within the framework of his communal system of ownership, distribution, and organisation of labour. Other aspects of pakeha economy, however, were more distasteful and also more difficult to reconcile with his own social and economic values. It was difficult for the task- and group-oriented Maori to accept the self-aggrandising aspects of pakeha primary status and the supportive traits that went with it; to become reconciled to the concepts of private profit and ownership of land and of individual economic responsbility and initiative; to grow accustomed to regular, monotonous, and uninterrupted work in a strange, impersonal context removed from his village and kinsfolk; to cultivate habits of thrift, and to live prudently within the demands of an unfamiliar money economy. These same individualistic and competitive features of pakeha primary status also threatened the Maori system of kinship obligations and mutual interdependence, and the very cohesiveness of the group that provided him with the derived status he valued so highly.

If open conflict and war with the pakeha had not intervened, it is quite possible that the Maori would have been able to resist most of these unpalatable and individualistic aspects of the European economic system, and to evolve a socialistic type of modern agrarian economy generally compatible with his tribal structure and cultural values. The colonists, however, wanted to own and control the major resources of New Zealand on their own terms, and were in no mood to accept Maori cultural autonomy and a genuinely dual economy. After the wars, acute demoralisation, rejection of pakeha technology and continued alienation of Maori land forever obliterated this possibility—even on a limited scale. Thus it soon became evident in the post-withdrawal period that if the Maori wished to adopt European technology it would largely have to be done within the framework of the prevailing pakeha economic system.

Even under the best of conditions, therefore, it was obvious that the Maori people would require considerable time in which to become familiar with the novel features of the pakeha economy and with the channels it provided for the achievement of primary status. Still more time was needed for internalising a new aspirational pattern and its supportive personality traits. In addition, however, many other factors operated against assimilation of all or part of the pakeha pattern and modification of the traditional pattern. First, lingering resentment towards the pakeha and disillusionment with pakeha values, motives, and practices, following the bitterness of the Maori wars and subsequent land confiscations, fostered an attitude of rejecting pakeha ways simply because they were pakeha. Secondly, any type of constructive reorientation of values was greatly hampered by the widespread demoralisation, lassitude, and feelings of hopelessness and impending cultural obliteration that gripped the Maori people in the first three decades following the civil wars. Thirdly, the residual vitality of the traditional value system created basic needs and provided basic satisfactions for those needs which the pakeha pattern could not easily gratify. This obviously cast the latter pattern in an extremely uncongenial light. Acceptance of pakeha ways not only threatened to isolate him from the support of his own people but also offered little certainty of acceptance on equal terms by the pakeha in return for the adoption of many alien values and distasteful habits. Finally, he was handicapped in utilising pakeha channels to primary status by lack of education and training for pakeha jobs, by lack of pakeha work habits, by lack of familiar indoctrination in pakeha values, by general unfamiliarity with pakeha vocational opportunities, and by prejudicial and discriminatory attitudes on the part of many pakehas.

The impact of these acculturation pressures on the traditional value structure led to four different types of aspirational patterns: (1) the predominant pattern of de-emphasising all kinds of primary status and placing exaggerated stress on derived status (see p. 15); and (2) the three less common patterns of (a) integrative compromise, (b) complete acceptance of the pakeha pattern, and (c) negativistic rejection of both the pakeha pattern and residual elements of the traditional pattern, and, in fact, of all the motivational goals of adult maturation.

The integrative compromise pattern was the least radical of the four in content because it drew on many of the features of the traditional Maori pattern that were perfectly compatible with the new system, i.e., emphasis on achievement motivation and the accompanying supportive traits. It also retained most of the task—and group-oriented aspects of Maori primary status since these aspects, although not characteristically pakeha, were not basically incompatible with success in the pakeha vocational world, and at the same time prevented complete alienation from the Maori people. The compromise lay in acceptance of pakeha channels of achieving primary status and of pakeha standards of more regular work with less constant personal-social support in familiar surroundings. The leaders of the Young Maori Party generally conformed to this pattern. They had high academic and vocational aspirations, and worked hard, responsibly, persistently, and often in isolation to achieve competence in pakeha vocations. At the same time, however, they were not compulsively driven by self-aggrandising, competitive, and anxiety- powered ambitions. They respected their kinship obligations, valued (but did not over-value) derived status, and used their attained position in the pakeha world for the welfare and betterment of the Maori people and for the perpetuation of the worthwhile elements of Maori culture.

It is quite understandable, however, why the integrative compromise pattern did not predominate. It presupposed a high level of personal morale, far-sighted willingness to reject the negative, self-defeating implications of deep-seated grievances, much steadfast self-direction in the face of group disapproval, and a high order of natural ability and determination to reach cherished goals despite many handicaps and obstacles. It had to overcome a blanket disposition to reject on principle all pakeha values and to perceive any type of primary status as pakeha in origin, as well as a natural tendency to react to the pakeha pattern as an all-or-none proposition. The latter tendency was strengthened by pakeha intolerance of deviations from the approved pattern.

In the light of these difficulties the easiest solution seemed to lie in de-emphasising the importance of primary status and making exaggerated use of the psychological support offered by derived status. The inclination to adopt this solution was bolstered by the fact that the segment of the pakeha population with whom the Maori people had most frequent contact and intermarried most frequently was, by and large, a group of lower-class pakehas with similar aspirational patterns. The same difficulties described above for the integrative compromise pattern applied in even greater force to complete acceptance of the pakeha pattern. Finally, a negativistic rejection of both the Maori and pakeha values and

goals of adult maturation, common enough as a transitory manifestation of adolescent emotional instability and generation conflict,
tended to persist in a minority of immature and aggressive young
Maori adults.

Childhood and Adolescent Experience*

After about the first two or three years of life, Maori children
tend to receive relatively little attention and affection from parents.
This casual treatment, by pakeha standards, is in marked constrast
to the affectionate indulgence they are given prior to this time.
The toddler and middle years children åre largely ignored and left
to their own devices or in the care of older siblings. The treatment
they receive during this latter period

> is the result of successive annual, or near annual, births, of
> certain beliefs about child development, and low level of
> household technology and labour resources. It does not mean
> that the mother is consciously hostile towards the child or that
> she wishes it ill. Nor does it mean that she does not value the
> child nor that she is purposely neglectful. She simply has not
> the time and believes that the development of walking with
> its consequent increased mobility is a sign of intrinsic inde-
> pendence in the child. She believes that the child is now ready
> to do without her assistance and that there is no longer any
> great need for his every whim to be immediately gratified.[9]

Hence, satellisation (dependent emotional identification) to
parents cannot constitute a significant source of derived status.
After an initial period of disorientation and resentment, however,
most children satellise quite satisfactorily in relation to siblings,
other relatives, and especially to a group of peers; and it is from
such identifications that they obtain the major portion of their
security and derived status. A comparable situation does not exist
in the pakeha world until adolescence. Pakeha children do form
satellising relationships with peers but generally satellise principally in relation to parents. The upshot of this difference in
experience is that Maori children from a very early age become
habituated to obtaining their derived status from diversified sources
and predominantly from peers rather than from parents, and
consequently develop greater needs for the continued receipt of
derived status from group sources. They are under less parental

---

* This section is based largely on data from the "Kowhai" and "Rakau"
districts.[8, 16, 30, 34, 36] In general, however, it conforms to the writer's own
observations in his urban and rural samples.

control and direction than pakeha children, and hence appear to be more mature for their age and more independent of adult direction.

Another consequence of the minimal degree of contact between Maori children and parents is that siblings and peers replace parents as the major socialising agents during childhood. Children experience adult attention, rewards and punishments only capriciously and unpredictably.[16, 34] Thus they tend to be wary and distrustful of the adult world. Since they are generally regarded as nuisances, they learn to avoid punishment from parents by keeping out of their way.[16, 34] For the most part they are excluded from the adult social world. Although they are expected to perform various chores, they receive and anticipate little praise or reward for their work and hence derive little satisfaction from it. Adult values, expectations, and models of role behaviour are transmitted only indirectly (and thus imperfectly) through the perceptions of older siblings and are enforced by the authority of the latter. This creates a special type of sibling rivalry: the older children frequently resent the responsibility thrust upon them and "take out" their aggressive impulses on their young charges, who in turn resent the arbitrary treatment to which they are subjected.[16, 36] In general, however, the equalitarian atmosphere of the peer group compensates for this situation and makes for greater reciprocity of obligations, less implicit acceptance of authoritarian values, and more functional (less absolutistic) concepts of the rules governing interpersonal relations than when adults are the principal socialising agents. The stage is thus set for a pattern of dependence on and conformity to the group at an earlier age than is typical of pakeha society.

The content of adolescent experience is also different for the Maori individual. Since satellisation to parents does not occur to begin with, the typical pakeha sequence of adolescent desatellisation from parents and resatellisation to peers is unnecessary. In fact, at least in rural areas, adolescence is partly a time of rapprochement with parents and the adult community, both of whom begin to take more interest in the adolescent individual and to communicate more effectively with him. Also, as already pointed out, the Maori adolescent is not expected to de-emphasise derived status to the same extent as is the pakeha or to aspire to much of and to as self-aggrandising a type of primary status. Hence the transition between Maori preadolescent and adolescent aspirational patterns is marked by less discontinuity than is characteristic of the comparable pakeha transition.

Social Class and I.Q.

The aspirational and motivational traits of Maori adolescents are undoubtedly influenced by the fact that Maoris are predominantly members of lower social class groups. By using matching procedures that controlled for social class, however, it was possible to eliminate the effects of relative social class status on our Maori-pakeha differences. These procedures, in fact, accounted for many of our intercultural uniformities by removing variance of social class origin that had formerly but erroneously been thought to be reflective of Maori cultural factors (see p. 20). In a comparable study of the "achievement syndrome" among Negroes, Jews, Greeks, Italians, French-Canadians and white Protestants in the United States, Rosen similarly found that "social class and ethnicity interact in influencing motivation, values and aspirations," and that "some of the differences between ethnic groups in motivations, values and aspirations are probably also a function of their class composition".[37] But just as in the present study, ethnic differences persisted when social class was controlled, and in some instances were greater than social class differences.

Intelligence is another variable that is significantly related to educational and occupational aspirations,[38] but the small Maori enrolment in our two schools precluded the possibility of matching pupils on this basis. It is extremely unlikely, however, that our Maori-pakeha differences in aspirational traits would have been materially reduced if it had been possible to adopt this procedure. Using a random sample of all high school seniors in Wisconsin, Sewell, *et al.* obtained significant relationships between social class status and educational and occupational aspirations when I.Q. was held constant.[38]

TRANSMISSION OF MAORI ASPIRATIONAL AND MOTIVATIONAL TRAITS

How can we account for the transmission of the distinctive Maori pattern of aspiration, motivational, and supportive traits from one generation to the next? Our logical point of departure in this inquiry must lie with the heritage of pervasive and interlocking cultural values regarding primary and derived status that functioned in the pre-pakeha Maori culture and was subsequently modified by the historical experience of acculturation (see pp. 120–124). As a result of the cumulative effects of (a) recurrent exposure to these achievement values and observation of culturally stereotyped role models, and (b) actual participation during childhood and adolescence in analogous types of role and status experience, this ideology is gradually internalised by the developing individual through the operation of the following mechanisms:[4] primacy and exclusiveness of exposure; pre-rational identification on the basis of personal and group loyalties; implicit and explicit indoctrination; the development of particular needs and the experience of particular satisfactions (canalisation); incidental learning; prestige suggestion; the pressure of group expectations and demands; and the application of internal and external sanctions (reward and punishment, shame and guilt, disapproval, threat of exclusion, induced anxiety).

Spiro[41] has suggested that "such psychological characteristics as emotions, attitudes and values which are acquired *early* in . . . life . . . are . . . most resistive . . . to acculturation forces". This is a plausible hypothesis in as much as these early acquisitions tend to be uncritically internalised on the basis of emotional loyalties to significant persons in the child's social environment. It is not necessary to assume, however, that during this period of development parent attitudes reflective of cultural values are transmitted solely through the type or tenor of specific child rearing practices.[4] A more credible view, in our opinion, is that parent attitudes are transmitted more directly through "recurrent explicit and implicit indoctrination (training, precept, example, incidental exposure), reinforced by [actual role and status experience], by appropriate external and internal sanctions, and by later experience with other socialising agents, during the entire period of childhood and adolescence".[4]

Distinctive cultural expectations with respect to primary and derived status also influence indirectly the nature of adolescent aspirational patterns by determining along parallel lines the kinds of childhood and adolescent role and status experience made available to children. Relevant to the Maori situation are such factors (see pp. 124-126) as the obtaining of the major portion of derived status from group rather than from parental sources, and hence greater dependence on and conformity to the group; the role of peers and siblings as the major socialising agents during childhood, with a resulting tradition of more equalitarian relationships and reciprocal obligations; no necessity for desatellisation from parents and resatellisation to peers during adolescence, since early satellising relationships to parents are weak or non-existent; less pressure to repudiate derived status and strive for a great amount and a self-aggrandising form of primary status; and less discontinuity in general between childhood and adolescence. Hence, reinforcing the direct influence of the cultural ideology on the types of aspirations adolescents internalise is actual experience with particular kinds of status satisfactions and equalitarian relationships in the peer group—experience that is consonant with the cultural value system and therefore sanctioned by it.

Examples of Transmitting Mechanisms in the Maori Situation

From our data it was clear that young Maori adolescents in our urban and rural samples had for the most part successfully assimilated the pakeha pattern of educational and vocational aspiration. These aspirations reflected both the prevailing pakeha achievement ideology to which they were exposed in school and in the wider culture, as well as the expressed but superficial desires of their parents. The latter, however, were basically identified with the Maori orientation towards primary and derived status and generally had no deep emotional commitment to pakeha achievement values. Hence, they did not *really* encourage the implementation of these aspirations by voicing appropriate expectations, making unequivocal demands, dispensing suitable rewards and punishments, and insisting on the development of the necessary supportive traits. But because of poor communication between parents and children, this situation was not clearly perceived by Maori secondary school pupils. Thus, during early adolescence, although they frequently revert to parental standards in the home environment, the influence of the school and of pakeha culture generally tends to predominate in the development of educational and vocational aspirations and in the matter of conforming to pakeha work standards.

Later on, however, as relationships and communication with parents and the adult community improve, the influence of Maori cultural values, as mediated through parents and peers, begins to prevail. Educational and vocational aspirations, achievement motivation, and essential supportive traits fail to become adequately internalised; and eventually, as the possibility of implementation progressively recedes, the aspirations are either lowered or abandoned. Concomitantly, Maori adolescents also become progressively more aware of the actual obstacles standing in the way of their vocational success because of pakeha prejudice and discrimination. This perception of the relative unavailability of the promised rewards of self-denial and striving similarly disposes them to abandon or modify their earlier aspirations. Other important factors that contribute to the lack of internalisation and implementation of educational and occupational aspirations include traditional Maori attitudes towards work, acute social demoralisation in some Maori communities, and the absence of adequate guidance and of traditions of high scholastic and vocational accomplishment in most Maori families.

The Role of Early Childhood Experience

A somewhat different view of the origin and transmission of the Maori non-achievement pattern has been advanced by the Beagleholes and by Ritchie in interpreting their "Kowhai" and "Rakau" data respectively.[8, 9, 34] They feel that the abrupt break in parental indulgence (i.e., "rejection") at the age of two to three (see pp. 124-126) has a lasting effect on the personality development of the Maori child and conditions his distinguishing characterological traits as an adolescent and adult. As a result of this experience, according to these observers, the latter not only develops inordinately potent needs for affection—needs which were never adequately satisfied and hence remain virtually insatiable—but also feels chronically threatened by the "expectation of further rejection".[9]

Thus, the Maori's extreme dependence on group psychological support, his acute fear of loss of this support, and his overwillingness to conform to group expectations are attributed by Beaglehole and Ritchie to his need to compensate for the early deprivation of parental affection.[9, 34] Non-achievement is similarly a defence against the possibility of rejection by the group, since conspicuous personal achievement constitutes a threat to group solidarity and challenges the individual's dependence on the group for his status and self-esteem. The Maori is engaged in a never ending quest to recapture the childhood security he lost in the trauma of rejection.[8, 9] His helpfulness, generosity, and hospitality are interpreted as efforts to purchase affection, to place others under obligation to him, and thus to provide a partial substitute for the parental love and solicitude from which he was so abruptly separated.[8]

Also attributed to the expectation of further rejection are signs of overvigilance, anxiety, depression, underlying feelings of hostility and aggression, superficial ego-involvement, and lack of ego-relatedness to others.[34]

Although much more intensive developmental research is required before a definitive answer to this problem can be attempted, there are two plausible *a priori* reasons for believing that the actual deprivation experienced by the Maori child is relatively mild in terms of its cultural and developmental contexts, is not directly comparable to rejection in pakeha culture, and hence leads only to *temporary* disorientation, resentment, and anxiety. First, since it is representative of the cultural norm, its origins are attributable more to an institutionalised way of handling children than to idiosyncratic narcissism, self-preoccupation, hostility, or inability to relate emotionally to others and extend affection. Hence, it not only lacks the characteristic affective properties and attitudinal substrate of parental rejection in our culture, but is also perceived by the child as a phenomenon implicating *all* children in the course of growing up rather than as a situation peculiar to him and his parents.

Secondly, the permanent, damaging effects of parental rejection in our culture inhere in the fact that it precludes the possibility of satellisation (dependent emotional identification with superordinate individuals or groups), and hence deprives the child of derived status and intrinsic feelings of security and adequacy. Family life and interpersonal relations are so organised in our society that only parents are in a position to provide children with the derived status they need. But satellisation need not necessarily occur in relation to parents in all cultures if other culturally institutionalised and sanctioned sources of adequate derived status are available. It is true that the Maori child cannot often satellise in relation to his parents, but can and does in relation to older siblings, other relatives, and especially the peer group. If the peer group and other kin were not available for this purpose, it is quite probable that the rejection experience would have lasting traumatic consequences, and would perhaps lead to exaggerated needs for *primary* status, as it does in our culture. But since satisfactory parent surrogates are available to make satellisation possible, dependence on derived status from group sources results, and no permanent traumatic effects ensue. *Overdependence* on derived status, however, is more likely a reflection of cultural overvaluation of this type of status rather than a compensatory reaction to the temporary trauma of early rejection.

Hence, if the rejection experience proved to be only of transitory developmental significance, it would be more parsimonious to believe that Maori dependence on group psychological support is a functionally autonomous need in its own right rather than a compensatory need stemming from traumatic deprivation. This need is reflective of a pervasive set of cultural values emphasising the continued importance of derived status throughout the life cycle, as well as a group-oriented type of primary status. Such values are internalised as a consequence of recurrent exposure, observation, indoctrination, canalisation, satisfying experience, imposition of group expectations and sanctions, etc. The Maori's "threat orientation", therefore, would not be interpreted as "fear of further rejection" but as an indication of his exaggerated dependence on the group for his self-esteem in view of cultural deprecation of primary status. Generosity, hospitality, and helpfulness would simply be supportive traits that are necessary for and consonant with a system of mutual emotional interdependence, and which are internalised along with other cultural values.

Outlook for the Future

What does the future hold for the Maori people? How will the post-withdrawal phase of acculturation end and by what will it be succeeded? Predictions about such matters are obviously highly speculative. We can only feel reasonably sure that certain alternatives are very unlikely and will probably not come to pass. These improbable alternatives include the following: (a) rapid and coercive assimilation, which is contrary to Government policy and distasteful to the majority of both Maori and pakeha citizens; (b) gradual racial amalgamation, which presupposes the eradication of more colour prejudice than is foreseeable for a long time to come; and (c) return to traditional patterns of village social life and organisation and to widespread communal economic enterprises, which would require an almost impossible reversal of the social and economic history of Twentieth Century New Zealand. Only two alternatives seem credible: gradual cultural assimilation of the Maori to the pakeha way of life without appreciable racial mixture, or the constitution of the Maori people as a highly and progressively more acculturated ethnic community within the larger framework of New Zealand social, political, and economic life, but enjoying a certain measure of cultural autonomy and separateness in a restricted range of activities. To the writer the latter alternative seems the more likely possibility in view of the residual vigour of various Maori psychological traits, the growing problem of colour prejudice, and the development of Maori supra-tribal nationalism.

Any realistic appraisal of the outlook for the future must take into consideration the following nine crucial factors: (1) the motivations for, and the effects of, cultural withdrawal following the Maori Wars, and their subsequent decline but residual presence in the post-withdrawal period; (2) the greater rate of natural increase in the Maori than in the pakeha population, coupled with a trend away from intermarriage; (3) the dwindling of Maori land resources and their present sufficiency for at best one-sixth of the Maori population; (4) the gradual disintegration of Maori village life and social organisation; (5) the increasing urbanisation of the Maori people; (6) the impressive degree of material, technological, social, and psychological acculturation that has already occurred in Maori life and which shows every indication of continuing; (7) the marked increase in colour prejudice and discrimination among pakehas and the growth of Maori racial nationalism; (8) the decline in traditional Maori culture and the failure of Maori youth to identify adequately with it; and (9) the predominantly lower social class status of the Maori in terms of their income, living standard, educational and vocational attainments, and achievement and child rearing ideology.

Maori Social and Economic Organisation

Some Maori leaders and pakeha theorists still nurture the hope that the Maori can adopt the material advantages of European civilisation (science, industry, technology, medicine, sanitation, housing, education, etc.) without relinquishing his traditional social-economic organisation and value system. This, in our opinion, is an idealistic but totally unrealistic long-term goal that ignores relevant social and economic factors as well as the lessons of Maori acculturational history. It is an objective that is feasible perhaps in adaptive acculturational situations (see p. 107) in which the original social structure largely remains intact, and dis-organisation and demoralisation due to precipitous resumption of culture contact are absent. It is even conceivable in certain resistive acculturational situations where considerable detribalisation has occurred, as long as physical, social, and psychological isolation can be maintained.

But once initial detribalisation has taken place as a result of calamitous defeat and demoralisation, and is followed at a later date by the disintegration of the conditions making for withdrawal (see pp. 109–110), by the disruption of village life, by rapid urbanisation, by disinvolvement of youth from traditional aspects of culture, and by further disorganisation stemming from overly abrupt acculturation, it is completely futile to expect that the traditional social order or the major outlines of the indigenous value system can be resuscitated and perpetuated. The remnants of Maori social structure, community life, and leadership patterns that survived during the period of withdrawal primarily owed their existence to the isolation and preservation of the Maori village. As the old-style village disappears, and with it the associated pattern of traditional social organisation, the cultural values it generated (i.e., emphasis on social goals, community values, kinship obligations, hospitality, derived status, group welfare and task-oriented achievement, mutual assistance, group psychological support) will for the most part be gradually superseded by corresponding values emanating from the pakeha way of life. It also appears likely that in the not too distant future—once their purposes will have been fully served—the special administrative and legislative devices, (e.g., Maori schools, Department of Maori Affairs, separate political representation in Parliament) which have served a "mediating function" in helping the Maori adjust to pakeha culture, will be abandoned.[7]

The possibility of large-scale communal agriculture or industry, organised along traditional *whanau, hapu* or tribal lines, has also been largely precluded by various developments preceding and following the Maori Wars (see p. 121). This does not mean, of course, that small-scale enterprises, such as the well-known Maori clothing factory at Opotiki, which utilise insightful knowledge of Maori work psychology (see pp. 155-156) to increase productive efficiency, are impracticable, or that greater stress cannot be placed on such non-material incentives as task-oriented and group welfare motivations in certain industrial settings where large numbers of Maoris are employed. But the Maori people have neither the capital nor the land resources to set up a parallel economic system, nor would such a move be welcomed or encouraged by the Government or by the pakeha population. It appears practically certain, therefore, that the vast majority of Maoris will earn their living in the future under circumstances not unlike those holding for the pakeha population.

As cultural differences between Maori and pakeha diminish, and as various social, economic, political and demographic factors lead to an intensification of colour prejudice in New Zealand (see p. 77), Maori racial nationalism will increase, and the problem of Maori-pakeha relations will largely hinge on the question of race and colour. The Maori will become less of a cultural minority and more of a racial-ethnic, lower social class minority group with a status similar to that of the Mexican in the southwest and of the Negro in the north of the United States. Their skin colour, their common ancestry, and their position as an underprivileged and victimised minority group will constitute the principal bases for their sense of racial identification. This is not to imply, of course, that colour prejudice is an ineradicable evil; but even at the very best a considerable length of time would be necessary before existing and growing prejudice could be counteracted, particularly when both the Government and people of New Zealand steadfastly refuse to acknowledge that a problem requiring amelioration exists.

Thus, although the Maori people will continue to assimilate pakeha values, standards, and ways of living and working, the two people will in the foreseeable future remain as separate communities. The voluntary social segregation that currently originates mostly from Maori preference will tend to become more and more a matter of extra-legal imposition, as in the northern states of America. Various overt and material expressions of *Maoritanga,* such as the Maori language, *hakas, huis* and *tangis,* will become less important as ends in themselves and more important as tangible symbols of Maori nationalism. Finally, as segregated living quarters in the urban slums become more squalid and overcrowded, and as Maoris find it increasingly more difficult to obtain jobs once the post-war boom in the national economy tapers off, it is inevitable (despite the current refusal of Maori leaders to face up to the situation) that a militant, self-protective organisation such as the National Association for the Advancement of Colored People, in the United States, will eventually arise in New Zealand.

Cultural Values Regarding Achievement

On the basis of our data it appears likely that significant Maori-pakeha differences in achievement orientation may be reasonably anticipated for at least another generation. They will be gradually obliterated, however, by the increasing urbanisation of the Maori people, and by progressive improvement both in the cultural level of the Maori home and in the concern of Maori parents for their children's educational and vocational advancement. The next generation of Maori parents will probably be able to sustain the internalisation and implementation as well as the instigation of pakeha aspirations for achievement. Racial discrimination will undoubtedly make it more difficult for Maoris to implement their aspirations; but depending on the magnitude of the handicap imposed, this situation may either stimulate greater striving, as in the case of the Jews and Greeks in the United States, or may promote an attitude of apathy and hopelessness, as is partly true in the case of the American Negro, who often perceives the cards as so overwhelmingly stacked against him that striving seems futile. In any event, the achievement ideology of the Maori will certainly reflect his predominantly lower social class status, becoming in time more and more similar to that of the lower-class pakeha.

What about the possibility of widespread adoption of the "integrative compromise" pattern described on pp. 122-124. This pattern places adequate emphasis on primary status and the necessary supportive traits, but lays greater stress on self-actualisation and group welfare goals than on the competitive and self-aggrandising features of personal achievement in pakeha society. This, after all, was the achievement pattern of the Maori of old and of the Young Maori Party, and is still characteristic of many contemporary Maori leaders who have successfully adapted to pakeha culture without cutting themselves off from their own people. There is no *inherent* incompatibility between individual competence and achievement, on the one hand, and community values, on the other. Yet it must be recognised that by virtue of the *particular* arrangement of urban social and economic life in Western civilisation, such incompatibility does exist—in fact if not in theory. Thus, although the Maori may eventually develop an achievement pattern which is slightly more task- and group-oriented than the pakeha's, it is unlikely—no matter how regrettable—that these latter elements can predominate indefinitely as in former times and even today. The leaders of the Young Maori Party and most of the current crop of Maori leaders had their roots in isolated and traditional village life—not in urban slums or in detribalised rural *pas*.

CHAPTER SIX

Recommendations

THE PREDICTIONS ABOUT THE MAORI'S ACCULTURATIONAL FUTURE hazarded in the last section of Chapter V represents speculative forecasts based on objective consideration of current research data and historical trends rather than expressions of what the writer would *like* or prefer to see happen. Laying no claims to prophetic vision, he has no professional stake whatsoever in the fulfilment of these predictions. All of his forecasts are implicitly qualified by the phrase, "provided that no *drastic* change occurs in the relevant factors bearing on this issue". In fact, the recommendations made in the present chapter are largely offered in the hope that they will encourage some such drastic action which may at least in part prevent one or more of these predictions (e.g., the persistence of the Maori low achievement pattern for at least another generation; the increase in colour prejudice; the decline in the Maori language and in certain Maori cultural values) from coming to pass.

The successful implementation of any programme of social amelioration must obviously be predicated on detailed and intimate knowledge of conditions in the field. At the end of every projected plan of social action is a human being with particular motivations and predispositions on whom various interpersonal and group forces are constantly impinging; and in the final analysis the success or failure of the programme can only be judged in terms of a change in *his* behaviour in the desired direction. Nobody, no matter how clever, sitting in an office in London, Washington or Wellington can dream up a programme, irrespective of how commendable its objectives are, and expect it to work unless it takes into account the actual motivations, predispositions, and social forces influencing the behaviour he is aspiring to modify.

Over the past few years the Maori Affairs Department has been engaged in a strenuous campaign to increase the number of Maori youths remaining in secondary school beyond the minimal leaving age and entering the skilled trades and professions. Unfortunately, however, this campaign was not preceded by any systematic attempt (such as was made on a small scale in this research study) to ascertain the actual educational and vocational aspirations of Maori youth, the motivations underlying these aspirations and the factors affecting their implementation. The Head Office has, in fact, largely lost touch with the real-life situation as it exists in the towns and villages. It is small wonder, therefore, that the results of this campaign have not been attended with resounding success.

Acculturational changes do not arise overnight. They are measured more in terms of generations than of years. Certain administrative steps can be taken to quicken the pace of change; but even if they are based on reliable and firsthand knowledge of conditions in the field, lasting change cannot be superimposed from above. Basically it can only be brought into effect gradually and from within. Like most ethnic groups—only more so in the light of their particular history—"the Maori can be led but not driven".* They cannot be pressured into any scheme, no matter how worthwhile or theoretically sound, that they do not really understand and wholeheartedly accept. The Maori Welfare Organisation appreciates this principle in theory but in practice often relies more on official directives and single visit exhortation than on patient, repeated and face-to-face explanation and discussion of its objectives with the people and their leaders on the *marae*. Like so many other organs of the Welfare State, in this investigator's opinion, it is top-heavy with head and district office staff who have a deep-seated aversion to leaving their desks, and is woefuly short of field workers.

VOCATIONAL GUIDANCE

The most important single measure currently required to counteract the prevailing low achievement pattern of Maori youth is an adequate programme of vocational guidance that would, at least in part, apply routinely to *all* Maori adolescents, and provide prolonged, intensive, and continuous coverage. Suitably trained Maori Vocational Guidance Officers are urgently needed in each

---

* *The Maori Today*. Wellington, Government Printer 1956, p. 37.

district to serve *in loco parentis* for the next two generations, in as much as the present generation of Maori parents lacks the necessary background, interest, sophistication, and emotional commitment to educational and vocational achievement to guide their children adequately along these lines. Pakeha adolescents could also benefit from an improved system of vocational guidance, but by and large they not only require vocational guidance less (because of more favourable home and cultural influences affecting occupational achievement), but also make more abundant use of existing facilities. By virtue of their predominantly urban residence, a much larger percentage of pakeha than Maori pupils has access to the six vocational guidance centres where the best guidance facilities in New Zealand exist; and even in town and country districts it is primarily the pakeha pupils who avail themselves of the services of visiting Officers from these centres.

Inadequacies of Present System

Vocational guidance in New Zealand is generally spread much too thinly in terms of the number of available personnel, their training, and the procedures employed, to be optimally effective. By overseas standards only a very small minority of the professional staff is adequately trained; and outside of the urban centres the activities of Vocational Guidance Officers are dispersed over such wide territories that they do not even have time to attend properly to pupils with the more urgent problems. It is questionable indeed what good a visiting Officer can accomplish with severe problem cases who are complete strangers to him, when he is required to interview about 15 boys in a single day and can only devote about 20 minutes to each. Yearly talks about careers to large groups of pupils are also rather pointless; they only constitute a good method of stimulating interest and building relationships when they are delivered by a local person working in the district and are followed up on an individual basis. The value of the career masters' work is similarly open to question in view of the fact that they have absolutely no training in guidance, have very little released time from teaching duties to devote to guidance work, and largely restrict their activities to dispensing occupational information.

Another serious inadequancy of the current system is lack of routine coverage of all pupils such as could be accomplished by periodic interviewing at crucial points in the pupil's school career, occupational information courses, supervised work experience programmes, and the routine administration of vocational interest tests. The only attempt in this direction is yearly talks to the entire school by visiting Vocational Guidance Officers (see above). Except in the urban centres, also, intensive guidance work with the more urgent cases (several lengthy interviews, interest and aptitude tests, interviews with parents and teachers) is virtually non-existent.

A related difficulty stems from the policy of only extending assistance to those pupils who take the initiative in asking for it. Although pupils obviously cannot be coerced into seeking guidance, they can quite legitimately be encouraged to do so by headmasters and teachers. The main disadvantage of the passive approach is that pupils requiring vocational guidance the least are precisely the ones most likely to ask for it, since their parents tend to be most sophisticated both about guiding their own children and seeking expert advice; and conversely, pupils needing it the most (e.g., Maoris from unsophisticated homes) are least likely to apply for it.

Lastly, there is much ambiguous overlapping of responsibility (and also some jurisdictional friction) regarding the vocational guidance and placement of Maori youth. Vocational Guidance Officers, Maori Welfare Officers, and the Labour Department all have a hand in the process; and although the functions of each are theoretically distinct, it is not completely clear to the personnel involved who is responsible for what. In any case it rarely happens that guidance and placement of a given youth are carried out by the same person.

Maori Vocational Guidance Officers

In the light of the urgent needs discussed above and the inadequacies of the present system of vocational guidance for Maori youth, it is essential that a special Maori Vocational Guidance Service be established within the existing vocational guidance programme of the Education Department. There is nothing new or radical about this suggestion. It was advocated as long ago as 1945 by H. C. McQueen.[25]

Because of the cultural emphasis on derived status, it is relatively easy for Maori adolescents to establish strong satellising relationships to admired adults whom they respect. Just to avoid disappointing these persons who have faith in them, they tend to persist in striving for long-term achievement goals. Such relationships exist today between many Maori youths, on the one hand, and Mormon elders and Roman Catholic clergymen,* on the other, and account in large measure both for the substantial improvement in social morale, school attendance, and care of home and children, and for the sharp reduction in alcoholism and delinquency that has taken place in some Maori communities. In some rural areas also, headmasters and teachers with strong feelings of social responsibility have played similar roles and have done valiant work in vocational guidance and placement. Such conditions, however, only apply in a sporadic way to a minority of the total Maori population.

If Maori Vocational Guidance Officers are to establish the intimate and long-term relationships with Maori adolescents envisaged above, it is essential that they be residents of the district, and preferably members of the Maori race. In the latter case it is also important that they belong to the local tribe, since, from my observation, Maori Welfare Officers who are not members of the tribal group with whom they work, labour under very great handicaps. They should be carefully selected on the basis of intelligence, character, sincerity, and experience, and given specially tailored training for their jobs.

The administrative advantages of locating this service in the Education Department are that a Vocational Guidance Division already exists in the Department and that much of the work of the Maori Vocational Guidance Officer will be done in schools with pupils and teachers. Maori Welfare Officers are not adequately trained for either guidance or placement functions, and already have too many other duties in connection with housing, tribal committees and executives, youth clubs, Women's League, marriage counselling, etc., to execute properly their educational and placement functions.

Maori Vocational Guidance Officers would have the following duties: (a) to maintain continuous relationships with pupils, parents, and teachers in the district; (b) to provide educational and vocational guidance to pupils on the basis of interest, ability, personality, motivation, and job opportunities; (c) to place young people in suitable jobs or apprenticeships, and to make the necessary transfer arrangements (when movement outside the district

---

* The clergy and leaders of other faiths adopt a more aloof approach in pastoral work.

occurs (for lodging and follow-up work; (d) to make periodic surveys of employment opportunities in the district; (e) to carry out race relations work with employers and civic groups, particularly with respect to Maori "work psychology" and the importance of not prejudging Maori job applicants on the basis of racial stereotypes; (f) to explain to Maori parents the existing system of available Government, tribal, and church bursaries and hostels; (g) to carry out follow-up work with Maori apprentices and junior employees they have placed, i.e., to ascertain whether both parties are satisfied (and if not, the reasons why), to remedy causes of dissatisfaction, and to investigate absenteeism and reasons for terminating employment; (h) to investigate cases of truancy; and (i) to secure the co-operation of tribal committees and executives and to use their community and disciplinary influence in maintaining high standards.

Hostels

The establishment of more and better hostels is an indispensable condition for increasing the number of Maori youths in apprenticeships and the universities. Suitable private lodging is difficult to obtain because of pakeha prejudice; and in slum areas unsophisticated Maori lads from country districts easily get into trouble with the law (see p. 76). Hostels help counteract homesickness, provide group atmosphere and community activities with other Maoris, and discourage drinking and brawling. By living with other apprentices who also earn little pay, Maori boys are less tempted to throw up their apprenticeship for higher paid unskilled labour. A hostel, however, fails to accomplish these purposes unless it is properly managed by someone who is firm but also understands Maori group life. It would also be helpful if apprentices were more highly paid. Both economically and motivationally it makes little sense to pay a partially skilled apprentice one-third as much as an unskilled workman simply on the pretext that he is being given an opportunity to learn a trade while he is working.

EDUCATION

Important as it is to increase the number of Maori pupils who continue in school beyond the minimal leaving age, it is even more important to make post-primary school a more rewarding and less frustrating experience for the large number of academically less capable Maori pupils who are currently only marking time in school until their fifteenth birthdays. Lacking the academic interests, the intellectual ability, the vocational incentives and the family background of upper- and middle-class pakeha youth that make the unfamiliar authoritarian regimen of the secondary school at least tolerable, many Maori pupils either take refuge in apathetic withdrawal or become aggressively anti-social. It is not sufficient in such cases merely to provide technical courses and expensive shop equipment, since disinterest in the school's programme typically extends to both trades and academic subjects. Thus, any changes that would make the disciplinary climate of the secondary school generally more compatible with the developmental needs and capacities of adolescent pupils would tend to make school work a happier and more productive experience not only for these boys, but also for more academically oriented pupils as well, both Maori and pakeha. Such necessary measures include "less authoritarian kinds of teacher-pupil relationships, the abolition of corporal punishment and school uniforms, the provision of more extra-curricular and school government activities, and a shift to more genuinely co-educational forms of classroom and social interaction between the sexes".[5] Harsh, authoritarian, and impersonal discipline tends to have an especially detrimental impact on Maori pupils from small village schools, in view of the warm, personal pupil-teacher relationships to which they were accustomed in such schools, and because of the special adjustive difficulties they face on entering secondary school (see pp. 87-89).

It would also be necessary to reduce the inordinate gap between levels of subject-matter difficulty in primary and secondary school [which is particularly marked in the case of Maori pupils (see pp. 88-89)], to minimise the stigma currently associated with low academic ability and to make some curricular changes. Adolescents with I.Q.'s below 90, whether Maori or pakeha, cannot possibly hope to do acceptable work in mathematics, French, English, science, and social studies as they are customarily taught, let alone pass the School Certificate Examination. In my opinion, it would make more educational sense to teach these pupils how to use oral and written English in everyday communication, and to give them a functional grasp of quantitative processes as employed in practical life situations, than vainly to attempt to make them memorise rote academic lessons in literature, grammar, algebra, and geometry that are utterly beyond their capacity.

It is manifestly unfair to send pupils (both Maori and pakeha) out into the world as parents, tradesmen, workers and citizens in the semi-literate state characteristic of the lower streams of third and fourth formers who currently leave New Zealand post-primary schools. This is not to imply that primary schools are any less successful than they used to be in instructing pupils in the three R's, as the critics of modern education so vociferously allege. All of the little empirical evidence that bears on the issue does not support this theory.* Much more credible is the explanation that the clientele of the secondary school is now representative of the general level of intellectual ability of the *entire* population rather than of a small, select minority, bound for the universities and the professions, as in pre-World War II days. Pupils who would never have gone beyond Standard Four in former times are now required to remain in school until they are 15. Yet, despite the fact that subject-matter content and methods of instruction which are suitable for pupils in the 110-130 I.Q. range are obviously inappropriate for pupils with I.Q.'s of 75-90, syllabi and instructional techniques in the academic subjects are still practically identical for these two groups of pupils.

By virtue of their language retardation Maori youth suffer a special handicap in the School Certificate Examination *over* and *above* the effect of this retardation on their general intellectual ability. Because of difficulty in expressing themselves they obtain lower marks than their knowledge of a given subject warrants. In many instances also, although they have sufficient functional grasp of the language to obtain passing marks in subjects like geography and history, they still fail in English because the formal academic aspects of the examination go beyond the pupils' knowledge of literature and his ability to communicate effectively. The following measures should be considered, therefore, to remedy this situation which has the undesirable effect of barring many Maori pupils from professional and sub-professional occupations: (a) greater use of "objective"-type (i.e., multiple choice matching, and completion) examination questions; (b) a more functional and less academic type of English examination for Maori pupils; and (c) the granting of a School Certificate on the basis of a pass in

---

* Reapplication of achievement tests used in earlier years shows improvement in silent reading and maintenance of standards in spelling, written English, and arithmetic. Statement of Minister of Education, *New Zealand Parent and Child,* 1959, 7, pp. 20-21.

three subjects plus mathematics but without English.*

In certain carefully selected instances a supervised work-study programme would be more desirable than full-time school attendance for those pupils (Maori or pakeha) with very resistive or apathetic attitudes towards education. Like apprentices they would have full-time jobs, but their work programmes would be supervised by the Education Department (to guard against exploitation and hazardous practices and to provide for optimally beneficial vocational experiences), and they would attend a specified number of afternoon and evening classes. Under these circumstances they are much more apt to appreciate the value and relevance of schooling for occupational life. But in cases where the school leaving age is not waived, the truancy law should be strictly enforced. Absences should be investigated promptly, and all irregularities should be brought immediately to the attention of the appropriate officer of the Education Board. In recalcitrant cases vigorous court action, severe penalties, and suspension of the family benefit are clearly warranted.

To facilitate the adjustment of Maori pupils to the "strange and alien post-primary school environment", Whakatane High School instituted a programme in 1958 which is worthy of emulation in other secondary schools with substantial Maori enrolments. This programme includes the teaching of the Maori language as a school subject, systematic study of Maori culture, the appointment of one teacher to counsel Maori pupils, meetings of Maori parents, discussions between teachers and Maori tribal officials, and lunchtime social activities for Maori and pakeha pupils. Holst[20] has also convincingly demonstrated the desirability of appointing tutors to help Maori pupils with language and scholastic difficulties, of making primary school buildings available to secondary school pupils for study purposes, and of scheduling "frequent and regular discussions between teachers of contributing schools and teachers of the post-primary school".[20]

Maori Schools

Maori village schools have served several important purposes in the past, and in many areas still have a useful function to perform in the present and immediate future. In isolated rural districts they provide necessary practical instruction in personal hygiene, sani-

---

* Some Trades' Boards accept this combination of passes in lieu of a School Certificate.

tation, agriculture, home science, mothercraft, cookery and wood-work; give Maori pupils some background in the songs, legends, history, and arts and crafts of their people; and generally serve as local centres of Maori culture, social advancement, and facilitation of adjustment to pakeha ways of life. Since Maori villages are gradually emerging from isolation, however, the special Committee on Maori Education appointed in 1955 wisely recommended that Maori schools be gradually absorbed into the regular system of Board schools as soon as the Maori people in the various districts feel that the need for the special school is no longer present.* Some Maori village schools as well as two Maori district high schools have, as a matter of fact, already become Board schools;[31] and present Education Department policy seems to indicate that if and when Maori district high schools become full secondary schools, they will be released from Department control and placed under their own Boards of Governors as are all other, full post-primary schools.

The gradual abolition of the Maori village school is especially important in view of the prospect of increased racial tension in the future. Although the existence of the Maori school system has only been used once in recent times (i.e., in 1952 at Pukekohe) as a means of segregating Maori from pakeha school children, much latent pakeha sentiment exists throughout the North Island for segregated schools and school buses. As long as a dual system of schools exists, it constitutes a potentially dangerous channel for the institutionalisation of segregated education as in the American South prior to the historic Supreme Court decision of 1954.

IDENTIFICATION OF YOUTH WITH MAORI CULTURE

The gradual attenuation of traditional Maori cultural values and practices seems inevitable as the social structure of the Maori village continues to distintegrate and as urbanisation proceeds apace. Concomitantly it appears likely that Maori youth, lacking deep emotional roots in the culture, will largely react with racial nationalism to the situation of becoming a victimised and under-privileged lower-class racial minority with second-class citizenship. That these developments will take place, as I have already emphasised, is only a prediction based on objective evaluation of past

* *Annual Report, 1956*, New Zealand Department of Education, pp. 29-31.

history, current trends, and the course of acculturation elswhere under analogous conditions. It is *not* a statement of advocacy. Quite the contrary! I think that the disappearance of various Maori cultural values will represent a genuine loss both to the Maori and the pakeha, because they offer something that Western man has yet been unable to attain—a genuine sense of belongingness in the community apart from his market value, and the capacity for living and working with fellow human beings other than as a stranger. Hence, since these latter values are not inherently incompatible with adjustment to pakeha life or with high standards of achievement, it is not simply sentimental or impractical idealism to recommend that the predicted process of cultural attenuation be rendered as gradual as possible by instituting active measures to enhance the identification of Maori youth with their culture.

But quite apart from this idealistic (but not unrealistic) reason for seeking to extend as long as possible the viability of certain selected Maori cultural values and traditions, are more pressing reasons stemming from the psychology of acculturation and racial minority groups. In almost every acculturational situation, not excluding New Zealand, a marked tendency exists for the indigenous people to feel or to be made to feel that their customs, beliefs, language, ways of life, etc., are inferior in comparison with their European counterparts, and hence are things to hide, disavow and be ashamed of. Maori youth can only overcome these feelings of inferiority by developing positive pride in and identification with their cultural background. Because their affiliation with Maori culture has genuinely deep roots, middle-aged and older Maoris tend to possess an impressive sense of "presence" or dignity which younger Maoris lack. This difference, I am convinced, is more than a difference in years or maturity. Nevertheless, some semblance of cultural identity can still be maintained through programmes in schools and youth clubs that teach Maori history, folk-lore, language, and arts and crafts.

Given the security of his cultural identity, the Maori is in a psychologically much stronger position to adapt with confidence to pakeha culture—without developing concomitant feelings of personal inadequacy. And in view of the impending increase in racial prejudice and discrimination in New Zealand, the best protection the Maori has against the irreparable damage to self-esteem and dignity as a person threatening all victims of a colour bar,* is a deep-seated sense of *cultural* pride and identification with his *cultural* traditions. Pride of *race* and *racial* nationalism are inadequate substitutes. Because he was forced to leave his African culture behind him when he was deported to America as a slave, the American Negro had no other choice than to develop racial pride. But enough Maori culture is still sufficiently vigorous to survive in attenuated form for one or more generations and to constitute a significant and psychologically constructive protective mechanism against the traumatic impact of militant colour prejudice.

This does not mean that I advocate a return to moribund traditions or to archaic ceremonial usages. An escapist orientation that emphasises cultural elements which no longer have any inherent vitality or current functional significance is either merely reactionary or is an opportunistic and potentially dangerous means of fanning racial nationalism and counter-chauvinism. In either case it distracts the Maori people from coming to grips with the real and urgent problems of cultural adaptation. It is favoured by some pakehas who, although they only know Maori life third-hand from a safe distance, are imbued with vague, sentimental, and romantic notions, and wish to preserve the Maori as an ethnological specimen or tourist attraction—not by those who have firsthand knowledge and a genuine understanding of the Maori situation.

TEACHING OF THE MAORI LANGUAGE

Much of the controversy regarding the perpetuation of Maori culture hinges on the issue of preserving and teaching the Maori language. Many persons who are in favour of instructing Maori and even pakeha children in the history, legends, songs, and arts and crafts of the Maori people, take an uncompromisingly negative position on the question of language.

There is no doubt about the fact that, apart from growing interest among some pakeha groups, Maori has been declining as a living language. This is merely a reflection and a concomitant of the general decline in traditional Maori cultural values and practices that has taken place in the post-withdrawal period, notwithstanding frequently reiterated claims about the post-war "renaissance" in Maori culture. Whether or not a language survives

---

* See D. P. Ausubel (3), pp. 328-330, and (4), pp. 430-431, for documentation on the detrimental effects of colour prejudice on the personality development of American Negro children and adolescents.

depends on whether it is transmitted to the younger generation. On the basis of this criterion the outlook for Maori is not very bright unless radical measures are instituted in the very near future. Generally speaking, Maori is a functional (although not the primary) language among the majority of the people only in the age group of 35-40 and above. In some Urewera and East Coast districts Maori is the mother tongue of most children; but in typical rural areas a fair estimate of the prevalence of Maori speaking children would be 20 per cent. In urban centres and town districts, five per cent would probably be an overestimate.

Unlike the children of many ethnic minority groups in the United States (e.g., Puerto Rican, Greek, Italian) who naturally and effortlessly absorb the language of their parents by hearing it spoken in the home, most Maori children have no real command of the language even though their parents speak it fluently. This situation is partly a function of the extremely little contact and poor communication between Maori parents and children. In part, however, it is a reflection of the fact that many parents not only make no effort to teach their children the language but also regard it as a badge of inferiority. Some parents discourage their children from learning Maori, either in the mistaken belief that by so doing they are helping them learn English, or because they themselves were punished in school for speaking it. In other instances they simply find it more convenient to converse in English, or claim that the children are disinterested, overly self-conscious, or fearful of being ridiculed by their age-mates.

Despite the declining use of the Maori language in the home and for everyday purposes of communication, instructional facilities in the language have expanded somewhat in recent years. Prior to World War II only the Maori denominational colleges taught it as a school subject. Now it is also offered by the University of Auckland, by various adult education groups, by most Maori district high schools, by the Correspondence School in Wellington and by a small number of full post-primary schools, both State and private. It is recognised as a degree subject and as meeting the foreign language requirement for the B.A. at the Victoria University of Wellington as well as at the University of Auckland, and as an approved subject for the School Certificate and University Entrance Examinations. But these steps obviously constitute no more than a mere beginning. It is necessary to extend instruction in the Maori language to all Maori primary and secondary schools and to all other schools with large Maori rolls. A convincing argument (see below) has also been put forward for making instruction in the Maori language available to both Maori and pakeha pupils in all schools, on a voluntary basis.

The biggest stumbling block in implementing these recommendations, of course, is the lack of qualified teachers. Partly as a result of the Education Department's earlier policy of first actively punishing children for speaking Maori in the school environment, and later remaining utterly indifferent to the question of providing instruction in the Maori language, a tremendous shortage exists in Maori-speaking teachers. This situation, however, can be remedied by first concentrating on the teaching of Maori in the post-primary schools and the Training Colleges so as to train new teachers; and in the meantime, until the latter are available, the part-time services of educated Maori parents and tribal committee officials can be enlisted.

The teaching of Maori in the schools has been opposed on four principal grounds. First, some ardent advocates of rapid assimilation argue that preservation of the language fosters "racial consciousness," which in turn allegedly encourages nationalism, provokes racial tensions, and impedes the process of integration with Europeans. All of the available overseas evidence, however, indicates that the preservation of cultural identity in an indigenous people, by enhancing self-confidence and self-respect, promotes successful integration, improves race relations, and prevents psychological trauma from exposure to colour prejudice. The alternative to *cultural* identification, namely, *racial* identification and counter-chauvinism, is both psychologically and socially a much less constructive type of ethnic self-protection. In any event, racial nationalism is preferable to demoralisation and feelings of racial inferiority.

Secondly, it is frequently stated that all formal attempts to preserve or revive languages artificially (e.g., Welsh, Gaelic and Erse in Wales, Scotland, and Eire respectively) have failed dismally in the past. But the analogy here is far-fetched because Maori is much more of a vigorous, functional and living language than the latter three tongues. Since Maori grandparents and middle-aged adults still speak the language fluently, Maori children would have ample opportunity for practice in everyday situations. Maori instruction in the schools would also tend to reduce the present conflict between home and school standards as well as the estrangement between Maori parents and children.

Thirdly, the example of the Scotch, Welsh and Irish is further invoked to deny that language is necessary for the perpetuation of Maori cultural identity. This analogy is also untenable because these latter peoples are more highly acculturated and better adjusted groups who dwell in their own national and ethnically homogeneous territories and who basically share a European cultural tradition not too different from the English. Furthermore, they have a long history of successfully preserving their cultural identity *before* their national tongues were gradually superseded by the English language. In the later stages of acculturation, once residual ethnic traditions are more stable and highly crystallised, language is a less indispensable condition than in the earlier stages for maintaining cultural cohesion. The present-day Maori is only half a Maori without his language, whereas Scotsmen are not *really* expected to speak Gaelic. Maori is the *only* acceptable language on the *marae* (except for visiting pakehas), and every Maori leader must be able to use it competently if he expects to have any influence with his people. Language is the most effective of all the "boundary maintaining mechanisms" (see pp. 106-107) in perpetuating the existence of a culture; and conversely, "there is no quicker way of killing a culture than of killing its language".*

Lastly, it is asserted that existing bilingualism impedes the educational and vocational achievement of the Maori by retarding his language development, and that instruction in the Maori language would only compound this damage as well as distract Maori children from the task of overcoming their handicap in English. To the arguments already adduced in countering the validity of these claims (see pp. 93-94), may be added the following statement by an experienced inspector of the Maori Schools:

> Although for many years the Maori Schools have catered for a minority of Maori children, it is an undeniable fact that most of the Maoris who have achieved professional status had their primary schooling at a Maori School.[21]

Plausible reasons also exist for believing that Maori would be a good optional subject for pakeha pupils. Pakehas do much glib talking about "amalgamating the two cultures into one nation," but they patronisingly expect Maoris to make one hundred per

---

* Colin Roderick, as quoted in the Sydney University *Union Recorder*, 11 July, 1957, p. 130.

cent of the effort and change in the integration process. They currently cannot even be bothered to learn how to pronounce Maori place names correctly. Hence, even a cursory knowledge of the Maori language on the part of pakehas would be a tangible expression of racial good-will and would go a long way towards improving mutual understanding in New Zealand. "If all New Zealanders had two mother tongues . . . it would chart a new course towards national homogeneity . . . and a new bond of sympathy and true fellowship would be forged between them." Enrichment of the English language and literature would also result from the incorporation of Maori vocabulary, idiom, and cultural tradition.*

I know from personal experience that the greatest compliment a pakeha guest can pay his Maori hosts on the *marae* is to address them in their own language. My limited efforts in learning to speak some colloquial Maori and to deliver the appropriate ceremonial speeches in Maori at *huis, tangis,* weddings, birthday celebrations, and *marae* welcomes, were more than amply repaid both in the warmth of personal relationships with Maori friends and in establishing rapport and goodwill for research purposes.

Making an effort to learn the Maori language is the most concrete way in which the research worker can manifest sincere interest and humility in the eyes of his Maori hosts. They invariably begin to wonder why a pakeha who professes to be so concerned with their welfare has managed to live a lifetime in New Zealand without acquiring the rudiments of their language. The fact that they know of some pakehas who *have* learned to speak Maori with considerable fluency provides a basis for the invidious comparisons that are frequently made. In fact, it can be stated quite categorically that a fluent command of the Maori language is an indispensable prerequisite for acquiring both the intimacy of rapport and the appreciation of nuances of thought and feeling that are necessary for a complete understanding of the cultural pattern. It must be remembered that although most Maoris have a functional grasp of the English language, some Maoris speak little or no English and relatively few are sufficiently conversant with the language to be able to express subtleties of thought with any fluency. The writer was always aware of the

---

* Summary of an interview with Colin Roderick reported in the *Waikato Times,* 17 April 1957.

research handicaps posed by his only rudimentary familiarity with the Maori language.[5]

Primary responsibility for perpetuating the Maori language obviously rests with the Maori people themselves—not with the schools or the Government. Unless Maori parents are sufficiently interested to transmit the language to their children, and unless the Maori community arranges suitable occasions for children to practise Maori conversation without self-consciousness, the efforts of the schools will certainly share the fate of experiments with Erse and Gaelic. At best the schools can only reinforce and solidify in a more grammatical form the basic word meanings and idioms acquired through daily use in the home.

IMPROVEMENT OF RACE RELATIONS

As already indicated, colour prejudice and discrimination constitute the most serious and prognostically least hopeful factors impeding the implementation of Maori educational and vocational aspirations. All of the other difficulties stemming from family, community, and cultural influences can be expected to diminish in intensity with the progress of acculturation, and to yield to intelligently applied administrative measures (e.g., vocational guidance, curricular, and disciplinary reforms in the school, improved housing conditions). Unfortunately, however, the various factors affecting race relations (see p. 77) threaten to become increasingly more unfavourable for at least another generation. Not the least unfavourable aspect of the entire situation—which currently prevents the organisation of fact-finding research studies and the application of preventive and remedial measures—is the prevailing complacency and self-deception of pakehas regarding racial matters, and the ostrich-like attitude of most Maori leaders and professionals, that if one only closes one's eyes and pretends that no problems exist, they will magically disappear by themselves.

The official position of the Government (including the Maori Welfare Organisation) is that genuine racial equality prevails, both as regards the spirit and the letter of the law, that a "behaviour" rather than a colour bar exists, and that all Maoris who conduct themselves in accordance with European standards are accepted and treated on exactly the same basis as pakehas. But if empirical evidence in support of these contentions is available, the Government has never bothered to publish it, whereas the present research report fairly bristles with contradictory evidence. The Bennett

Affair* was officially deplored, but regarded as an isolated incident rather than as symptomatic of a steadily deteriorating racial situation, and as representative of widely prevalent practices that in one form or another are daily occurrences throughout the North Island, but are not reported in the Press because the victims do not happen to be senior Government physicians, sons of the late Bishop Bennett, or brothers of the New Zealand High Commissioner to Malaya. If ordinary people as well as governments and dramatists could live indefinitely by the dictum that "Nothing is but thinking makes it so", there assuredly would be no cause for concern or for the recommendations that are offered below. In spite of the pessimistic outlook I still believe that it is morally indefensible to adopt a defeatist attitude towards this problem.

Equality of Vocational Opportunity

Equality of vocational opportunity in New Zealand exists only in political oratory and in propaganda to the outside world—not in fact. Maoris are not explicitly barred by law from any occupation, but neither are they legally guaranteed equal access to employment (as, for example, racial minorities are in many northern states of America), despite New Zealand's self-congratulatory claim of being the most advanced nation in the world in the sphere of race relations and social legislation. If equality did exist in fact, one might argue that legislation is superfluous; but we have already seen that anti-Maori discrimination is rampant in banks, shops, commercial establishments, skilled trades, apprenticeships, private offices, and managerial and supervisory positions (see p. 44 and p. 50).

Hence it should be clear to all men of goodwill that a vigorous campaign is urgently required to ensure equality of occupational opportunity in New Zealand. If Maoris were guaranteed equal access with pakehas to all kinds of jobs, the vicious cycle of vocational and social maladjustment could be broken. Maoris who are satisfactorily adjusted occupationally can afford better housing, clothes, and sanitation, are more likely to provide adequate care and supervision for their children, and are less likely to become

---

* An ugly and highly publicised incident in February 1959, in which Dr H. R. Bennett, a Maori physician, was refused service in the Papakura Hotel lounge on the grounds that he was a Maori. Only four months prior to this incident, the Minister of Education publicly branded as "fatuous" the writer's fully documented conclusion in a magazine article that a colour bar prevailed in most parts of the North Island.

socially demoralised and implicated in crime and alcoholism. By earning their own self-respect and the respect of their pakeha neighbours, race relations are improved and adaptation to pakeha ways is enhanced. If, on the other hand, they are prejudged on the basis of the racial stereotype and denied jobs on the grounds that the *statistical* probabilities of unreliability are greater among Maoris than among pakehas, the opposite social consequences can be anticipated, i.e., social demoralisation and the "Maori" traits that pakehas find objectionable will be perpetuated, racial strife, and bitterness will be intensified, and the moral basis of a democratic society that rests on the right of each individual to be judged on his *own* merits will be destroyed.

This campaign for equality of vocational opportunity can be furthered through both legislative and educational means. The legislative approach has its obvious limitations in the sense that only the negative manifestations of intolerance as reflected in employment and other types of discriminatory practices can be proscribed by law;* the positive aspects of tolerance, goodwill and fair play cannot be similarly inculcated. Nevertheless we should not underestimate the tangible benefits of placing the moral and legal force of society squarely against the colour bar. "Fair Employment Practices Commissions which are empowered to investigate complaints of discrimination, to persuade offending employers to mend their ways and, where necessary, to issue 'cease and desist' orders that are enforceable by the courts," have substantially improved the economic status of Negro and other ethnic minorities in the United States.[5] "The availability of . . . legal remedies brings many bigots into line, provides minority groups with an orderly channel for the redress of real or fancied grievances, . . . and forces timid employers to abandon unwarranted fears or rationalisations regarding discriminatory practices."[5]

Educational activities sponsored by schools, churches, and civic groups constitute the positive complement to the legislative approach. "To be effective, however, they must go beyond the vague generalities, the customary platitudes, the familiar exhortations about 'loving thy brother', and the mystical belief that if peoples of different races 'only got together more often and learned to know each other better' all inter-racial conflict would magically

---

* Scope for similar legislation exists in housing, hotel accommodation, bars, restaurants, cinemas, dance halls, credit, prices, etc.

disappear."[5] It is important to explain the origins and mechanisms of prejudiced thinking and to point out its pernicious moral, political, social, and economic consequences. But "even more important, perhaps, is to provide practical guidance in the application of racial tolerance. . . . Pakeha employers, for example, could be taught how greater understanding of Maori work psychology could be utilised in obtaining more efficient and reliable performance from Maori employees."[5] By varying the monotony of their work, by allowing for greater informality and more group participation in management, by making reasonable alowances for Maori social customs, and by letting group responsibility and discipline handle such problems as absenteeism, shirking of work and inefficiency, some firms have achieved phenomenally good records of work attendance and production. If employees know more than one job and are willing to work overtime so that a fellow-worker can attend a relative's *tangi,* the disruptive influence of the latter practice on production schedules is eliminated, and at the same time a Maori is not made to feel that he has let his kinsmen down in an important matter just to earn a few more pounds. "This patient and enlightened type of approach eventually pays greater social and economic dividends than a policy of not hiring . . . [Maoris] at all or firing them abruptly for their first offence of absenteeism."[5]

The establishment, wherever practicable, of rural industries in areas of dense Maori population can also do much to improve living standards in Maori villages and to relieve some of the problems caused by excessively rapid urbanisation. The transition to urban life can be rendered much less traumatic if experience in industrial work can first be obtained in a more familiar setting. Being able to remain in his ancestral home is a matter of much deeper emotional significance to the Maori than to the pakeha.

Equality in Housing

Second only to the urgency of providing equality of vocational opportunity is the need for bringing Maori housing up to European standards. In its own *Annual Report* for 1956, the Department of Maori Affairs has this to say about Maori housing conditions:

Housing of a good modern standard is enjoyed by only a minority of Maoris, and well over half the population of many settlements live under conditions not much better than those of pre-European times. Far too many are literally in shelters no better than huts. We cannot expect those who live in this way to prosper economically, we cannot expect from them sound standards of social conduct, we cannot expect their children to be successfully educated especially at high school level (p. 16).

More might also have been said about the effects of such housing on health, delinquency, alcoholism, community morale, and race relations.

Although "part of this deplorable situation can be attributed to the inevitable consequences of prolonged withdrawal in remote and backward villages, to the high Maori birth rate and to traditions of Maori hospitality, to confusion about land titles, and to vocational maladjustment, social demoralisation, and individual improvidence",[5] successive Governments have been at fault in failing to sponsor housing programmes of adequate scope. It is not enough merely to construct sufficient new units to keep pace with the growth in population without remedying the cumulative housing deficit of eight decades of economic stagnation. The Maori people must be provided with "the necessary guidance and financial assistance they require to overcome their special cultural handicaps in this matter".[5]

The Government has also conveniently closed its eyes to the disgraceful discriminatory practices of pakeha landlords which (apart from State rental houses and housing projects) have had the effect of virtually segregating urban Maoris in the least desirable slum districts. That radical legislative and educational measures are required to rectify this situation is evident from the public response to a recent statement[11] by the secretary of the Orakei Tribal Committee which charged that many Maoris in Auckland were living in tents, that as many as twenty persons often occupied a three-bedroom house, that seven children of both sexes sometimes slept in one bed, and that many Maoris sought solace in excessive drinking because of the endless delays and frustrations involved in obtaining Government housing loans. The correspondence columns of the newspapers were flooded with irate letters from self-righteous pakeha readers blaming everything on Maori laziness, improvidence, and unwillingness to help themselves. Even his conclusion that "when landlords refuse accommodation to Maoris because of their colour and force them into hovels, the proud statement to the world that Maori and pakeha

---

* *New Zealand Herald*, 10th April, 1958.

are equal becomes a mockery" failed to prick any consciences—public or private.

The Maori's Responsibility in Improving Race Relations

Just because he is the principal victim of, rather than the major guilty party in instigating, racial intolerance in New Zealand does not mean that the Maori has no responsibility in improving race relations. By the same token, because he has the most to gain from harmonious inter-racial attitudes and behaviour, he should and must be willing to assume much of the initiative in furthering this objective.

This implies a willingness realistically to come to grips with the situation and to seek constructive legislative, judicial, and educational remedies rather than [to bury his head in the sand], to react with counter-chauvinism, or to exploit the racial conflict for nationalistic purposes. Compared to other racial minorities in comparable circumstances the Maori people have been relatively apathetic about taking any kind of organised self-protective action in response to the very real colour bar . . . confronting them. This becomes immediately apparent when it is realised that organisations such as the National Association for the Advancement of Coloured People are currently spearheading the drive for racial equality in the United States.[5]

Maori groups themselves are most strategically placed to further the educational, vocational and social advancement of the youth, and hence to establish a sound basis for self-respect and respect from the pakeha. They are also best able to cope with

those symptoms of incomplete or inadequate adjustment to pakeha culture—[over-reliance on Government assistance], alcoholism, tardiness, absenteeism, juvenile delinquency, boisterousness in public places and at late hours, inattention to personal grooming and hygiene—that further aggravate Maori-pakeha relations. Just such a simple step as making sure that every Maori school child had a handkerchief and knew when and how to use it would, for example, make for an immediate improvement of race relations in New Zealand. Lastly, the Maori people themselves rather than the Government . . . are primarily responsible for perpetuating the Maori language and other basic cultural symbols without which it becomes impossible for young Maoris to identify with their culture.[5]

Some type of national, supra-tribal organisation is needed to speak and act for all the Maori people in these crucial matters affecting the welfare and future of the entire race. Tribal executives cannot serve this function because they are intra-tribal, statutory bodies with specified limits of authority. The King Movement is too regional, parochial, authoritarian, and moribund in outlook to represent all of Maoridom in a modern and progressive programme of social action that must of necessity have a strong grass roots basis; and the Ratana Movement is too sectarian, is too involved in Labour Party politics, and lacks the necessary vigour and leadership.

Clearly the time is ripe for a new movement and for new leaders to appear. And just as the necessary leadership arose in the Land Leagues of 1858, and again in 1897 with the formation of the Young Maori Party, when the fortunes of the Maori race were at their lowest ebb, it can be confidently predicted that from the cauldron of the forthcoming crisis in race relations, enlightened and effective leadership will emerge.

CHAPTER SEVEN

Summary and Conclusions

PROBLEM AND RESEARCH DESIGN

IN GENERAL THIS RESEARCH STUDY WAS CONCERNED WITH culturally determined uniformities and differences in the personality structure and development of Maori and pakeha adolescents and how they are transmitted to the developing individual. More specifically it sought (a) to identify Maori-pakeha uniformities and differences in expressed and internalised levels of academic and vocational aspiration and in the kinds of motivations underlying these aspirations; (b) to identify Maori-pakeha uniformities and differences in supportive personality traits important for the realisation of achievement goals; and (c) to relate these motivational and other personality differences to cultural and interpersonal factors and mechanisms that account for their transmission from one generation to the next.

Another focus of research concern was on urban-rural differences in aspirational pattern among Maori adolescents and on the relative magnitude of Maori-pakeha differences in urban and rural areas. An attempt was also made to assess the relative magnitude and significance of Maori-pakeha differences by comparing them to urban rural-differences.

In addition to their theoretical significance for general problems of adolescent personality development (e.g., cross-cultural uniformities and differences; the impact of acculturation), findings such as these obviously have important implications for the direction and organisation of education and vocational guidance for Maori youth. The data have particular relevance for the serious problem of keeping Maori youth in school beyond the age of fifteen and of increasing Maori representation in the professions and skilled trades.

The general plan was to utilise a rural and an urban group of Maori male adolescents and comparable groups of pakeha adolescents from the same localities. Partly because of the advantage of ready accessibility to subjects, and partly because one focus of inquiry was on academic aspirations, only young adolescents attending school were studied. Fifty Maori and 50 pakeha subjects in each sample (urban and rural) were drawn from the same secondary schools and were matched individually on the basis of form, course, ability group, and father's occupation. The purpose of using matched groups of Maori and pakeha pupils and both urban and rural samples was to distinguish between distinctively Maori personality traits, on the one hand, and traits assimilated from pakeha culture, on the other, and to isolate the effects of Maori culture on personality from the effects induced by the unequal operation of such factors as occupation, social class status, urban-rural residence, and academic aptitude on Maori and pakeha populations. Because of generally higher pakeha than Maori I.Q.'s in the same ability groupings, and the unavailability of sufficient subjects, it was not possible to match subjects on the basis of I.Q. Separate matchings were conducted for the Maori-pakeha and the urban-rural comparisons.

The procedures and instruments used in this study included: (1) structured academic and vocational interviews with pupils; (2) Test of Occupational Prestige Needs; (3) Achievement Imagery Test; (4) Vocational Tenacity Test; (5) Responsiveness to Prestige Incentives Test; (6) Teachers' Ratings of motivational and aspirational traits; and (7) participant observation at community functions (tribal committee and tribal executive meetings, *huis, tangis,* weddings, sports meetings, birthday parties, etc.), and informal interviews with parents, teachers, Vocational Guidance Officers, Maori Welfare Officers, community leaders and clergymen.

The methods of participant observation and informal interview were used to obtain supplementary data and relevant background information of general and regional cultural significance that would facilitate the interpretation of the more quantitative findings. They were primarily employed with adults, and in relation to those kinds of data for which structured interviews and test procedures were inappropriate, e.g., community morale and leadership, attitudes towards work and achievement, race relations, employment practices. Because of the importance of protecting the identity of informants, and because primary reliance was placed on more rigorous quantitative data, participant observation and informal interview materials were reported in general rather than in specific terms.

The validity of the generalisations derived from these latter qualitative materials is obviously limited by such methodological shortcomings as unrepresentativeness of sample, inapplicability of statistical treatment to data, indeterminability of observer reliability, and variability in content and sequence of interview questions. Nevertheless, since it was frequently possible to cross-check informants both against each other and against observational data and since the generalisations mirror overwhelming and unambiguous trends in the direction of the evidence, it is highly unlikely that they are completely unreflective of actually prevailing attitudes and behaviour in the particular communities under investigation. In certain instances (e.g., race relations), the extension of participant observation and informal interview techniques to a wide variety of other North Island districts adds national perspective to the data.

Since there is no such thing as a "typical" Maori community, and since no attempt was made in this study to use a stratified sample representative of the Maori population in New Zealand, the quantitative findings of this study may be properly generalised only to Maori communities similar to those described herein, i.e., to urban provincial centres, and to relatively prosperous Maori rural districts with roughly equal numbers of Maori and pakeha inhabitants and better than average race relations. Implications from these findings for the educational and vocational achievement of Maori youth *as a whole* are only tentative and suggestive, and would have to be confirmed by research on a more representative sample of Maori adolescents (i.e., drawn from the various main types of Maori districts) before they could be generalised more widely.

The Findings

Matched groups of Maori and pakeha secondary school pupils exhibited a striking measure of overall similarity in educational and vocational aspirations, underlying motivations for achievement, supportive traits, and perceptions of both prevailing opportunities and family and peer group pressures for achievement. This finding supports the view that many (but by no means all) of the traits commonly regarded as typically Maori are largely reflective of low occupational and social class status, predominantly rural residence, and environmentally stunted verbal intelligence. Some Maori-pakeha differences may have been obscured in part either because of insufficient sensitivity of the measuring instruments or because of their transparency to the subjects. This possibility, however, is discounted both by the adequate range of variability obtained for the various instruments, and by the substantial degree of intercultural uniformity found in relation to those measures where transparency was impossible. In fact, obtained Maori-pakeha differences are probably overestimates of true differences since the pakeha sample was favoured by several factors that could not be controlled by matching.

The major finding of this study was the much greater similarity between Maori and pakeha pupils with respect to their expressed educational and vocational aspirations than with respect to those factors necessary for the internalisation and implementation of these aspirations, namely, underlying needs and motivations for achievement, supportive traits, and perceived pressures and opportunities for academic and occupational success. In terms of overall magnitude and prestige of academic and vocational aspirations, Maoris and pakeha samples were not significantly different. But although the stated aspirations of Maori pupils are not later internalised and implemented to the same extent as are those of pakeha pupils—because of the absence of suitable cultural, family, and peer group pressures and supports—there is no reason to believe that they were insincere or did not correspond to genuine intentions at the time that they were reported. Maori aspirations were especially expansive in relation to more remote goals (i.e., School Certificate, university, hypothetical vocational ambitions) unconstrained by current reality considerations, and were more restrained in relation to less distant goals, i.e., end of the year marks, improvement of scholastic standing in the class.

Assimilation of pakeha academic and vocational aspirations by Maori pupils—despite inadequate later internalisation and implementation—is a datum of tremendous cultural and psychological significance. It constitutes an all-important first step in the taking over of pakeha achievement patterns, and is indicative of a degree of acculturation that undoubtedly was not present 20 or even 10 years ago. Maori acculturation has evidently proceeded to the point where it can sustain the generation—if not the implementation—of European educational and occupational ambitions. The development of these aspirations during late childhood and early adolescence is facilitated by considerable contact with the school and with the wider pakeha culture, and by relatively poor communication with parents and the Maori adult community. As this communication improves and as Maori adolescents begin to perceive more accurately the lack of strong cultural and family pressures for educational and vocational achievement, their ambitions not only fall far short of realisation but are also drastically lowered.

Pakeha pupils had higher occupational prestige needs than Maori pupils and considered vocational achievement a more important life goal. They also gave higher ratings to such factors as prestige, wealth, and advancement as reasons for seeking occupational and academic success. Maori pupils, on the other hand, were more highly motivated by task-oriented ("interest in studies", "liking job") and group welfare (" to help others") considerations. Urban pakeha pupils were more highly rated by teachers than their Maori counterparts were on such supportive traits as persistence, attentiveness, conscientiousness, planning capacity, and initiation of activity; and in the rural school pakeha pupils did more studying for examinations.

Because of poor parent-child communication in our Maori sample, obtained Maori-pakeha differences in *perceived* family pressures and opportunities for educational and vocational achievement were less striking than those actually prevailing and noted in the course of participant observation and informal interviews. Nevertheless, pakeha parents were still perceived as demanding higher school marks than Maori parents and as prodding more about homework. Pakeha pupils were more optimistic than their Maori age-mates about the chances of achieving occupational success and saw fewer obstacles in their path. Another indication of defective parent-child communication was the fact that only about one-quarter of the Maori pupils had any insight into the existence of blatant anti-Maori discriminatory practices in employment.

As predicted, Maori-pakeha differences were greater in the urban than in the rural environment. Despite being more highly acculturated than rural Maoris, urban Maoris have not yet assimilated the urban pakeha pattern as completely as rural Maoris have assimilated the rural pakeha pattern. This, of course, is largely a function of the recency of Maori migration to the cities. In addition to the fact that rural life is much closer than urban to his indigenous pre-pakeha culture, the Maori has had at least a hundred years more time in accustoming himself to it.

With progressive urbanisation of the Maori population, urban-rural differences among Maori adolescent pupils are becoming increasingly more important, even though these differences in aspirational and motivational traits are currently less conspicuous than corresponding uniformities. Many factors undoubtedly contributed to the finding that Maori pupils in our urban sample were closer to pakeha norms in these traits than were rural Maori pupils. These factors include selective migration to the city of vocationally more ambitious youth, the greater acculturation of long-standing urban residents, the difficulty of practising Maori cultural values in the city, and less exposure to traditional practices and to the influence of Maori elders and of the Maori peer group.

Differences between urban and rural Maori pupils were most marked with respect to expressed educational and vocational aspirations, prestige motivation, desire for occupational success, and supportive traits. Urban pupils strove more for top marks and were more desirous of improving their class standing, had higher occupational prestige needs, made higher scores on the Achievement Imagery Test, and valued occupational achievement more highly. They also spent more time on homework and in studying for examinations. Although they perceived more obstacles in their path they were more hopeful of eventually achieving vocational success. Consistent urban-rural differences were not found in relation to task-oriented and group welfare motivation and perceived family pressures for achievement. It seems, therefore, that urban surroundings may encourage pakeha aspirations, motivations, and supportive traits without immediately attenuating Maori motivations. Since Maori parents were only recent arrivals to the city they apparently did not play an important role in transmitting pakeha achievement patterns to their children; they were not perceived by the latter as demanding higher educational and vocational achievement than were the parents of rural pupils. Urban parents, however, gave the impression of being less authoritarian than their rural counterparts, seemed to have less contact with and control over their children, and generally played a less important role in determining their children's choice of career.

Contrary to our hypothesis, urban-rural differences were slightly greater in the Maori than in the pakeha sample. The original prediction was based on the assumption that because of relative recency of urban residence, the Maori population would have assimilated the urban pattern of achievement less completely than their pakeha countrymen. Although this factor was undoubtedly operative, it was apparently more than offset by the fact that movement to the city constituted a much greater change, and hence had more of an impact on a Maori than a pakeha population.

With the progressive advance of Maori acculturation and migration to urban centres, the increasing importance of urban-rural differences among the Maori people has been paralleled by a corresponding decrease in the magnitude of Maori-pakeha differences. A credible hypothesis supported by our data would be that Maori acculturation with respect to aspirational patterns has proceeded to the point where, in rural areas, Maori and pakeha pupils are more similar to each other than are urban and rural Maori adolescents. In the city, however, Maori youth are, *relatively speaking,* not quite as far along on the acculturation continuum: Maori and pakeha pupils are still more different from each other than are matched urban and rural pupils within the Maori population.

Factors Affecting Maori Vocational Achievement

Parental Influences. Maori parents are less sophisticated than their pakeha counterparts about vocational matters, and are accordingly less capable of assisting their children with appropriate information, advice, and guidance. Even if they were more capable in these respects, however, they would still be handicapped in transmitting helpful insights from their own life experience because of the conspicuous estrangement and lack of adequate communication existing between them and their children, especially in urban centres. In view of their smaller incomes and larger families, Maori parents are also more reluctant to commit themselves to supporting plans requiring long-term vocational preparation. Many are greatly confused about the standards of behaviour they should properly expect and demand from their adolescent children, and others are ambivalent about letting the latter leave home in search of better vocational opportunities.

Maori parents tend to adopt more permissive and laissez-faire attitudes than pakeha parents towards their children's vocational careers. Despite occasional and inconsistent displays of authoritarianism in this regard, they are usually content to let them drift. They apply fewer coercive pressures and extend less support and encouragement in relation to the long-term occupational ambitions of their children. Their own values concerning vocational achievement, and the example they set their children also tend to encourage the adoption of a short-term view. In practice they make few demands for the deferment of immediate hedonistic satisfactions and for the internalisation of supportive traits consistent with high academic and occupational attainment. It is small wonder, therefore, that Maori adolescents are unable to resist the lure of immediate "big money" in unskilled labouring jobs. Although they tend in early adolescence to lack adequate insight into their parents' lack of genuine commitment to educational and vocational achievement, Maori pupils in our sample still perceived fewer family pressures regarding these matters than did pakeha pupils.

Peer Group Influences. Maori pupils also receive less encouragement from their peers than pakeha pupils do to strive for vocational achievement. Not only is occupational success less highly valued in the Maori than in the pakeha peer culture, but the greater availability of *derived status*—based solely on membership in and intrinsic acceptance by the group—also removes much of the incentive for seeking *primary status* on individual competence and performance. In districts where community morale is low and bodgieism flourishes, vocational achievement tends to be negatively sanctioned.

Cultural Influences. Greater emphasis on derived than on primary status, and on the task-oriented and group welfare features of primary status (rather than on its self-aggrandising aspects) is generally characteristic of Maori culture. Less concerned with achieving occupational prestige, the Maori is less willing than the pakeha to internalise traits important for implementing achievement goals, i.e., to practise initiative, foresight, self-denial and self-discipline, to persevere in the face of adversity, and to defer immediate hedonistic gratification in favour of remote vocational goals. Valuing personal relationships, derived status, and kinship ties above material possessions and occupational prestige, helpfulness, generosity, hospitality, and sociability count for more in his eyes than punctuality, thrift, and methodicalness.

Many Maori attitudes towards work, stemming both from his indigenous and current value system as well as from his pre-pakeha organisation of economic life, impede his vocational adjustment. In the first place he is less accustomed than the pakeha to regular and steady employment. Secondly, he finds dull, monotonous labour less congenial than the pakeha does. Thirdly, the concept of thrift for vocational or economic purposes is more foreign to him. Fourthly, he has greater ties of kinship and senti-ment to the locality of his birth and is less eager to migrate to other districts. Fifthly, he does not value work as an end in itself, as a badge of respectability or as a means of getting on in the world. Lastly, he is more dependent than the pakeha on the psychological support of an intimate group in his work environment.

Another factor limiting the vocational achievement of Maori youth is the relatively low occupational status and morale of Maori adults. Young people lack the encouragement of a tradition and a high current standard of vocational accomplishment in the ethnic group. They are also denied the practical benefits of guidance and financial backing that would follow from the exist-ence of such a standard and tradition. On the other hand, they are discouraged by the marginal economic position of their elders, by social demoralisation (i.e., wretched housing and sanitation, alcoholism, apathy, neglect of children) in many communities, and by the institutionalisation of a period of occupational drifting during late adolescent and early adult life. Compounding this situation is the overly casual, "She'll be right" attitude that is generally rampant in New Zealand, and the absence of sufficient incentive for a young person to acquire a trade or profession. This is largely a function of an undifferentiated national wage scale which places a tremendous premium on unskilled manual labour.

Racial Prejudice. Finally, discriminatory employment practices deriving from colour prejudice and from the popular stereotype of the Maori as lazy, undependable, and capable of only rough, manual labour tend to bar Maoris from many higher status occupations in banks, commercial establishments, private offices, shops and skilled trades. Maori boys desiring apprenticeships are usually required to migrate to the principal centres where they face further discrimination in obtaining suitable board and lodging. The denial of equal occupational opportunity to Maori youth con-stitutes the most serious and prognostically least hopeful factor impeding Maori vocational achievement, since colour prejudice is not only deeply ingrained and increasing in the pakeha population as a whole, but its existence is also categorically denied by both the people and Government of New Zealand.

Factors Affecting Maori Educational Achievement

Home Influences. Despite their high educational aspirations, incomparably fewer Maori than pakeha pupils sit or pass the School Certificate Examination, enter the upper forms of post-primary school, attend the university, or obtain a university degree. Home factors are largely responsible for this situation. Many Maori parents have had little schooling themselves, and hence are unable to appreciate its value or see much point in it. Although they accept the necessity for post-primary education, they do not provide active, wholehearted support for high level academic performance by demanding conscientious study and regular attendance from their children.

Maori pupils tend to lead two discrete lives—one at school, and one at home in the *pa*. There is little carry-over from school to home, but probably much more in the reverse direction. Conflict between home and school standards exists until middle adolescence and is resolved by the dichotomisation of behaviour: each standard prevails in its own setting. Thereafter, parental values, reinforced by increased contact with the Maori adult community, tend to predominate over the influence exerted by the school and the wider pakeha culture.

In addition to the fact that Maori parents are less vitally concerned with their children's educational achievement than are pakeha parents, they are less capable of helping them with their lessons. Because of their larger families they also have less time to do so. Living more frequently in outlying rural areas they are less able than pakeha parents to consult with headmaster and teachers. Divided responsibility for children, because of the common Maori practice of adoption and the greater informality and irregularity of marital arrangements, further compounds this situation.

Keeping a large family of children in secondary school constitutes a heavy economic burden on Maori parents in view of their low per capita income and the substantial hidden costs of "free" education. Maori pupils have more onerous household, dairying, and gardening chores to perform than their pakeha classmates, and seldom have a quiet place in which to do their home-work. Their parents may also remove them to another district during the shearing season. They are further handicapped by inadequate lighting and late hour social activities in the home, and frequently by serious malnutrition.

Cultural Influences. Maori cultural values regarding achievement have had a less adverse effect on the educational than on the vocational accomplishments of Maori youth. In the first place, acculturational progress has been greater in the educational than in the vocational sphere. Secondly, since motivations for educational achievement are referable to the less remote future, they are influenced less by the values of the peer group and of the adult Maori community. But although Maori intellectual traditions and traditional respect for learning have been seriously eroded, the loss has not been adequately compensated for by a corresponding acquisition of European intellectual values and pursuits. The modern Maori tends to be distrustful of book learning, intellectuals, and higher education. This attitude is in part a reflection of residual disenchantment with pakeha education stemming from the Maori Wars and subsequent withdrawal.

Other limiting factors in the current cultural situation of the Maori include the relatively low educational attainment of most Maori adults, the absence of a strong academic tradition, residence in remote areas where there are only district high schools or no post-primary facilities whatsoever, and serious staffing problems in most Maori district high schools. But since the percentage of Maoris attending secondary schools is progressively increasing, many of these problems will gradually disappear.

Adjustive Difficulties. Coming as they frequently do from small rural schools where they are in the majority, know all of their fellow-pupils, and enjoy intimate personal relationships with their teachers, Maori pupils experience more difficulties than their pakeha classmates in adjusting to the new secondary school environment. Less well prepared academically for post-primary studies, and less accustomed to impersonal and authoritarian teacher attitudes, they often tend to develop serious feelings of personal inadequacy. In many secondary schools also, teachers frequently adopt covertly antagonistic and overtly patronising attitudes towards Maori pupils. They often accept them on suffer-ance only, feeling that it is a waste of time, effort, and money to educate Maoris since they "only go back to the mat". Hence they offer the latter little encouragement to remain in school beyond the minimal leaving age. Some university lecturers also manifest similar intolerant and unsympathetic attitudes. Maori students at the universities encounter colour prejudice in seeking board and must often contend with patronising treatment and social aloofness from their fellow-students.

Stunting of Verbal Intelligence. Maori pupils are undoubtedly handicapped in academic achievement by a lower average level of intellectual functioning than is characteristic of comparable pakeha pupils. In both our urban and rural samples, particularly the latter, Maori pupils had significantly lower Otis I.Q.'s than their pakeha classmates. They were also retarded in arithmetic, English usage, and ability to handle abstract concepts. This retardation is attributable to two main factors: (a) the status of the Maori people as a generally underprivileged lower-class minority group with unusually large families, and (b) special disabilities associated with problems of acculturation. Pointing to the environmental rather than to the genetic origin of these differences is the fact that urban I.Q.'s were higher than rural I.Q.'s in both Maori and pakeha samples, and that the Maori-pakeha difference was significantly lower in the urban than in the rural sample. The extreme intellectual impoverishment of the Maori home *over and above* its rural or lower social class status reflects the poor standard of both Maori and English spoken in the home and the general lack of books, magazines, and stimulating conversation.

The low average level of intellectual functioning among Maori pupils cannot be dismissed simply as a function of test bias or of "language difficulty". The inability to handle verbal concepts that leads to low intelligence test scores is undoubtedly of environmental origin; nevertheless it renders individuals no more competent to handle analogous verbal materials in educational and vocational situations than if it were hereditary in origin.

Bilingualism. No research has been conducted in New Zealand to test the widely held view that the bilingualism of the Maori child is responsible for his educational retardation. In our particular post-primary schools, no relationship was found between bilingualism, on the one hand, and school marks or passes in School Certificate English, on the other. Cook Island, Fijian, and

ɔan pupils (although constituting a highly selected group in
ɪs of intellectual ability) also tend to be more bilingual than
ɪᴧᴧoris, but still do quite well academically in New Zealand
secondary schools and universities. Although rigorous research is
urgently needed in this area, it may be tentatively concluded that
the language retardation of Maori secondary school pupils is
attributable to the poor standard of English spoken in the home
and to the generally impoverished intellectual environment in
Maori rural districts rather than to bilingualism per se. When
Maori children grow up in the intellectually more stimulating
urban environment, mental and language retardation are markedly
reduced.

Acculturational History and Personality Development

Acculturational History. The source of current Maori values
regarding educational and vocational achievement lies in the pre-
pakeha Maori culture and in the distinctive features of Maori
acculturational history since contact with Europeans was established by Captain Cook in 1769. In the early phases of Maori
acculturation, pakeha goods and technical processes were simply
incorporated into the traditional Maori system of social and
economic organisation. The Maori sought to retain as far as
possible his land, his social institutions, and his distinctive way
of life, while at the same time acquiring all of the benefits of
European technology. But in accepting colonisation and British
sovereignty he naively placed his trust in treaty guarantees and
failed realistically to reckon with the predatory designs of the
colonists who were determined to obtain the most desirable land
in New Zealand and to establish the supremacy of their own
economic and political system. When no more land could be
obtained by sharp practices, or through questionable, coercive, or
frankly illegal means, the colonists finally resorted to war and
confiscation, and after a dozen years of bitter conflict eventually
gained their ends.

The war and the confiscations left bitterness, disillusionment,
and resentment in the Maori camp. The Maori lost confidence in
himself and in the pakeha. European motives, values, customs,
education, and religion became suspect. The Maori withdrew
from contact with the pakeha and surrendered to apathy, despondency, demoralisation and stagnation. He lived in isolated

villages and reverted to a subsistence type of agricultural economy supplemented by land clearing and seasonal labour for pakeha farmers and for the Railways and Public Works Departments. Various messianic, superstitious, and nationalistic "adjustment cults" flourished during this period of withdrawal. Although the old communal system of common ownership, co-operative labour organised under the direction of chief and *tohunga,* and sharing of the harvest among the kinship group was largely abandoned, much of Maori social organisation and cultural values tended to remain intact.

The perpetuation of Maori culture during this period (1872-1939) was possible because of (a) the vigorousness and adaptive qualities of indigenous cultural institutions; (b) strong needs, nourished by smouldering bitterness and resentment, arbitrarily to reject pakeha ways of life; (c) organised efforts to preserve as far as possible the central values and institutions of pre-pakeha culture; and (d) semi-complete physical, social, and psychological withdrawal, in reservation-like areas, from erosive contact with European culture. This is the classical pattern of *resistive acculturation* in post-defeat withdrawal situations that contrasts so sharply with *assimilative acculturation,* such as has taken place in Hawaii. Between these two extremes is *adaptive acculturation,* i.e., incorporation of material and ideational elements of the new culture into the existing social and ideological structure (e.g., Fiji, Western Samoa).

Emergence from withdrawal was facilitated by the convergence of several factors—the gradual weakening of bitterness, resentment, and suspicion of the pakeha, the paternalistic policies of the New Zealand Government, the desire of the better educated younger generation to obtain pakeha-type jobs, overseas experience during World War II, the effect of new highways, schools, automobiles, telephones, and the wireless in reducing the isolation of the Maori village. The phenomenally rapid growth of the Maori population and the shrinking of Maori land resources had also created a serious problem of unemployment in rural areas. Thus when attractive new jobs opened up in the cities during World War II, young Maoris were ready to enter the mainstream of New Zealand life.

Yet neither the emergence-from-withdrawal process nor the reversal of 70 years of experience in actively resisting pakeha culture were phenomena that could be accomplished overnight.

A strong residuum of traditional values, of ingrained mechanisms of resistance to acculturation, and of deep-seated tendencies indiscriminately to reject pakeha values still remained among the older generation. Thus, even though young Maori adolescents are currently able to assimilate the pakeha pattern of educational and vocational aspiration, they still fail to internalise and implement it adequately, largely because of insufficient support and pressures from their parents, older siblings, and peers, and the adult Maori community.

The post-withdrawal phase of Maori acculturation has been characterised by the following major developments stemming from the re-establishment of contact with the pakeha: (a) gradual disintegration of Maori village life and social organisation as isolation decreased and the young people migrated to the cities; (b) the growth of a youthful urban proletariat and of serious youth and social problems (crime, juvenile delinquency, bodgieism) associated with excessively abrupt urban acculturation; (c) the revival of latent anti-Maori racial prejudice in the pakeha population as a result of suddenly increased inter-racial contact under unfavourable conditions; (d) the growth of supra-tribal racial nationalism as a manifestation of national self-consciousness, as a reaction against colour prejudice, and as a compensation for the weakening of tribal loyalties and of traditional cultural practices; (e) notable advancement along many social and economic fronts, i.e., income, health, education, entrance into industrial and skilled occupations and into some professions, and (f) the establishment of self-government at a community level.

Regarding the future, only two alternatives seem credible: gradual cultural assimilation of the Maori to the pakeha way of life without appreciable racial mixture, or the constitution of the Maori people as a highly and progressively more acculturated ethnic community within the larger framework of New Zealand social, political, and economic life, but enjoying a certain measure of cultural autonomy and separateness as well as the status of underprivileged, second-class citizens. To the writer the latter alternative seems the more likely possibility in view of the residual vigour of various Maori psychological traits, the growing problem of colour prejudice, and the development of Maori supra-tribal nationalism. Indefinite perpetuation of the indigenous value system hardly seems likely now that village life is decaying and withdrawal is no longer possible, that rapid urbanisation is taking place, and that youth is becoming disinvolved from traditional practices. Overt expressions of *Maoritanga* will become less important as ends in themselves and more important as tangible expressions of racial nationalism.

Sources of Maori Motivational Traits. The ultimate source of Maori-pakeha differences in adolescent personality development may be attributed to two core aspects of traditional Maori value structure dealing with the basis of self-esteem: (a) greater emphasis on *derived status* throughout the entire life cycle of the individual, and (b) less emphasis on the self-aggrandising aspects and greater emphasis on task- and group-oriented aspects of *primary status*. The Maori of old highly valued primary status as a proper source of self-esteem and fostered achievement motivation in youth by encouraging appropriate supportive traits. But the self-aggrandising features of primary status (i.e., personal ambition, individualism, competitiveness, compulsive need to work, relentless anxiety-driven drives to succeed), although not unknown, were not as highly emphasised as in pakeha society. Greater stress was laid on mastery of skills for its socio-economic importance, on pride of craftsmanship, and on the personal satisfactions of meritorious accomplishment; on kinship obligations, on the enhancement of group welfare and prestige, on the personal-social values of co-operative effort towards a common goal, and on *inter-tribal* competition; and on the satisfactions associated with working together in an intimate, personal context of reciprocal psychological support. These characteristics of primary status and the continued importance of derived status engendered and made valuable in turn traits of mutual helpfulness and co-operative effort in bearing economic burdens, generosity, hospitality, and concern for the welfare of kinsmen.

This cultural orientation towards status and self-esteem was modified by the Maori's subsequent acculturational history. Several factors militated against acceptance of the pakeha achievement pattern. In the first place, lingering resentment towards the pakeha and disillusionment in pakeha values, motives, and practices fostered an attitude of rejecting pakeha ways simply because they were pakeha. Secondly, it was difficult for the task- and group-oriented Maori to accept the self-aggrandising aspects of pakeha primary status and the supportive traits that went with it, and to grow accustomed to pakeha working conditions. Thirdly, he was handicapped in utilising pakeha channels to primary status by lack of education and training for pakeha jobs, by lack of familial indoctrination in pakeha values, by general unfamiliarity with pakeha vocational opportunities, and by discriminatory attitudes on the part of many pakehas. Lastly, the residual vitality of the traditional value system created basic needs and provided basic satisfactions for those needs which the pakeha pattern could not easily gratify. On the other hand, traditional channels for implementing the Maori pattern of primary status, and the associated social organisation and leadership devices, were no longer functional; and any type of constructive achievement was greatly hampered by the widespread demoralisation, lassitude, and feelings of hopelessness and impending cultural obliteration that gripped the Maori people in the first three decades following the civil wars. Hence, the easiest solution for most Maoris seeemed to lie in de-emphasising the importance of *all kinds* of primary status and achievement motivation and in making exaggerated use of the psychological support offered by derived status.

Distinctive cultural expectations with respect to primary and derived status also influenced indirectly the nature of adolescent aspirational patterns by determining along parallel lines the kinds of childhood and adolescent role and status experience made available to children. Relevant to the Maori situation were such factors as habituation to procurement of the major portion of derived status from group rather than from parental sources, and hence greater dependence on and conformity to the group; the role of peers and siblings as the major socialising agents during childhood, with a resulting tradition of more equalitarian relationships and reciprocal obligations; no necessity for desatellisation from parents and resatellisation to peers during adolescence, since early satellising relationships to parents were weak or non-existent; less pressure to repudiate derived status and strive for a great amount and self-aggrandising form of primary status; and less discontinuity in general between childhood and adolescence. Hence, reinforcing the direct influence of the cultural ideology on the types of aspirations adolescents internalised was actual experience with particular kinds of status satisfactions and equalitarian relationships in the peer group—experience that was consonant with the cultural value system and therefore sanctioned by it.

The aspirational and motivational traits of Maori adolescents are undoubtedly influenced by the fact that Maoris are predominantly members of lower social class groups. By using matching procedures that controlled for social class, however, it was possible to eliminate the effects of relative social class status on our Maori-pakeha differences. Intelligence is another variable that is significantly related to educational and occupational aspirations, but the small Maori enrolment in our two schools preclude the possibility of matching pupils on this basis. It is extremely unlikely, however, that our Maori-pakeha differences in aspirational traits would have been materially reduced if it had been possible to adopt this procedure.

Transmission of Maori Aspirational and Motivational Traits. In accounting for the transmission of the distinctive Maori pattern of aspirational, motivational, and supportive traits from one generation to the next, our logical point of departure must lie with the heritage of pervasive and interlocking cultural values regarding primary and derived status that functioned in the pre-pakeha Maori culture and was subsequently modified by the historical experience of acculturation. As a result of the cumulative effects of (a) recurrent exposure to these achievement values and observation of culturally stereotyped role models, and (b) actual participation during childhod and adolescence in analogous types of role and status experience, this ideology is gradually internalised by the developing individual through the operation of the following mechanisms: primacy and exclusiveness of exposure; prerational identification on the basis of personal and group loyalties; implicit and explicit indoctrination; the development of particular needs and the experience of particular satisfactions (canalisation); incidental learning; prestige suggestion; the pressure of group expectations and demands; and the application of internal and external sanctions (reward and punishment, shame and guilt, disapproval, threat of exclusion, induced anxiety).

From our data it was clear that young Maori adolescents in our urban and rural samples had for the most part successfully assimilated the pakeha pattern of educational and vocational aspiration. These aspirations reflected both the prevailing pakeha achievement ideology to which they were exposed in school and in the wider culture, as well as the expressed but superficial desires of their parents. The latter, however, basically identified with the Maori orientation towards primary and derived status and generally had no deep emotional commitment to pakeha achievement values. Hence, they did not *really* encourage the implementation of these aspirations by voicing appropriate expectations, making unequivocal demands, dispensing suitable rewards and punishments, and insisting on the development of the necessary supportive traits. But because of poor communication between parents and children, this situation was not clearly perceived by Maori secondary school pupils. Thus, during early adolescence, although they frequently revert to parental standards in the home environment, the influence of the school and of pakeha culture generally tends to predominate in the development of educational and vocational aspirations and in the matter of conforming to pakeha work standards.

Later on, however, as relationships and communication with parents and the adult community improve, the influence of Maori cultural values, as meditated through parents and peers, begins to prevail. Educational and vocational aspirations, achievement motivation, and essential supportive traits fail to become adequately internalised; and eventually, as the possibility of implementation progressively recedes, the aspirations are either lowered or abandoned. Concomitantly, Maori adolescents also become progressively more aware of the actual obstacles standing in the way of their vocational success because of pakeha prejudice and discrimination. This perception of the relative unavailability of the promised rewards of self-denial and striving similarly disposes them to abandon or modify their earlier aspirations. Other important factors that contribute to the lack of internalisation and implementation of educational and occupational aspirations include traditional Maori attitudes towards work, acute social demoralisation in some Maori communities, and the absence of adequate guidance and of traditions of high scholastic and vocational accomplishment in most Maori families.

On the basis of our data it appears likely that significant Maori-pakeha differences in achievement orientation may be reasonably anticipated for at least another generation. They will be gradually obliterated, however, by the increasing urbanisation of the Maori people, and by progressive improvement both in the cultural level of the Maori home and in the concern of Maori parents for their children's educational and vocational advancement. The next generation of Maori parents will probably be able to sustain the internalisation and implementation as well as the instigation of pakeha aspirations for achievement. Racial discrimination will undoubtedly make it more difficult for Maoris to implement their aspirations; but depending on the magnitude of the handicap imposed, this situation may either stimulate greater striving, as in the case of the Jews and Greeks in the United States, or may promote an attitude of apathy and hopelessness, as is partly true in the case of the American Negro, who often perceives the cards as so overwhelmingly stacked against him that striving seems futile. In any event, the achievement ideology of the Maori will certainly reflect his predominantly lower social class status, becoming in time more and more similar to that of the lower-class pakeha.

RECOMMENDATIONS

The need for obtaining more representative data about the actual educational and vocational aspirations of Maori youth, the motivations underlying these aspirations, and the factors affecting their implementation cannot be stressed too highly. Such systematic research efforts should logically precede rather than follow the organisation of Government campaigns to increase the number of Maori youths remaining in secondary school beyond the minimal leaving age and entering the skilled trades and professions. The greatest weaknesses of these campaigns, in my opinion are, first, the fact that they are not based on detailed first-hand knowledge of the situation in the field, and secondly, the failure of Government officials to engage in patient, face-to-face explanation and discussion of the proposed programme with the people on the *marae, before* launching it.

The following specific recommendations were offered in the hope that they might help advance the educational and vocational achievement of Maori youth:

1. In order to overcome the present lack of adequate support, encouragement and guidance from parents, peers, and the adult community for the long-term occupational ambitions of Maori youth, Maori Vocational Guidance Officers are urgently needed in each district to serve *in loco parentis,* i.e., to provide prolonged and intensive guidance for all young people. The present system of vocational guidance is much too superficial, does not provide routine coverage, is staffed by inadequately trained personnel, and is too passive in its orientation. Maori Vocational Guidance Officers, working in the existing vocational guidance set-up of the Education Department should combine the guidance and placement functions currently performed by

three separate Government Departments. More hostels are also required to reduce the high drop-out rate among Maori apprentices and university students.

2. Post-primary education should be made a more rewarding and less frustrating experience for the large number of academically less capable boys who are currently only marking time in school until their fifteenth birthdays. To do this it would be necessary to render teacher-pupil relationships less impersonal and authoritarian, to provide more coeducational and extra-curricular activities, to reduce the inordinate gap in difficulty level between forms II and III, and to minimise the stigma currently associated with low academic ability. Teaching methods and subject-matter content should be appropriately adjusted to the varying intellectual capacities of pupils. Emphasis on a functional grasp of oral and written English and of arithmetical processes would be more appropriate for some low ability pupils than such subject-matter as algebra, geometry, literature, poetry, and French.

3. To reduce the special language handicap under which Maori pupils are labouring in relation to the School Certificate Examination, objective-type examination questions should be used more frequently, and the English examination should either be made less academic in content or a pass should not be mandatory for certain occupational fields.

4. Pupils who are genuinely incapable of profiting from full-time schooling should not be required to attend post-primary school but should be enrolled in supervised work-study programmes. In all other instances, however, the truancy law should be conscientiously enforced.

5. More attention should be given to the special adjustment problems of Maori pupils entering secondary schools. Greater liaison between primary and secondary school teachers and between the latter teachers and Maori tribal officials and Welfare Officers would be desirable. Because they have inadequate study facilities at home, Maori post-primary pupils should be permitted to do their homework in primary school buildings.

6. Once its special functions are no longer required, the Maori School system should be speedily dismantled to prevent the institutionalisation of latent sentiment for segregated education

that is gradually becoming more vocal in the face of increasing racial tension. The situation at Pukekohe should not be permitted to become the national pattern of education in New Zealand. The provision of more public health nursing, D.D.T. powder, antibiotic ointments, and improved housing and sanitation would be a socially more enlightened way of handling impetigo, pediculosis, scabies, and dysentery in Maori pupils than to segregate them in special schools.

7. Certain Maori cultural values should be kept alive as long as possible not only because of their intrinsic value, but also because the strong identification of an ethnic minority with its cultural traditions protects it from the serious damage to self-esteem threatening all acculturating peoples, and especially the victims of a colour bar. This does not imply, however, that an escapist reversion to moribund traditions or archaic ceremonial usages is advocated.

8. The Maori language should be taught in all primary and secondary schools—particularly those with large Maori enrolments. Knowledge of the language by children and adolescents is an indispensable prerequisite for the perpetuation of Maori cultural identity at the present stage of acculturation. It would also reduce the serious "generation conflict" between Maori parents and children. The groundwork for learning the language, however, must be laid in the home. Even a cursory knowledge of the Maori language on the part of pakehas would constitute a tangible expression of racial goodwill that would go a long way towards improving mutual understanding in New Zealand.

9. Vigorous measures must be adopted to improve the steadily deteriorating racial situation. Discriminatory practices in employment, housing, hotel accommodation, bars, restaurants, cinemas, credit, prices, etc., should be made illegal, and schools, churches, and civic organisations should sponsor realistic educational campaigns to promote racial tolerance and goodwill. The establishment of rural industries, wherever practicable, would also alleviate some of the problems caused by excessively rapid urbanisation.

10. The Maori people should be provided with Government assistance of adequate scope so that they can overcome in the

Has achieved much of this but can't use it

near future their serious cultural handicap in housing. The present housing position not only impedes the educational and vocational achievement of youth, but also encourages disease, delinquency, alcoholism, social demoralisation, and racial tension.

11. The Maori people themselves must be willing more realistically to come to grips with the growing problem of colour prejudice instead of burying their heads in the sand. They must be willing to take more responsibility in combating the symptoms of incomplete or inadequate adjustment to pakeha culture, in furthering the educational and vocational advancement of youth, and in perpetuating worthwhile elements of their cultural heritage. The time is ripe for the emergence of a new national movement with strong grass roots support dedicated to the accomplishment of these objectives.

APPENDIX I

Procedures and Instruments

Three principal methods of obtaining data were employed: (1) structured interview with pupils; (2) tests and rating scales; and (3) participant observation and informal interviews. Only the first two methods are considered below, since the latter methods were described in detail in Chapter 1.

Structured Interview

Each pupil was interviewed individually in a small school office during regular school hours. The investigator adhered closely to a cyclostyled interview schedule covering expressed academic and vocational aspirations, underlying motivations, perceived motivational pressures and influences in the environment, and traits important for implementing achievement goals.* Interview questions were so constructed as to yield quantifiable answers. Wherever feasible, for example, subjects were asked to rate their responses along a designated scale of intensity or frequency, or to rank various factors in order of importance. The average length of the interview was approximately one hour.

The establishment of rapport presented no special problems. The investigator was introduced to the pupils by the headmaster (and also introduced himself) as a vocational guidance specialist whose purpose was to discuss with them their occupational plans and to help them with any problems they might have in connection with those plans. Pupils were also assured that the substance of the interviews would be held in strictest confidence.

Partly perhaps because they were familiar with the functions of the careers master and were accustomed to the periodic visits of the vocational guidance officer from the Education Department,

* The actual content of the interview is specified under a listing of different categories of variables at the end of this appendix.

almost all of the pupils responded naturally and matter-of-factly to the interview situation. None of them appeared disturbed or inhibited by the recording of their replies. Many of the boys seemed to welcome the opportunity of talking freely about themselves and their plans in a permissive and non-threatening setting. Being a foreigner, I felt, was a distinct advantage in obtaining valid responses in this situation, since the pupils were not only unsure about the kinds of answers I preferred to receive, but also lacked previous experience in behaving deviously or evasively with American adults. The disposition to tell the interviewer what they thought he wanted to hear was also counteracted to some extent by frankly informing pupils at the outset that I was not unaware of this temptation.

Within this particular school context, therefore, the structured interview presented fewer difficulties than it does in clinical settings with adults. It also yielded more comparable and reliable data than could be obtained through an unstructured interview in which the content, sequence, and phraseology of the questions necessarily vary from one interviewee to another. The data, furthermore, were directly quantifiable without any need for subjecting interview protocols to subjective and inferential methods of content analysis.

One measure derived directly from the interview data was the Academic Goal Discrepancy Score,[6] representing the pupil's degree of optimism about improving his current class standing. It was calculated by subtracting the ordinal place he earned in his class the previous year (or, in the case of third-formers, the approximate place he currently occupied) from the place he was striving to attain by the end of the year.

According to the original plan, the parents of each boy in our sample were to be given a structured interview. For several reasons, however, this idea had to be abandoned as unfeasible. In the first place, sufficient time was not available to interview all of the parents. Secondly, in many instances the language barrier was sufficiently formidable to preclude obtaining precise replies to questions unless the investigator became didactic and defined his terms to an extent that adults outside a school setting would certainly find offensive. Thirdly, it was discovered that valid and sincere replies could not ordinarily be obtained from Maori adults until initial suspiciousness was broken down and a good personal relationship established; hence, answers given to structured interview questions during a first meeting were little better than worthless. It was decided, therefore, that it would be more fruitful to cultivate a limited number of more intimate relationships with certain key Maori parents and other leading figures in the community, and to obtain, on an informal basis their views on desirable academic and vocational aspirations for Maori youth.

Instead of systematically soliciting statements from parents regarding the aspirations they had for their adolescent sons, the latter's perceptions of these aspirations were obtained. The advantages of this procedure were twofold. First, pupils' perceptions in this area were probably less coloured than corresponding parental reports by desire to impress the interviewer favourably. Secondly, they were undoubtedly a more proximate determinant of the pupils' aspirational behaviour, since adolescent boys were presumably more influenced by their own perceptions of their parents' attitude in these matters than by their parents' actual or self-reported attitudes.

Tests and Rating Scales

Although group administration was technically feasible, each of the following tests (except for "Responsiveness to Prestige Incentives") was administered individually to the subjects so that possible language difficulties on the part of Maori pupils could be handled more effectively. The tests were administered during the course of a second individual session with the subject after completion of the interview schedule.

Test of Occupational Prestige Needs

In this test, which is identical with the level of interests portion of the Lee-Thorpe Occupational Interest Inventory,[22] the subject is presented with thirty triads of occupational activities. In each triad the area of work involved is held constant while level of job prestige (i.e., professional, subprofessional, skilled, unskilled) is varied. Total score is computed from the subject's preference in each triad appropriately weighed in terms of occupational prestige. The test-retest reliability of this test is .88.[22]

Achievement Imagery Test[23]

This is a measure of degree of achievement motivation derived from the relative amount of imagery concerned with success in competition with some standard of excellence. Subjects write stories in response to four standard pictures; each story is written on a separate page and entered under four printed questions. A time limit of four minutes per story is imposed, and the investigator announces time at the end of each minute.

The stories were scored for total achievement imagery according to the very explicit set of criteria supplied by the authors of the test.[23] The product-moment correlation between the scores given by the invesigator on 60 test protocols and those given independently by a doctoral candidate in psychology was .98.

Vocational Tenacity Test[6]

In this test the subject reacts successively to three hypothetical vocational situations in which he is asked to imagine that he is preparing for careers in engineering, fine arts, and medicine respectively, and that in the course of his studies he encounters serious obstacles of a designated nature. In each situation, four alternatives are presented, ranging from maintenance of the original goal at all costs (high vocational tenacity) to complete abandonment of the original goal (low vocational tenacity). The subject's choices in the three situations, appropriately weighted, are summated to yield a composite score.

Responsiveness to Prestige Incentives (Group Test)[2]

Responsiveness to a prestige incentive is defined as the difference in work output under ostensibly anonymous motivational conditions, on the one hand, and intensively competitive conditions, on the other hand. The work tasks consist of simple arithmetic, letter cancellation, and digit-symbol speed tests, each consisting of six separately timed pages of material. Under the anonymous conditions the work material is surreptitiously coded to permit identification of subjects. Under the competitive conditions (one week later), subjects are informed in advance that a rank-order list of scores will be read aloud to the group after the test papers are corrected. The split-half reliability coefficient of this test is .89 and the generality coefficient is .42.[2]

Teachers' Ratings

Each pupil was rated by four of his teachers on ten motivational traits. These traits are specified in the listing of categories of variables below.

CATEGORISATION OF VARIABLES

To facilitate subsequent analysis of the data, all of the interview items, test scores, and teachers' ratings were classified under eleven categories of variables in four principal areas. All of the categories except one (perceived influence of others on vocational choice) are related to the substantive content of the hypotheses listed in Chapter 1. The following is a complete listing of variables:*

I. Expressed Aspirations
  1. Stated Academic Aspirations: marks desired for current school year; Academic Goal Discrepancy Score; intention of remaining in school after the age of 15, and of trying for the

---

* All variables not explicitly designated as *test* scores or as teachers' ratings were derived from the structured pupil interview.

School Certificate; intention of attending the university and working towards a degree; teachers' ratings on academic aspirations and on motivation to succeed in university studies.

2. Stated Vocational Aspirations: type and prestigefulness of vocational choice; relative importance of vocational success as a life goal; similarity of vocational aspiration to "ideal" choice of occupation.

II. *Type of Motivation Underlying Aspirations*

3. Prestige Motivation: scores on Test of Occupational Prestige Needs, Achievement Imagery Test, Vocational Tenacity Test, and Test of Responsiveness to Prestige Incentives; teachers' rating on scholastic competitiveness; rank values of "prestige" and "monetary reward" as factors in vocational choice; frequency of mentioning prestige, wealth, advancement and respect as reasons for desiring occupational success; rank values of "importance for career" and "excelling classmates" as reasons for desiring school success.

4. Task-Oriented Motivation: rank values of "interest in job" and "aptitude" as factors in occupational choice; frequency of mentioning "liking the job" as a reason for seeking vocational success; rank value of "interest in studies" as a reason for wanting high marks in school.

5. Group Welfare Motivation: teachers' rating on "co-operativeness in group enterprises"; rank value of "to help others" as a factor influencing vocational choice; frequency of mentioning "to help others" as a reason for desiring occupational success.

III. *Supportive Traits*

6. Traits Important for Implementing Achievement Goals: teachers' ratings on attentiveness, conscientiousness, persistence, initiation of activity, planfulness of work habits; time spent on homework and study for end of the year examinations; worry about examinations.

IV. *Perceived Motivational Pressures and Influences in the Environment*

7. Perceived Family Pressures for Academic Success: family attitude towards the School Certificate; parents' academic aspirations for pupil (current year); parents' reactions to pupil's failure in school (anger; disappointment; loss of love, respect, and confidence); relatives' reaction to pupil's failure in school; rank value of "parents' approval" as a reason for

seeking school success; frequency of parental help with and prodding about homework.

8. Perceived Family Pressures for Vocational Success: parents' vocational aspirations for pupil; parents' reaction to pupil's occupational failure (anger; disappointment; loss of love, respect, and confidence); frequency of mentioning "family approval" as a reason for desiring vocational success.

9. Perceived Influence of Others in Vocational Choice: influence of parents and others in occupational choice; rank value of "family approval" as a factor in vocational choice; agreement between parent and child in choice of a career; whether parent leaves occupational choice to pupil; extent to which pupil asks for and is influenced by parents' vocational advice.

10. Perceived Peer Group Pressures for School Success: rank value of "pupils' approval" as a reason for desiring high marks in school; friends' reaction to pupil's school failure.

11. Perceived Opportunity for Vocational Success: predicted chances of attaining occupational success; obstacles in path of vocational success, effect of anti-Maori bias on Maori boys' opportunity for vocational achievement; optimism about entering and remaining in occupation of choice.

Comparison of Maori and Pakeha Aspirational Patterns

On the basis of general theoretical propositions and consideration of the relevant literature, it was hypothesised that pakeha secondary school pupils would express higher academic and vocational aspirations than Maori secondary school pupils, and would be more highly motivated by prestige considerations and less highly motivated by task-oriented and group welfare factors. It was also hypothesised that pakeha pupils would manifest to a greater degree those personality traits important for implementing high achievement goals, and would perceive greater family and peer group pressures as well as greater opportunity for such achievement. Lastly, it was hypothesised that Maori-pakeha differences would be more conspicuous in the urban than in the rural sample, but that the direction of the differences would be similar.

Maori-Pakeha Uniformities and Differences

After presenting the findings separately for urban and rural samples under our eleven categories of variables, we will conclude this appendix by examining to what extent the above hypotheses are or are not supported by the data.

Stated Academic Aspirations

Urban Sample

Generally speaking, Maori and pakeha pupils were very similar in their stated academic aspirations. The majority of boys in each group aspired either to "top" marks or to marks "well above average". The mean academic goal discrepancy scores of the two groups of subjects were practically identical. The members of each group desired to improve an average of approximately five "places" over their previous year's or current academic standing in the class.

In terms of more long-range academic aspirations, about 87 per cent of each group intended to remain in school after the age of fifteen. A suggestively larger number of Maori pupils indicated that they desired to sit the School Certificate Examination (p. 15)* and enter the university (p. 20). All of the nine pakeha and thirteen Maori boys who hoped to pursue university studies expected to work towards degrees.

These aspirational findings contrast sharply with the fact that in actual practice a much larger percentage of pakeha than Maori pupils in this district remain in school after the minimal leaving age, complete fifth- and sixth-form work, sit and pass the School Certificate and University Entrance Examinations, enter the university, and obtain degrees.

Pakeha pupils were rated by teachers as having higher academic aspirations (t almost .05) and as being more highly motivated to succeed in university studies.

Rural Sample

The academic aspirations of Maori and pakeha pupils in the rural sample were also generally similar in most respects. Aspirations for the current school year were practically identical for boys in the two culture groups, but were concentrated in the "slightly above average" and "well above average" categories rather than in the latter and "top" categories as in the case of the urban sample. Pakeha pupils in the rural sample, however, aspired to significantly greater improvement than Maori pupils in their end of the year class standing (t .01).

Maori and pakeha boys in the rural sample were slightly more similar with respect to long-term academic aspirations than were Maori and pakeha boys in the urban sample. Over ninety per cent of the subjects in each cultural group indicated that they wished to remain in school after the age of fifteen. Somewhat more Maori than pakeha pupils were desirous of sitting the School Certificate Examination (p. 20), but the relative number of pupils in each culture group who expressed a desire to enter the university and pursue a degree course was practically identical.

In terms of actual long-term academic *accomplishments* (i.e.,

---

* *Statistical Note:* The letters "t" or "p" in parenthesis, respectively, indicate that either a "t" or chi-square test of statistical significance was performed. An accompanying decimal refers to the level of confidence qualifying the significance of the difference in question. The letters "n.s." indicate that a given difference was not signficant at the 0.5 level. In instances where the "F" test on the radio of the variances of two groups was significant for a particular measure, the Cox-Cochran procedure and correction were used in performing the "t" test on the difference between the means.

number of years completed in secondary school; percentage of
pupils sitting and passing the School Certificate and University
Entrance Examinations; percentage of pupils entering the university
and obtaining degrees), pakeha pupils in this district are incomparably superior to their Maori age-mates.

Maori-pakeha differences in teachers' ratings, noted above for
the urban sample, were not present in the rural sample.

Stated Vocational Aspirations

Urban Sample

As shown in Table IV, Maori and pakeha boys in the urban
sample did not differ significantly with respect to the prestige
associated with their stated vocational aspirations. The differences
that did emerge in the pattern of occupational choices, namely,
the more frequent choice of farming by pakeha pupils and the
more frequent choice of skilled trades by Maori pupils ,are self-
evidently attributable to the greater possession of land by pakeha
families in this district.

In the case of approximately three-quarters of the pupils in

TABLE IV
STATED VOCATIONAL ASPIRATIONS
OF URBAN AND RURAL SAMPLES

| | Frequency of Choice | | | |
| | Urban Sample | | Rural Sample | |
Vocational Choice	Maori	Pakeha	Maori	Pakeha
Professional	6.5	7.0	7.5	7.0
White Collar, Commercial	6.0	6.0	4.5	10.0
Skilled Trades	25.0	18.0	23.5	14.0
Farmer	7.0	13.0	8.5	17.0
Farm Labourer	3.5	1.0	5.0	1.0
No Decision	0	3.0	1.0	1.0
TOTALS	48.0	48.0	50.0	50.0

each culture group, expressed occupational choice was the same
as "ideal" vocational choice. Pakeha boys, however, rated future
vocational success as significantly more important in their lives
than did Maori boys (p. .01).

Rural Sample

In addition to exhibiting the same differences in choice of
farming and skilled trades respectively as noted above for the
urban sample, Maori and pakeha boys in the rural sample also
differed slightly in the prestige of their occupational aspirations. More pakeha pupils aspired to white collar and commercial

occupations, whereas more Maori boys aspired to farm labouring jobs (see Table IV). As in the urban sample, stated occupational aspiration and ideal vocational choice were the same for about 75 per cent of the pupils in each culture group. The Maori-pakeha difference in the importance attached to future vocational success was in the same direction as in the urban sample, but the difference in favour of pakeha pupils was less significant (p. 15).

Prestige Motivation

Urban Sample

With respect to some criteria of degree of prestige motivation underlying the achievement drive, the pakeha urban group, as hypothesised, was significantly superior to the Maori urban group. In regard to most other criteria, however, only slight or non-significant differences in favour of the pakeha group emerged; and in some few instances, Maori pupils showed greater evidence of prestige motivation.

Pakeha pupils tended to make higher scores than Maori pupils on the Test of Occupational Prestige Needs (t almost .05). On the other hand, only slight and inconsistent differences respectively between the two groups were found on the Achievement Imagery Test and on the Vocational Tenacity Test. Teachers rated pakeha boys as scholastically more competitive than Maori boys, but the difference was not significant at the .05 level.

TABLE V
MEAN RANK VALUE OF FACTORS INFLUENCING VOCATIONAL CHOICE

| | Mean Rank Value | | | |
| | Urban Sample | | Rural Sample | |
Factor	Maori	Pakeha	Maori	Pakeha
Interest in Job	1.56	1.60	1.92	2.08
Aptitude	3.98	4.26	3.86	3.90
Family Approval	3.85	3.96	4.28	4.14
Prestige	5.50	5.79	5.32	5.20
Monetary Reward	4.56	4.62	4.83	4.58
Security	3.94	3.28	3.86	3.34
Help Others	4.60	4.51	3.93	4.76

Note: A rank of 1 signifies "most important".
A rank of 7 signifies "least important".

In the test of responsiveness to immediate prestige incentives, Maori pupils made consistently higher scores than pakeha pupils on all three subtests (t. .05 for one subtest and almost .05 on the other two subtests). Maori boys also rated "prestige" somewhat higher (t-n.s.) than pakeha boys as a factor influencing vocational choice, but "monetary reward" received practically the same rank value from subjects in the two culture groups as a factor bearing on this issue (see Table V). In each group, "prestige" received the lowest rank of all factors influencing choice of occupation.

Pakeha pupils mentioned prestige factors (i.e., "prestige", "wealth", "advancement", "respect") consistently more frequently than Maori pupils (t-n.s.) as reasons for desiring vocational success (see Table VI).

TABLE VI

REASONS GIVEN FOR DESIRING VOCATIONAL SUCCESS

Reason	Frequency of Mention (Percentage of Total)			
	Urban Sample		Rural Sample	
	Maori	Pakeha	Maori	Pakeha
Prestige	4.9	10.3	11.0	9.4
Wealth	10.7	15.1	16.1	21.5
Advancement	14.6	18.3	20.7	17.4
Respect	31.0	37.3	30.4	32.9
"Like Job"	18.3	3.9	8.4	4.7
To Help Others	7.8	1.0	1.9	2.0
Family Approval	2.9	1.6	3.2	2.7
Security	3.9	7.1	7.1	8.1
Others	5.9	5.4	1.2	1.3
TOTAL	100.0	100.0	100.0	100.0

Although "importance for career" ranked first for both Maori and pakeha pupils as the chief reason for wanting to do well in school, it was significantly more important (t .05) for the pakeha group (see Table VII). "Excelling classmates" was a slightly but not significantly more important reason for striving for academic success among Maori than among pakeha pupils (see Table VII).

Rural Sample

Except for a significantly higher (t .05) total Vocational Tenacity score in favour of the Maori group, all of the criteria of prestige motivation showed either nonsignificant or inconsistent mean differences between subjects in the two culture groups. Pakeha pupils scored somewhat higher than Maori pupils on the Test of Occupational Prestige Needs, but the direction of intercultural differences was reversed on the Achievement Imagery Test and on teachers' ratings of scholastic competitiveness. Degree of responsiveness to immediate prestige incentives varied inconsistently for the two groups depending on the type of test material employed.

Pakeha pupils ranked "prestige" and "monetary reward" slightly and somewhat higher respectively than Maori pupils did as factors influencing vocational choice (see Table V). As in the urban sample, both Maori and pakeha boys ranked "prestige" as the least important consideration influencing choice of occupation (see Table V). Differences between pupils in the two culture groups were slight and inconsistent regarding the various prestige reasons offered for desiring vocational success (see Table VI).

Both Maori and pakeha pupils rated "importance for career" highest among the reasons for seeking success in school. Intercultural differences were negligible on this item (see Table VII). The two groups gave approximately the same rank value to "excelling classmates" as a reason for aspiring to high marks in school (see Table VII).

TABLE VII
MEAN RANK VALUE OF REASONS FOR DESIRING SCHOOL SUCCESS

| | Mean Rank Value | | | |
| | Urban Sample | | Rural Sample | |
Reason	Maori	Pakeha	Maori	Pakeha
Importance for Career	1.79	1.36	1.88	1.82
Interest in Studies	3.00	3.21	2.46	3.18
Excel Classmates	4.29	4.53	4.48	4.69
Parents' Approval	3.06	3.11	3.42	2.76
Pupils' Approval	4.35	4.19	4.40	4.37
Teachers' Approval	4.50	4.60	4.36	4.18

Note: A rank of 1 signifies "most important".
A rank of 6 signifies "least important".

Task-Oriented Motivation

Urban Sample

Although Maori and pakeha groups were not significantly different with respect to most criteria of task-oriented motivation, obtained differences were invariably in the hypothesised direction (i.e., in favour of the Maori group). "Interest in job" and "aptitude" were ranked first and fourth respectively (in order of importance) by both Maori and pakeha pupils as factors influencing vocational choice; in both instances, however, the differences between the two groups were slight and not significant (see Table V). Maori boys mentioned "liking the job" more frequently (t .01) than pakeha boys did as a reason for desiring vocational success, and also ranked "interest in studies" as a slightly more important reason for seeking success in school (t-n.s.).

Rural Sample

Maori-pakeha differences among the rural pupils paralleled quite closely the picture reported above for the urban sample. Intercultural differences with respect to task-oriented factors in vocational choice were similarly negligible (see Table V). Maori pupils more often (t-n.s.) than pakeha pupils, however, mentioned "liking the job" as a reason for seeking vocational success (see Table VI), and also considered "interest in studies" a significantly more important reason (t .01) for doing well in school (see Table VII).

Group Welfare Motivation

Urban Sample

Intercultural differences were inconsistent in direction. Teachers rated pakeha pupils as more co-operative than Maori pupils in group enterprises (t .05), but Maori pupils mentioned "helping others" more frequently (t .01) as a reason for desiring vocational success (see Table VI). The two groups gave only slightly different mean rank values to "helping others" as a factor influencing vocational choice (see Table V).

Rural Sample

Intercultural differences in favour of Maori pupils were significant in only one of three instances, but were not inconsistent in direction as in the urban sample. Maori pupils ranked "helping others" as a more influential factor (t .05) in vocational choice than did pakeha pupils (see Table V); they did not, however, mention this item more frequently than their pakeha schoolmates as a reason for desiring vocational success (see Table VI). Teachers rated Maori boys as more co-operative than pakeha boys in group enterprise (t-n.s.).

Traits Important for Implementing Achievement Goals

Urban Sample

All of the significant differences in this category were in favour of the pakeha group, as predicted. Teachers rated pakeha pupils significantly higher than Maori pupils on all traits important for implementing achievement goals: initiation of activity (t .05); planfulness of work habits (t .05); conscientiousness (t .05); attentiveness (t almost .05); and persistence (t .05). Maori pupils, however, claimed that they spent slightly more time (t-n.s.) studying for end of the year examinations (7.5 hours per examination as against 6.8 hours claimed by pakeha pupils). They also reported slightly more worry regarding these examinations than did pakeha pupils (p-n.s.). Each group of pupils spent an average of 1.5 hours daily on homework.

Rural Sample

Intercultural differences in this category were, with one exception, practically non-existent. Pupils in the two culture groups received almost identical mean ratings from teachers on traits important for implementing achievement goals. Pakeha pupils reported studying longer for end of the year examinations, i.e., 7.4 hours per examination as against 4.8 hours reported by Maori pupils (t almost .05). Maori pupils, on the other hand, reported slightly more worry about examinations (p-n.s.) and slightly more time spent on daily homework (t-n.s.).

Perceived Family Pressures for School Success

Urban Sample

Data bearing on this issue were generally inconsistent in direction and provided no clear support for the hypothesis that pakeha pupils would perceive greater family pressures than Maori pupils for achieving school success. Pakeha parents were perceived by their sons as demanding somewhat higher school achievement than were Maori parents by their sons (p .10), but the reverse held true with respect to perceived parental desire for School Certificate attainment (p .15). Pupils in both groups gave approximately the same mean rank value to "parent approval" as a reason for asiring to school success (see Table VII).

Maori and pakeha pupils perceived their respective parents as reacting similarly to their (the pupils') school failure in terms of anger and degree of disappointment. In both groups parental reactions, in order of frequency, were slight disappointment, great disappointment, and anger. More Maori than pakeha pupils, however, felt that their parents would respond to their low school marks with loss of love and respect (p .02). Loss of parents' confidence as a reaction to failure in school was perceived with approximately equal frequency by both groups. About 40 per cent of the boys in each group thought that relatives other than parents would feel disappointed if they (the pupils) did poorly in school.

More pakeha than Maori pupils (83 as against 33 per cent) reported receiving parental help on their homework (p .01), but slightly more Maori pupils stated that their parents prodded them into doing homework (p-n.s.).

Rural Sample

Although the data for the rural sample were not completely consistent, they generally supported the hypothesis that perceived family pressures for academic success were greater in the pakeha group. Maori and pakeha parents were perceived by their respective children as equally desirous of School Certificate attainment, but pakeha parents were perceived as demanding higher marks in school (p .10). Pakeha pupils ranked "parent's approval" significantly higher (t .05) than did Maori pupils as a reason for desiring to do well in school (see Table VII).

The intercultural comparison with respect to perceived family reactions to school failure was identical with that reported above for the urban sample except that more Maori than pakeha pupils (70 as against 52 per cent) thought that relatives would be disappointed if they obtained low marks in school (p almost .05).

More pakeha than Maori pupils (64 as against 50 per cent) reported receiving parental help on homework (p .20) and being prodded by parents into doing homework (p .10).

Perceived Family Pressures for Vocational Success

Urban Sample

The data provided no support for the hypothesis that pakeha pupils would perceive greater parental pressures than Maori pupils for vocational success. Maori-pakeha differences in pupils' perceptions of the occupational preferences their parents had for them paralleled almost exactly the intercultural differences reported above in pupils' own vocational choices. Differences between the two culture groups, therefore, inhered in the pattern (relative prominence of farming and skilled trades) rather than in the relative prestige of perceived parental preferences.

More Maori than pakeha pupils perceived their parents as reacting to their (the pupils') vocational failure with anger (p .05), loss of love (p .01), and loss of respect (p .01), whereas the opposite held true with respect to reactions of disappointment (p-n.s.). Parental loss of confidence in response to pupils' vocational failure was perceived with equal frequency by both groups.

"Family approval" was infrequently mentioned by both groups as a reason for desiring vocational success (see Table VI).

Rural Sample

Findings for the rural sample were generally similar to those reported above for the urban sample except in two instances where rural and urban intercultural differences were in the same direction but unequal in magnitude. Compared to the urban sample, pakeha parents were perceived as reacting relatively more strongly with disappointment to their sons' vocational failure; the rural intercultural difference in favour of the pakeha group (p .05) was greater than the urban intercultural difference (p-n.s.) in this respect. Maori and pakeha pupils in the rural sample were more similar than in the urban sample in perceiving their respective parents as reacting with loss of respect to their vocational failure; the rural intercultural difference in favour of the Maori group (p-n.s.) was less than the urban intercultural difference (p .01) on this item.

Perceived Influence of Others in Vocational Choice

Urban Sample

Differences between Maori and pakeha pupils in the degree of influence they perceived other persons exerting on their occupational choices tended to be small in magnitude and inconsistent in direction. About forty per cent of the boys in each group reported that they were influenced by others (principally by parents) in deciding on a future career. More pakeha than Maori boys (49 as against 29 per cent) stated that they solicited occupational advice from their parents (p .15), and that they would be influenced "greatly" or to "some" extent (100 as against 88 per cent) by such advice (p-n.s.). More Maori than pakeha pupils, however, said that they would be influenced "greatly" or "not at all" by parental advice (p .01). "Family approval" received a slightly higher (t-n.s.) mean rank value from Maori than from pakeha pupils as a factor influencing vocational choice (see Table V).

More pakeha than Maori parents (43 as against 31 per cent) were perceived by their sons as being satisfied with letting the latter make their own occupational choices (p-n.s.), and as agreeing (74 as against 63 per cent) with their sons' vocational preferences (p-n.s.).

Rural Sample

With one exception, Maori-pakeha differences in the rural sample were negligible for this category of variables. More Maori than pakeha pupils (58 as against 23 per cent) acknowledged that they were influenced by other persons (principally by parents and teachers) in their choice of vocation (p .01). Slightly more pakeha than Maori pupils (50 as against 40 per cent), on the other hand, said that they asked their parents for occupational advice (p-n.s.) and would be influenced by such advice (96 as against 90 per cent) if given (p-n.s.). Pakeha boys also ranked family approval slightly higher (t-n.s.) than did Maori boys as a factor influencing choice of occupation (see Table V).

An identical percentage of parents in each cultural group was perceived by their sons as leaving vocational choice entirely up to them (34 per cent) and as agreeing with the latter's choice of occupation (53 per cent).

Perceived Peer Group Pressures for School Success

Urban Sample

No significant or consistent intercultural differences were obtained. Approximately one-third of the pupils in each group thought that their friends would be disappointed if they (the pupils) made poor marks in school. Pakeha boys ranked "pupils' approval" slightly higher (t-n.s.) than did Maori boys as a reason for doing well in school (see Table VII).

Rural Sample

"Pupils' approval" received almost identical mean rank values from boys in both culture groups. Significantly more Maori than pakeha pupils (50 as against 28 per cent), however, thought that their friends would be disappointed if they (the pupils) did poorly in school (p .05).

Perceived Opportunity for Vocational Success

Urban Sample

Pakeha pupils were generally more optimistic than Maori pupils about available opportunities for vocational success. Both in terms of appraising their chances of succeeding in their occupation of choice (t .05), and of perceiving fewer obstacles in their path, pakeha pupils were more confident than their Maori classmates. Seventy-eight per cent of the pakeha pupils and 56 per cent of the Maori pupils saw nothing whatsoever blocking their path to occupational success (p .02). Obstacles mentioned most frequently were "job market" and "studies" (Maori boys), and "ability" (pakeha boys).

Approximately 95 per cent of the boys in each group expected to enter and be engaged ten years later in their occupation of choice. More Maori than pakeha boys (29 as against 8.5 per cent), when asked explicitly about this factor, thought that anti-Maori bias would hinder the Maori's chances of achieving vocational success (p .05).

Rural Sample

Maori-pakeha differences were similar to those found for the urban sample. Pakeha pupils were significantly more confident than Maori pupils about achieving vocational success (p. .01), and perceived fewer obstacles (primarily "studies" in both groups) standing in the way of their success. More pakeha than Maori pupils (68 as against 60 per cent) saw no obstacles whatsoever in their path(p-n.s.).

Slightly more pakeha than Maori pupils (95 as against 84 per cent) expected to enter and remain in their occupation of choice (p-n.s.). As in the urban sample, more Maori than pakeha pupils (22 as against 2 per cent) perceived anti-Maori bias as a factor obstructing Maori vocational success (p .01).

Summary of Maori-Pakeha Uniformities and Differences

On the whole, taking into consideration all major categories of variables for which intercultural comparisons were made, the component variables and subvariables in each category, and both urban and rural samples, Maori and pakeha pupils were generally more similar than different in their aspirational patterns. Principal findings are summarised below for each of the categories considered in the inter-cultural hypotheses:*

(1) *Stated Academic Aspirations:* Few significant Maori-pakeha differences were found. Pakeha pupils in the rural sample were more confident than Maori pupils about improving their current class standing. In the urban sample, pakeha pupils were rated by teachers as having higher academic aspirations than Maori pupils. A suggestive tendency in favour of Maori pupils was evident regarding *expressed* desire to attain the School Certificate.

(2) *Stated Vocational Aspirations:* The two culture groups were generally more similar than different. In accordance with the much greater amount of pakeha than Maori-owned land in both districts, more pakeha pupils aspired to farming and more Maori pupils aspired to the skilled trades. In both samples pakeha boys placed greater weight on the importance of achieving vocational success.

---

* In each case, only significant or near-significant differences are listed. Unless a particular variable is explicitly mentioned, it can be assumed that a significant intercultural difference was not found. See Appendix I for a listing of variables in each category.

(3) *Prestige Motivation:* Intercultural differences were absent for most criteria of prestige motivation, but when such differences did occur they were more often than not in favour of pakeha pupils. Most of the obtained significant or consistent Maori-pakeha differences were in the urban sample. Pakeha pupils in the latter sample made higher scores than Maori pupils on the Test of Occupational Prestige Needs and ranked more highly prestige reasons for achieving both vocational and academic success. In the same sample, however, Maori pupils were more responsive than pakeha pupils to immediate prestige incentives; and in the rural sample, Maori boys manifested greater goal tenacity than pakeha boys in hypothetical vocational situations.

(4) *Task-Oriented Motivation:* Significant intercultural differences were not found in most categories. Maori pupils in the urban sample ranked "liking the job" more highly than did pakeha as a reason for desiring vocational success, and in the rural sample ranked "interest in studies" more highly as a reason for desiring school success.

(5) *Group Welfare Motivation:* Intercultural differences occurred as frequently as intercultural uniformities. Differences were in the hypothesised direction (Maori > pakeha) for "helping others" as a reason for vocational choice (rural sample) and for desiring occupational success (urban sample). In the urban sample, however, pakeha pupils (contrary to prediction) were rated by teachers as more co-operative than Maori pupils in group enterprises.

(6) *Traits Important for Implementing Achievement Goals:* Maori and pakeha groups were generally more similar than different. Significant differences were all in the hypothesised direction and occurred mostly in the urban sample. Teachers rated pakeha pupils in the urban sample more highly than Maori pupils on persistence, attentiveness, conscientiousness, planfulness of work habits and initiation of activity. Pakeha pupils in the rural sample reported studying more hours than Maori pupils for end of the year examinations.

(7) *Perceived Family Pressures for School Success:* Maori-pakeha uniformities were more conspicuous than Maori-pakeha differences. Somewhat more frequently than not, the latter differences were in the predicted direction (pakeha > Maori). Compared to their Maori schoolmates, pakeha pupils perceived their parents as demanding higher marks in school (urban and rural samples), and rated "parents' approval" as a more important reason for desiring high marks (rural sample). Pakeha parents were also reported as helping more than Maori parents with home-

work (urban sample) and as prodding more with respect to homework (rural sample). Contrary to expectation, more Maori than pakeha pupils perceived their parents as reacting with loss of love and respect (both samples) and their relatives as reacting with disappointment (rural sample) to low marks in school. Maori parents in both samples were also perceived as suggestively more desirous than pakeha parents of their sons attaining the School Certificate.

(8) *Perceived Family Pressures for Vocational Success:* Few significant intercultural differences were found. Maori-pakeha differences regarding perceived parental preferences for sons' vocations paralleled almost exactly intercultural differences between pupils' own occupational choices. More pakeha than Maori parents in the rural sample were perceived by their sons as reacting to the latter's vocational failure with disappointment. More Maori than pakeha parents, on the other hand, were perceived as reacting to the same situation with anger (urban sample), loss of love (both samples), and loss of respect (urban sample).

(9) *Perceived Influence of Others on Vocational Choice:* In most instances, differences between the two groups of pupils were slight in magnitude and inconsistent in direction. More Maori than pakeha pupils in the rural sample thought that they were influenced by others (particularly by parents and teachers) in their vocational choices. In the urban sample, more pakeha than Maori pupils reported that they solicited their parents' advice regarding choice of occupation; Maori boys indicated more frequently than pakeha boys, however, that they would either be influenced a great deal or not at all by such advice.

(10) *Perceived Peer Group Pressure for School Success:* Data for Maori and pakeha groups were similar except for the fact that more Maori than pakeha pupils in the rural sample believed that their friends would be disappointed if they (the pupils) failed in school.

(11) *Perceived Opportunity for Vocational Success:* Intercultural differences were more conspicuous than intercultural similarities and were in the hypothesised direction (pakeha > Maori). Pakeha pupils in both samples were more optimistic than Maori pupils about achieving vocational success, and in the urban sample perceived fewer obstacles in their path. In both samples more Maori than pakeha boys thought that anti-Maori bias would hinder the Maori's chance of achieveing occupational success.

Conclusion

Except for two categories (group welfare motivation; perceived opportunity for vocational success) intercultural similarities were more pronounced than intercultural differences. Where significant differences between Maori and pakeha pupils did occur, they were, by and large, in the hypothesised direction in eight categories, and opposite to the hypothesised direction in only two categories (perceived family pressures for vocational success; perceived peer group pressures for school success).

Thus, compared to the typical pakeha pupil, the typical Maori pupil was verbally more desirous of attaining the School Certificate, but was rated by his teachers as having lower academic aspirations. He was also less confident than the pakeha pupil about improving his current class standing. Vocationally, he was more apt than the pakeha pupil to aspire to a skilled trade rather than to farming, and to consider occupational success a less important life goal. Although he was more responsive to immediate prestige incentives and manifested higher goal tenacity in hypothetical vocational situations than did the pakeha pupil, he had lower occupational prestige needs and offered fewer prestige reasons for desiring both vocational and academic success. He manifested more task-oriented motivation than the pakeha pupil in the reasons he gave for seeking success in his job and in school, and more group welfare motivation in the reasons he offered for choice of a career and striving for occupational success. His teachers, however, rated him as less co-operative than pakeha pupils in group enterprises. He was also rated by teachers as less attentive, conscientious, and presistent than pakeha pupils, as less planful in his work habits, and as less highly disposed to initiate activity by himself.

The typical Maori pupil perceived his parents as less demanding of high marks but as more desirous of the School Certificate than the pakeha pupil perceived his parents. Parental approval was a less important reason to him than it was to the pakeha pupil for desiring school success. More often than his pakeha schoolmate the Maori pupil perceived his parents as reacting to low marks in school with loss of love and respect, and his friends and relatives as reacting with disappointment. He reported receiving less help and prodding from his parents about homework than pakeha pupils did.

The Maori pupil perceived his parents as reacting to his (the pupil's) vocational failure with less disappointment but with more loss of love and respect than the pakeha pupil perceived his parents. Although claiming to be more influenced by his parents in the choice of a career than was true of his pakeha classmates, he less frequently solicited their advice in vocational matters. He was less optimistic than the pakeha pupil of achieving occupational success and saw more obstacles in his path. When asked explicitly he acknowledged more frequently than the pakeha boy that anti-Maori bias would constitute an occupational handicap to Maori youth.

Urban versus Rural Intercultural Differences

The hypothesis that intercultural differences would be greater in the urban than in the rural area or that Maori and pakeha aspirational patterns would be more similar in the rural than in the urban sample was generally confirmed. In seven categories (stated academic aspirations; prestige motivation; group welfare motivation; traits important for implementing achievement goals; perceived family pressures for vocational success; perceived influence of others in vocational choice; perceived opportunities for vocational success), the number of significant and suggestive Maori-pakeha differences was greater in the urban than in the rural sample. In two categories (perceived family pressures for school success; perceived peer group pressures for school success), the corresponding number of Maori-pakeha differences was greater in the rural sample; and in still two other categories (stated vocational aspirations; task-oriented motivation), the number of Maori-pakeha differences was the same for both samples. The total number of significant and suggestive intercultural differences in the urban sample was 28; the corresponding figure in the rural sample was 18.

In the vast majority (83 per cent) of instances,* Maori-pakeha differences in urban and rural samples were in the same direction. The net balance of intercultural differences in urban and rural samples was also in the same direction in each of the categories except one (perceived peer group pressure for school success)

---

* This included both instances when the Maori-pakeha difference in a given variable was significant and in the same direction for both samples, as well as instances when the Maori-pakeha difference in a particular variable within a category was significant for only one of the two samples but was in the hypothesised direction.

Comparison of Urban and Rural Aspirational Patterns

On the assumption that urbanisation would have much the same effects on aspirational patterns as a shift from Maori to pakeha culture, it was hypothesised that, by and large, urban-rural differences would be in the same direction as hypothesised pakeha-Maori differences (that is, "urban" could be substituted for "pakeha" and "rural" for "Maori" in the list of hypotheses concerning pakeha-Maori differences). It was also hypothesised that urban-rural differences (although similar in direction in Maori and pakeha samples) would be less marked in the Maori than in the pakeha sample, and that intercultural differences would overshadow inter-locational differences.

Urban-Rural Uniformities and Differences

Urban-rural comparisons will be presented separately for Maori and pakeha samples. But since we are primarily concerned with contrasting (a) the relative magnitude and direction of Maori-pakeha differences with (b) the relative magnitude and direction of urban-rural differences within the Maori sample, urban-rural findings will be presented more comprehensively for the Maori than for the pakeha sample.

Because the original matching of pupils attempted to equate Maori and pakeha pupils within each location with respect to form, course, stream, and father's occupation, rematching of urban and rural pupils within each culture group was necessary before interlocational comparisons could be made. Rematching was performed on the basis of form, course, and stream only, since it was not practicable to match paternal occupation interlocationally. The much greater percentage of third-formers in the urban than in the rural sample reduced to 37 on rematching the number of rural pupils that could be matched with urban pupils in each of our Maori and pakeha samples.

Stated Academic Aspirations

Maori Sample

Urban-rural differences in stated academic aspirations were in the same direction but were greater in magnitude than corresponding Maori-pakeha differences. The majority of boys in the urban group aspired to "top" and "well above average" marks, whereas the majority of boys in the rural group aspired to marks either "well above average" or "slightly above average". Although there was a significant difference (p .02) between urban and rural groups in the distribution of academic aspirations, the difference between group means was not significant. Urban pupils were also more confident than rural pupils about being able to improve their current class standing (t almost .05).

Almost identical percentages of pupils in both groups indicated that they intended to remain in school after the age of 15 (95 per cent) and sit the School Certificate Examination (77 per cent). The two groups were only slightly different with respect to the number of pupils desiring to pursue university studies and work towards degrees.

Urban pupils were rated by teachers as being more highly motivated to succeed in university studies (t almost .05) and as having slightly higher academic aspirations (t-n.s.).

Pakeha Sample

Significant urban-rural differences were in the hypothesised direction and were generally similar to those reported above for the Maori sample. Urban pupils aspired to higher marks in school (t .05) than did rural pupils, and were rated by teachers as having higher academic aspirations (t .05) and as being more highly motivated with respect to university studies (t .05).

Stated Vocational Aspirations

Maori Sample

The two groups were generally more similar than different. Urban-rural differences were smaller but in the same direction as Maori-pakeha differences. Urban and rural groups exhibited strikingly similar patterns of occupational choice. Fifty per cent of the boys in the rural group and 55 per cent of the boys in the urban group aspired to the skilled trades. Slightly more urban than rural groups chose the professions, whereas the reverse held true with respect to "farmer" and "farm labourer".

Stated occupational aspiration and "ideal" vocational choice were the same for 81 per cent of the urban pupils and 69 per cent of the rural pupils (p-n.s.). Urban boys rated future vocational success as significantly more important to them than did Maori boys (p .01).

Pakeha Sample

Urban-rural findings were practically the same as corresponding findings for the Maori sample. Except for a slightly higher percentage of rural boys choosing farming, the pattern of occupational choices in rural and urban groups was almost identical. The only significant differences between the two groups was the greater importance attached to future vocational success by pupils in the urban group (p .01).

Prestige Motivation

Maori Sample

On most criteria of prestige motivation, urban and rural groups were similar. Urban-rural differences in this category of variables were approximately of the same order of magnitude as Maori-pakeha differences, and were generally in the same direction.

Urban pupils tended to make higher scores than rural pupils on the Test of Occupational Prestige Needs (t almost .05) and on the Achievement Imagery Test (t .05). Differences between the two groups on the Vocational Tenacity Test and on teachers' ratings of scholastic competitiveness were negligible. In the test of responsiveness to immediate prestige incentives, differences between urban and rural pupils on the component subtests were inconsistent in direction.

Both groups ranked "prestige" lowest of all seven factors influencing vocation choice, but the urban group gave it a higher mean rank value (t-n.s.). "Monetary reward" received a slightly higher mean rank value from rural than from urban pupils as a factor affecting choice of occupation (t-n.s.).

Contrary to expectation, rural pupils mentioned "prestige", "wealth" and "advancement" consistently more frequently (t-n.s.) than urban pupils as reasons for desiring vocational success.

"Importance for career" ranked highest for both urban and rural pupils among the various reasons for doing well in school. The two groups were only slightly different (t-n.s.) with respect to the mean rank value they gave both to this latter factor and to "excelling classmates" as reasons for seeking high marks in school.

Pakeha Sample

The few significant differences that prevailed between urban and rural groups were all in the hypothesised direction. Urban pupils made higher scores than rural pupils on the Test of Occupational

Prestige Needs (t .01). They also ranked "prestige" as a more significant consideration in choosing an occupation than did rural pupils (t .05), and ranked "importance for career" as a more significant reason for seeking high marks in school (t .05).

Task-Oriented Motivation

Maori Sample

Although urban-rural differences were greater than corresponding Maori-pakeha differences, they were inconsistent in direction. "Interest in job" and "aptitude" were ranked first and fourth respectively by both urban and rural pupils as reasons for choosing a vocation. Contrary to hypothesis, however, the urban group gave a higher mean rank value to the former reason than did the rural group (t-n.s.) and a slightly higher mean rank value to the latter reason. Also contrary to expectation, more urban than rural pupils mentioned "liking the job" as a reason for desiring occupational success (t .01).

Rural pupils, as hypothesised, ranked "interest in studies" more highly than did urban pupils as a reason for seeking high marks in school (t almost .05).

Pakeha Sample

Urban and rural groups yielded almost identical findings with respect to this category of variables.

Group Welfare Motivation

Maori Sample

Interlocational differences were similar in magnitude to intercultural differences but were more inconsistent in direction. Rural pupils ranked "helping others" higher than did urban pupils as a factor influencing vocational choice (t almost .05),but more urban than rural pupils mentioned the same factor as a reason for desiring occupational success (t .01). Teachers rated both groups almost equally regarding co-operativeness in group enterprises.

Pakeha Sample

The only significant difference between urban and rural groups —the higher rating urban pupils received from teachers for co-operativeness in group enterprises (t .05)—was not in the hypothesised direction.

Traits Important for Implementing Achievement Goals

Maori Sample

Urban-rural differences in this category were somewhat less prominent and consistent than corresponding Maori-pakeha differences. Teachers rated rural pupils consistently but only slightly more highly (t-n.s.) than urban pupils on the five traits relevant for the implementation of achievement goals. Urban pupils, however, claimed that they spent more time (1.5 as against 1.15 hours) daily on homework (t .05) and in studying (6.9 as against 3.4 hours) for each end of the year examination (t .05). The two groups reported the same amount of worry for these examinations.

Pakeha Sample

Interlocational differences for this category of variables were greater and more consistent with the hypothesis in the pakeha than in the Maori sample. Urban pupils not only reportedly spent more time on homework (t .05) and studying for end of the year examinations (t-n.s.) but were also rated more highly by teachers on conscientiousness (t .05), attentiveness (t .05) and persistence (t .05).

Perceived Family Pressures for School Success

Maori Sample

Interlocational differences in this category were less striking and more inconsistent than corresponding intercultural differences. Also, more often than not, urban-rural differences were not in the hypothesised direction.

Urban parents were perceived by their sons as demanding slightly higher school achievement (p-n.s.) and as more desirous of School Certificate attainment (p-n.s.) than were rural parents by their sons. Urban pupils gave a slightly higher mean rank value to "parent approval" as a reason for aspiring to school success (t-n.s.).

Urban and rural pupils perceived their respective parents as reacting similarly to their (the pupils') school failure in terms of disappointment, loss of love, and loss of respect. Significantly more rural than urban parents, however, were perceived as reacting with anger to low marks (p .05). More rural than urban pupils (73 as against 38 per cent) also thought that their relatives would feel disappointed if they (the pupils) did poorly in school (p .01).

Slightly more rural than urban parents (49 as against 35 per cent) reported receiving help from their parents with their homework (p-n.s.), but more urban than rural pupils (41 as against 19 per cent) stated that they were prodded by their parents into doing homework (p .05).

Pakeha Sample

Urban and rural groups in the pakeha sample were strikingly similar. Interlocational differences were less pronounced than in the Maori sample. The only near significant difference between the two groups was in the greater number of urban than rural boys who reported receiving help with their homework (p .08).

Perceived Family Pressures for Vocational Success
Maori Sample

Interlocational differences occurred rarely in this category and were less conspicuous than corresponding intercultural differences. Urban-rural differences in pupils' perceptions of their parents' occupational preferences for them were very slight, and paralleled in direction the interlocational differences reported above in pupils' own vocational choices. "Family approval" was infrequently mentioned by both urban and rural groups as a reason for seeking vocational success. Differences between the two groups in perceived parental response (anger; disappointment; loss of love, respect, and confidence) to pupils' occupational failure were negligible.

Pakeha Sample

Urban-rural differences in the pakeha sample were as inconspicuous as in the Maori sample for this category of variables. The only significant interlocational difference was the more frequently perceived loss of respect on the part of rural parents in response to pupils' vocational failure (p .05).

Perceived Influence of Others in Vocational Choice
Maori Sample

Urban-rural differences were small in magnitude, inconsistent in direction and slightly less pronounced than the intercultural differences in the same category reported in Appendix II.

More rural than urban Maori pupils (48 as against 38 per cent) indicated that they were influenced by others (principally by parents) in deciding on their future careers (p-n.s.), and that they (35 as against 27 per cent) solicited occupational advice from their parents (p-n.s.). Urban pupils, on the other hand, indicated that they would be influenced more strongly by such advice if it were given (p-n.s.), and also gave "family approval" a slightly higher mean rank value as a factor influencing choice of vocation (t-n.s.).

A higher percentage of urban than rural parents (72 as against 46 per cent) was perceived as agreeing with the occupational choices of their children (p .10). Approximately one-third of the pupils in each group felt that their parents were satisfied with letting them make their own choice of career.

Pakeha Sample

More urban than rural pupils acknowledged that they were

influenced by others (principally by parents) in their occupational choices (p .05). They indicated more frequently than did rural pupils, however, that their parents agreed with their choice of career (p .10).

Perceived Peer Group Pressures for School Success

Maori Sample

Only one significant interlocational difference was obtained in the Maori sample for this category of variables, and (as was similarly true of the single significant intercultural difference in the same category) it was not in the hypothesised direction. More rural than urban Maori pupils (52 as against 33 per cent) thought that their friends would be disappointed if they (the pupils) made low marks in school (p .10). "Pupils' approval" received only a slightly higher mean rank value from urban than from rural pupils (t-n.s.).

Pakeha Sample

No noteworthy or significant differences were found between urban and rural groups in this category.

Perceived Opportunity for Vocational Success

Maori Sample

Urban-rural differences were both less pronounced and less consistent than corresponding intercultural differences in this category of variables.

Urban pupils were more optimistic than rural pupils about the possibilities of achieving vocational success (p .05), but paradoxically perceived more obstacles in their path. Seventy per cent of the rural pupils and 49 per cent of the urban pupils saw nothing whatsoever blocking their path to occupational success (p almost .05).

Slightly more urban than rural pupils (95 as against 88 per cent) expected to enter and remain in their occupation of choice (p-n.s.). More urban than rural Maori boys (33 as against 24 per cent) saw themselves handicapped by anti-Maori bias in their pursuit of vocational achievement (p-n.s.).

Pakeha Sample

Rural and urban groups were not significantly different except for the more confident prediction by the latter group of future occupational success (p .01).

Summary: Comparison of Urban and Rural Maori Pupils

Difference versus Uniformities

As was similarly true of the relative number of intercultural uniformities and differences, urban-rural uniformities in the Maori sample were much more pronounced than urban-rural differences. Urban and rural Maori pupils, in other words, (just as Maori and pakeha pupils in either location) were alike in many more ways than they were different. The number of urban-rural uniformities was greater than the corresponding number of differences in seven of the eleven categories and equal to the number of differences in three categories (task-oriented motivation; perceived peer group pressure for school success; perceived opportunity for vocational success). Only in one category (group welfare motivation) was the number of urban-rural differences greater than the number of urban-rural uniformities.

Direction of Differences

The hypothesis that the aspirational pattern of urban Maori pupils would be more highly Europeanised than the aspirational pattern of rural Maori pupils (i.e., that the urban pattern would differ from the rural pattern in the same ways that the pakeha pattern differed from the Maori pattern) was confirmed for the most crucial four of the ten categories of variables bearing on this hypothesis—those dealing with expressed academic and vocational aspirations, prestige motivation, and traits implementing achievement goals. In each of these four latter categories, significant urban-rural differences were more often than not in the hypothesised direction. In four other categories (task-oriented motivation; group welfare motivation; perceived family pressures for vocational success; perceived opportunities for vocational success), half of the significant urban-rural differences were in the hypothesised direction and half were not. In still two other categories (perceived family pressures for school success; perceived peer group pressures for school success), less than half of the significant urban-rural differences were in the hypothesised direction.

Thus, compared to Maori-pakeha differences, urban-rural differences in the Maori sample were much less frequently in the hypothesised direction. The effects of Europeanisation and urbanisation appeared to parallel each other with respect to expressed academic and vocational aspirations, prestige motivation, and traits implementing achievement; but with respect to non-prestige (task-oriented and group welfare) motivation, perceived family pressures for school success and perceived opportunity for vocational success, the effects of an urban environment failed to overlap consistently in the hypothesised direction the effects of a European environment. In two other categories (perceived family pressures for vocational success; perceived peer group pressures for school success), *neither* Maori-pakeha *nor* urban-rural hypotheses were confirmed.

"Typical" Urban and Rural Maori Pupils Compared

Compared to the typical Maori pupil in our rural sample, the typical urban Maori pupil strove more for top marks and was more optimistic about improving his current class standing. His teachers also rated him as more highly motivated to succeed in university studies. He was somewhat more likely than his country cousin to aspire to a skilled trade or profession rather than to farming or farm labour, and regarded occupational achievement as a more important life goal. Although he tended to offer slightly fewer prestige reasons for desiring occupational success than the rural pupil did, he made significantly higher scores on the Test of Occupational Prestige Needs and on the Achievement Imagery Test. He spent more time on homework and on studying for the end of the year examinations than did the rural pupil, but he was rated slightly yet consistently lower by teachers on initiation of activity, planfulness of work habits, conscientiousness, and persistence.

The urban pupil was prodded more frequently by his parents about doing his homework than the rural pupil was, but perceived them as becoming less angry when he did poorly in school. More commonly than the typical rural pupil, he perceived both his friends and relatives as not feeling disappointed if he received low marks in school. He perceived greater agreement between his parents and himself regarding the choice of a career than did the rural pupil, and was more optimistic about achieving vocational success. Paradoxically, however, he saw more obstacles in his path.

Findings with respect to task-oriented and group welfare motivation were inconsistent in direction. No significant differences were obtained with respect to perceived family pressures for vocational success.

Summary: Comparison of Urban and Rural Pakeha Pupils

The predominance of urban-rural uniformities over differences was even more true of the pakeha than of the Maori sample. The number of urban-rural uniformities was greater than the corresponding number of differences in ten of the eleven categories. In one category (traits important for implementing achievement goals), the number of uniformities and differences was the same.

Urban-rural differences were in the hypothesised direction (i.e., parallel to the hypothesised direction of Maori-pakeha differences) in six of the ten categories.* No significant differences whatsoever occurred in two categories (task-oriented motivation; perceived peer group pressures for school success); and in two other categories (group welfare motivation and perceived family pressures for vocational success), less than half of the significant differences were in the hypothesised direction. In general, therefore, the correspondence between urban-rural and Maori-pakeha differences was higher in the pakeha than in the Maori sample.

Compared to the typical pakeha pupil in our rural sample, the typical urban pakeha pupil aspired to higher marks in school and was rated by teachers as having higher academic aspirations and was more highly motivated to succeed in university studies. Less commonly than the rural pupil he chose farming as a future career. He tended to place greater weight on the achievement of vocational success than the rural pupil did, to make higher scores on the Test of Occupational Prestige Needs, and to rank prestige factors more highly as reasons for choosing a vocation and striving for success in school. Teachers rated him more highly than the rural pupil both on co-operativeness in group enterprises and on conscientiousness, attentiveness, and persistence. He reportedly spent more time on and received more help from his parents with homework than the rural pupil did. More often than the latter he perceived his parents as both influencing and agreeing with his choice of career and as retaining respect for him even in the event of vocational failure. Finally, he was more confident than the rural pupil of ultimately attaining occupational success.

Maori versus Pakeha Interlocational Differences

Contrary to our hypothesis, urban-rural differences were slightly greater in the Maori than in the pakeha sample. Urban and rural pakeha pupils resembled each other more closely with respect to the variables under investigation than did urban and rural Maori pupils. Twenty-one of the 38 significant or near significant urban-rural differences occurred in the Maori sample.

Urban-rural differences were more numerous in the Maori than in the pakeha sample in five of the eleven categories (task-oriented and group welfare motivation; perceived family and peer group pressures for school success; perceived opportunity for vocational success). In three categories (traits important for implementing achievement goals; perceived family pressures for vocational success; perceived influence of others on vocational choice), the

---

* In two of the four categories in which the direction of urban-rural differences failed to support the hypothesis (i.e., perceived peer group pressures for school success and perceived family pressures for vocational success), Maori-pakeha differences were not in the hypothesised direction.

number of urban-rural differences was greater in the pakeha than in the Maori sample; and in three other categories (stated academic and vocational aspirations and prestige motivation), the number of urban-rural differences was the same in both Maori and pakeha samples.

Generally speaking, the *direction* of interlocational differences tended to be the same for Maori and pakeha samples. Seventy-one per cent of the significant urban-rural differences in the Maori and pakeha samples were in the same direction. Hence, although urbanisation tended to have similar kinds of effects on both Maori and pakeha pupils, the effects were greater in the Maori than in the pakeha sample, and were less consistently in the hypothesised direction.

Urban-Rural versus Maori-Pakeha Differences

One of the main objectives of this study was to appraise the relative magnitude of differences between the aspirational patterns of Maori and pakeha secondary school boys. In order to do this it was necessary to have available a standard that could be used as a basis for comparison. Urban-rural differences serve this purpose admirably since they constitute for many persons a familiar and easily identifiable point of reference for evaluating inter-group comparisons.

By using a research design which (a) matched Maori and pakeha pupils in both an urban and rural sample, and (b) matched urban and rural pupils in both a Maori and a pakeha sample, it was possible to ascertain whether those aspects of acculturation under investigation had proceeded to the point where intercultural differences were less than or approximately equivalent to urban-rural differences. Although preliminary consideration of the literature led to the hypothesis that intercultural differences would overshadow urban-rural differences, actual comparison of the number of significant and near significant differences that emerged from the two intercultural and the two interlocational comparisons supported the view that Maori-pakeha and urban-rural differences were approximately of the same order of magnitude. The number of intercultural differences was 28 and 18 respectively for the urban and rural samples, and the number of interlocational differences was 21 and 17 respectively for the Maori and pakeha samples. Thus, aspirational differences between Maori and pakeha boys in the *urban* area tended to be somewhat greater than corresponding differences between urban and rural boys in the Maori sample. On the other hand, differences in aspirational pattern between Maori and pakeha pupils in the *rural* area tended to be slightly less than urban-rural differences in the Maori sample.

References

The numbers in the text refer to these books

1. ANDERSEN, J. C. and PETERSEN, G. C. *The Mair Family*. Wellington: Reed, 1956.
2. AUSUBEL, D. P. Prestige motivation of gifted children. *Genet. Psychol. Monogr.*, **43**, 1951, 53-117.
3. AUSUBEL, D. P. *Theory and Problems of Adolescent Development*. New York: Grune & Stratton, 1954.
4. AUSUBEL, D. P. *Theory and Problems of Child Development*. New York: Grune & Stratton, 1958.
5. AUSUBEL, D. P. *The Fern and the Tiki*. Sydney: Angus & Robertson, 1960.
6. AUSUBEL, D. P., *et al*. Real-life measures of academic and vocational aspiration in adolescents: relation to laboratory measures and adjustment. *Child Development*, **24**, 1953, 155-168.
7. BEAGLEHOLE, E. The Maori in New Zealand: A case study of socio-economic integration. *Int. Lab. Rev.*, **76**, 1957, 103-123.
8. BEAGLEHOLE, E. and BEAGLEHOLE, P. *Some Modern Maoris*. Wellington: New Zealand Council for Educational Research, 1946.
9. BEAGLEHOLE, E. and RITCHIE, J. E. The Rakau Maori studies. *J.Poly.Soc.*, **67**, 1958, 132-154.
10. BEALS, R. Acculturation. *In* A. L. Kroeber (ed.), *Anthropology Today*. Chicago: University of Chicago Press, 1953, pp. 621-641.
11. BELSHAW, H. Economic circumstances. *In* I. L. G. Sutherland (ed.), *The Maori People Today*. Wellington: Whitcombe & Tombs, 1940, pp. 182-228.
12. BEST, E. *The Maori*. 2 v. Polynesian Society Memoir, Vol. 5, 1924.
13. BOARD OF MAORI AFFAIRS. *Report for the Year Ended 31 March 1958*. Wellington: Government Printer, 1958.
14. BUCK, P. *The Coming of the Maori*. Wellington: Maori Purposes Fund Board, 1952.
15. *Census of 17 April 1956: Interim Return of Populations and Dwellings*. Wellington: Government Printer, 1956.
16. EARLE, M. J. *Rakau Children from Six to Thirteen Years*. Wellington: Department of Psychology, Victoria University of Wellington, 1958.
17. FIRTH, R. *Economics of the New Zealand Maori*. 2nd ed. Wellington: Government Printer, 1959.
18. FREED, S. A. Suggested type societies in acculturation studies. *Amer. Anthropol.*, **59**, 1957, 55-68.
19. HAWTHORN, H. B. The Maori: A study in acculturation. *Amer. Anthropol. Memoir*, **64**, 1944.
20. HOLST, H. The Maori child's first year at post-primary school. *Education*, **6**, no. 3, 1957, 45-8.
21. HOLST, H. The Maori schools in rural education: an historical survey. *Education*, **7**, no. 1, 1958, 53-9.
22. LEE, E. A. and THORPE, L. P. *Occupational Interest Inventory, Advanced Form A*. Los Angeles: California Test Bureau, 1946.

23. McCLELLAND, D. C. *et al. The Achievement Motive.* New York: Appleton-Century-Crofts, 1953.

24. McCREARY, J., and RANGIHAU, J. *Parents and Children of Ruatahuna.* Wellington: School of Social Science, Victoria University of Wellington, 1958.

25. McQUEEN, H. C. *Vocations for Maori Youths.* Wellington: New Zealand Council for Educational Research, 1945.

26. METGE, J. The urban Maori. Paper read at Auckland Institute and Museum, October 1953.

27. METGE, J. Urbanisation and the pattern of Maori life. Paper read at the Eighth New Zealand Science Congress, Auckland, 1954.

28. MILLER, H. G. Maori and Pakeha, 1814-1865. *In* I. L. G. Sutherland (ed.) *The Maori People Today.* Wellington: Whitcombe and Tombs, 1940, pp. 75-95.

29. MILLER, J. *Early Victorian New Zealand.* London: Oxford University Press, 1958.

30. MULLIGAN, D. G. *Maori Adolescence in Rakau.* Wellington: Department of Psychology, Victoria University of Wellington, 1957.

31. NEW ZEALAND DEPARTMENT OF EDUCATION. *Annual Report, 1957.* Wellington: Government Printer, 1957.

32. *New Zealand Official Year Book, 1956.* Wellington: Government Printer, 1956.

33. PIDDINGTON, R. Emergent development and cultural symbiosis with special reference to the Maori and French Canadians. Paper read at Section F of the Australian and New Zealand Association for the Advancement of Science, Dunedin, 1957.

34. RITCHIE, J. E. *Basic Personality in Rakau.* Wellington: Dtpartment of Psychology, Victoria University of Wellington, 1956.

35. RITCHIE, J. E. Some observations on Maori and pakeha intelligence levels. *J.Poly.Soc.,* **66,** 1957, 351-356.

36. RITCHIE, JANE. *Childhood in Rakau: The First Five Years of Life.* Wellington: Department of Psychology, Victoria University of Wellington, 1957.

37. ROSEN, B. C. Race, ethnicity, and the achievement syndrome. *Amer. Sociol. Rev.,* **24,** 1959, 47-60.

38. SEWELL, W. H., *et al.* Social status and educational and occupational aspiration. *Amer. Sociol. Rev.,* **22,** 1957, 67-73.

39. SINCLAIR, K. *The Origins of the Maori Wars.* Wellington: New Zealand University Press, 1957.

40. SMITH, L. M. *Educational Assessment of Maori Children.* Unpublished M.A. Thesis, University of Auckland, 1958.

41. SPIRO, M. E. The acculturatioⁱ of American ethnic groups. *Amer. Anthropol.,* **55,** 1955, 1240-1252.

42. SUTHERLAND, I. L. G. (ed.) *The Maori People Today.* Wellington: Whitcombe and Tombs, 1940.

Glossary

THIS GLOSSARY includes only those Maori terms used but not defined in the text. Place names and names of persons, religions, and social movements have not been included. In general, the accent in Maori falls on the first syllable. Vowels are pronounced as in Latin or Italian, and consonants are mostly pronounced as in English.

atua god, in pluralistic sense of traditional Maori pantheistic religion.

Fleet The fleet of seven Maori canoes comprising the third and major colonising expedition to New Zealand from central Polynesia about 1350 A.D. The canoes mentioned in the text are the *Aotea*, the *Kurahaupo*, and the *Matatua*.

haka a stirring and warlike posture dance with accompanying chant.

hangi Maori earth oven; feast cooked in earth oven.

hapu a sub-tribe, or the largest sub-division of a tribe including several *whanau*.

hongi traditional Maori greeting by pressing noses.

hui a large gathering, meeting or assembly to greet visitors, celebrate important events or anniversaries, etc.

kaumatua elder.

kotahitanga unity, oneness, Maori supra-tribal solidarity.

kumara sweet potato.

makutu sorcery.

mana prestige, power, authority, influence.

Maori the indigenous Polynesian inhabitants of New Zealand.

Maoritanga "Maorihood" or Maori way of life.

marae open courtyard or green space in front of Maori meeting house; the ceremonial centre of Maori social life.
or higher studies.

mate Maori illness attributable to traditional Maori theory of disease causation; believed only amenable to treatment by *tohunga*.

pa a Maori village or nucleated type of settlement typically centred around a *marae*.

pakeha a person in New Zealand of predominantly European ancestry.

piupiu Maori kilt, primarily used for action songs and dances.

poi a Maori action dance performed by women in which balls attached to short or long strings are twirled.

puha sow thistle; a favourite Maori vegetable.

rangatira a person of chiefly hereditary rank or noble birth.

taihoa "by and by"—a dilatory policy of "wait and see".

tangi Maori ceremonial mourning rites; a prolonged wake with feasting and speechifying.

taniko ornamental border work of traditional Maori garments; now used mostly in the form of bands for head and waist.

tapu forbidden; sacred.

tohunga formerly a Maori priest or expert craftsman; in more recent times a practitioner of Maori folk medicine and magic.

whanau the Maori extended family group or clan.

whare wananga formerly the Maori sacred school of learning

whare runanga carved Maori meeting house.

Index

absenteeism, 94, 145
acculturation, 17, 163
"... continuum", 18
Maori, 20
stages in, 96ff
resistance to, 105
achievement
cultural values on, 134
educational, 13, 78ff
ideology of Maori, 119-20
Imagery Test, 90
vocational, 13, 53ff
adolescence, 15, 124
Maori, 21ff
"cultism", 67
aspirations
educational and vocational, 13,
24, 60, 78ff, 163
importance of adolescent
changes, 14, 22
differences in traits, 118ff

Beaglehole, Ernest [foreword], 14,
90, 129
Beaglehole, Pearl, 14, 129
Best, Elsdon, 14
bilingualism, 93, 150, 171
Buck, Sir Peter, 14, 101

control group, 17, 19
cross-cultural approach
values, 16
in acculturational setting, 17
cultural factors, general, 74
related to personality differences
13
cultural factors, Maori, 68
achievement values, 68
attitudes to work, 69
occupational status, 71
social demoralisation, 73
attitudes to education, 84
school adaptation difficulties, 87,
170
causes of intellectual retardation,
91
bilingualism, 93, 150, 171
absenteeism, 94, 170

derived status, 15-16, 22-3, 25, 68,
83, 119ff, 175

Earle, M., 14

early colonisation period, 39, 47,
85, 98, 114, 172
education, 142ff, 180
educational achievement, 78ff
ethnological research, 17, 30
equality
of vocational opportunity, 154
of housing, 156, 182

findings, 53, 163ff
Firth, Raymond, 13
Freed, S. A., 106, 108, 109
future of the Maori, 131ff, 174

Hawthron, H. B., 14
Holst, H., 145
home influences 80ff, 169
(see also parental influences)
hostels, 142
housing
urban, 42
rural, 48
improvement, 156, 182
hypotheses, research, 26-7

identification, 18, 146
intelligence quotient, 20, 126, 171
verbal, 90-3
interviews, 28ff

language, 19, 32, 93, 144, 148, 181

McQueen, H., 14
Maori adolescence, 124, 176-8
general characteristics, 21
aspirational pattern, 22
supportive traits, 24, 69
urban, 25
"cultism", 67
Maori arts and crafts, 19, 181
Maori ceremonial, 19, 30
Maori child care and early experi-
ence, 65, 124, 129
Maori crime, 113
Maori King movement, 100
Maori language, 19, 181
problem of, 32
teaching of, 148
Maori schools, 88, 145, 180
Maoritanga, 19, 25, 113
Maori traditions, 19, 26
Maori values, 175
Maori Wars, 100, 172

Metge, J., 14
motivation, 13, 118ff, 175–7
Mulligan, D., 14, 21

nationalism, racial, 100, 115

occupations
    Maori representation in, 13
    of subjects' fathers, 38
    intended, 60–3
    attitudes to, 70
    status and morale, 71
    improvement of opportunity, 154
organisation of book, 51

parent-child communication, 63–4,
    81, 124
parents
    influences, 63ff
    expectations, 81
    values concerning education, 80
participant observation, 28ff
peer group influences, 67, 83
personality
    change, 15, 18, 20
    structure, 13
    study, 16
    traits, 13, 24–5, 69, 175
pre-colonisation culture, 14, 39, 47,
    84, 96, 172
primary status, 15–6, 23–4, 25, 68,
    119ff, 175
prior research, 14, 20
problem, research, 13ff

racial prejudice, 75–7, 89, 114, 168
racial relations
    urban, 42–5
    rural, 49–51
    improvement of, 153–155
    Maori's responsibility for, 158,
        181–2
recommendations, 137ff, 177
religion
    affiliations, 40–2, 48
    "adjustment cults", 102
reporting of material, 34
research methods, 19ff
    control groups, 19
    design, 27ff
    hypotheses, 26
    procedures, 28ff

sampling, 20
    validity, 35
residence of pupils
    urban, 37–8
    rural, 46–7
Ritchie, James E., 14, 21, 90, 129
Ritchie, Jane, 14

sampling considerations, 20
satellisation, 124ff
school environment
    urban, 44–8
    rural, 50
setting
    urban, 36ff
    rural, 45ff
social anthropology, 13
social class, 20, 126
social life
    urban, 39–40
    rural, 47–8, 50
    demoralisation, 73, 111–3
    and economic organisation, 103,
        116–7, 132ff
Spiro, M. E., 127
stages in Maori acculturation, 96ff
    pre-colonisation, 96, 172
    colonisation, 98, 172
    war, 100, 172
    withdrawal, 103, 173
    post-withdrawal, 109, 174
subjects
    experimental, 27
    attitudes of, 30–2
    selection of, 32–4
supportive traits, 24, 69

tribal organisation
    urban, 39–40
    rural, 47–8
    disruption of, 111

uniformities, Maori-Pakeha, 13, 53
urban-rural uniformities and dif-
    ferences, 13, 25–26, 56–8 112
    general trends, 58

variables, 17, 19, 27
vocational guidance, 13, 138–40,
    179

work, Maori attitudes to, 70–71